Table of Contents

£16

PLANNING CONTROLS AND THEIR ENFORCEMENT

Planning Controls and their Enforcement

BY

A. J. LITTLE, LL.B., D.P.A.
Solicitor of the Supreme Court.

LONDON:
Printed and Published by
SHAW & SONS LTD.,
Shaway House,
London, SE26 5AE
1983

Under the title: "The Enforcement of Planning Control"

First Edition	*March, 1964*
Second Edition	*November, 1969*
Third Edition	*August, 1972*
Fourth Edition	*October, 1977*

As "Planning Controls and their enforcement"

Fifth Edition	*February, 1983*

ISBN 07219 0492 0

Printed in Great Britain.

PAGE

Part II
Additional Controls

PREFACE TO THE FIFTH EDITION

In the period of over four years since the Fourth Edition of this book appeared under the title "The Enforcement of Planning Control", there has been a continued steady stream of judicial decisions, interpreting, elaborating and refining the already complex field of law concerned with town and country planning controls.

Towards the end of that period Parliament once again changed the statute law on the subject by recasting the control machinery. The Local Government Planning and Land Act 1980 made changes in the law relating to Tree Preservation Orders and to Listed Buildings. It also provided for Urban Development Corporations and Enterprise Zones. In 1981 the Local Government and Planning (Amendment) Act brought about substantial changes by repealing sections 87 and 88 of the 1971 Act, containing the statutory machinery relating respectively to enforcement notices and enforcement appeals, and substituting significantly altered provisions, at the same time effecting further and similar changes in the machinery relating to listed building enforcement controls. The penalties for a number of offences were increased and the appeal provisions for enforcement of tree planting requirements and for enforcement of waste land notices were amended. Nor was this all, for the Secretary of State was empowered by the 1981 Act to make regulations relating to the issue of enforcement notices and to enforcement appeals, and that power has been exercised. The Lord Chancellor has also made Regulations governing the procedure for Local Inquiries into enforcement appeals. Another effect of the 1981 Act has been effectively to restrict further the right to challenge before magistrates the validity of an enforcement notice, thus abrogating the decision in *Smith v. King*. The Town and Country Planning (Minerals) Act 1981 effects important changes in the law relating to the control of mineral workings.

Whilst the judicial decisions in the period mentioned are too numerous to mention in detail here, the Courts have (*inter alia*) considered further the difficult question of estoppel, the doctrine of the planning unit, established use rights, and the effects of outline permissions. There have been further decisions concerned with the possibility of challenging in the High Court, decisions of the Secretary of State or his Inspectors and others in which the meaning of the important phrase "material considerations" has been further illustrated.

The material to be incorporated in this edition was therefore considerable and it was thought opportune to take a fresh look at the general layout of the book. It is hoped that the resulting re-arrangement of sections and Chapters will result in an improved presentation of the subject. It has also been considered useful to include a section on the question of planning agreements. As a further result of this rethinking the title of the work has been changed so that (it is considered) it now reflects more accurately the content of the book.

Any errors are mine, but my thanks are due, as always, to Mr. Gordon Morris, Publishing Consultant to the publishers for his unfailing help and guidance in presentation.

The book attempts to state the law as at the 1st October 1982.

A. J. LITTLE

Chelmsford, Essex.

TABLE OF STATUTES

PAGE

TABLE OF STATUTORY INSTRUMENTS

TABLE OF CASES

A

C

I

R

Y

ABBREVIATIONS

(unless otherwise stated)

The Act	means the Town and Country Planning Act 1971.
The Act of 1947	means the Town and Country Planning Act 1947.
The 1962 Act . . .	means the Town and Country Planning Act 1962.
The 1968 Act . . .	means the Town and Country Planning Act 1968.
The 1980 Act . . .	means the Local Government Planning and Land Act, 1980
The 1981 Act . . .	means the Local Government and Planning. (Amendment) Act, 1981.
The Secretary of State	means the Secretary of State for the Environment, or in Wales, the Secretary of State for Wales.

References to sections are, unless otherwise indicated, to those of the 1971 Act.

Planning Controls and their Enforcement

INTRODUCTION

The Town and Country Planning Act 1971 (a consolidating measure), imposes extensive controls upon owners and occupiers of land. Other enactments concerned with planning matters add to those controls, but for convenience one may usefully divide all controls of this nature in the way adopted by the 1971 Act itself.

That Act, in Part III, deals first with what it calls "General Planning Control" and then, in Part IV, with "Additional Control in Special Cases". Part V deals with the enforcement of controls in both groups.

One of the most important concepts in our town and country planning legislation is that a permission must generally be obtained before any **development** of land can lawfully be carried out. It is that concept which is given statutory force under the heading **General Planning Control**. This control of development and the **enforcement of that control** is dealt with in Part I of this work.

Part II deals with the **additional controls** (and their enforcement) applying to special cases. These relate to Buildings of Special Architectural or Historic Interest, Trees, Advertisements, and what the 1971 Act calls "Waste Land".

Part I
General Planning Control

CHAPTER 1

DEVELOPMENT

WHAT IS DEVELOPMENT

Development is defined in section 22 of the 1971 Act as meaning (subject to exceptions to be mentioned hereafter) "the carrying out of building, engineering, mining or other operations in, on, over or under land[1] or the making of any material change in the use of any building or other land.

Mining operations include—

(a) the removal of material of any description—

(i) from a mineral-working deposit;
(ii) from a deposit of pulverised fuel ash or other furnace ash or clinker; or
(iii) from a deposit of iron, steel or other metallic slags; and

(b) the extraction of minerals from a disused railway embankment.[2]

There is a clear distinction between the two types of development, *i.e.* between **operations** on the one hand and **uses** on the other. By Section 290 the word **use** is expressly defined to exclude use for building or other operations. The Court of Appeal in *Parkes v. Secretary of State for the Environment*[3] has held that "use" of land comprises activities done in, alongside, or on land but which do not interfere with the actual physical characteristics of the land, whereas

---

[1] Land includes buildings unless the contrary is stated. See the definitions of "land" and "buildings" in section 290.

[2] Section 23(3A) of 1971 Act inserted by the Town and Country Planning Act (Minerals) Act 1981. Effective on a day to be appointed.

[3] [1978] 1 W.L.R. 1308, C.A.

"operations" comprise activities resulting in some physical alteration to the land which has some degree of permanence. This case concerned storing and sorting of scrap metal, held to be a use rather than an operation. The Court of Appeal in *Bilboe v. Secretary of State for the Environment*[1] held that "operations" and "material change of use" were distinct and mutually exclusive forms of development.

The question of whether there has or has not been development is a matter of fundamental importance, but it is a question not always capable of easy answer, although the Courts have given some guidance.

WHAT IS NOT DEVELOPMENT

The following operations or uses of land[2] are declared by the Act **not** to involve development for the purposes of the Act[3]:—

(1) The carrying out of works for the maintenance, improvement, or other alteration of any building, provided they affect only the interior of the building or do not materially affect the external appearance of the building and (in either case) are not works for making good war damage, but, if begun on or after *6th December* 1968 the carrying out of works for the alternation of a building by providing additional space in it, below ground *does* involve development.

(2) Works by a local highway authority required for maintenance or improvement of a road and carried out on land within the boundaries of the road.

(3) Works by local authorities or statutory undertakers for the purpose of inspecting, repairing or renewing sewers, mains, pipes, cables or other apparatus.

---

[1] (1980) 39 P. & C.R. 495, C.A.

[2] This includes buildings unless the contrary is stated. *See* the definition of "land" and "building" in s. 290.

[3] Section 22 (2).

(4) Use[1] of any buildings or other land within the curtilage[2] of a dwellinghouse for any purpose incidental to enjoyment of the dwellinghouse as such

(5) Use of land for agriculture or forestry (including afforestation) and use for any of these purposes of any building occupied together with land so used.[3]

(6) In the case of buildings or other land which are used[4] for a purpose of any class **specified in an order made by the Secretary of State**, the use thereof for any other purpose of the same class.

Under the last mentioned provision there has been made the Town and Country Planning (Use Classes) Order 1972.[5] The effect of this particular provision and the Order appears to be very far-reaching. Where a building[6] or other land is used for a purpose within a Use Class and a change is made to another use which is within the Use Class it is expressly declared[7] that such a happening is for the purposes of the Act not to involve development. This being so, the author had, in earlier editions, submitted that the enforcement provisions could have no application, because development is an essential pre-requisite of an enforcement notice.

It was suggested that (subject to possible exceptions) a grant of planning permission for a use within a particular

---

[1] As noted earlier "use" excludes the carrying out of building or other operations.

[2] The bringing of agricultural land into the curtilage of a dwellinghouse involves a material change of use of the land. *Per* Goddard, C.J. in *Sampsons Executors v. Nottinghamshire County Council* [1949] 2 K.B. 439.

[3] This does not include breeding and keeping horses, except for farming purposes. *See Belmont Farm Ltd. v. Minister of Housing and Local Government* (1962) 13 P. & C.R. 417, D.C. For a case concerning grazing of horses see *Sykes v. Secretary of State for the Environment.* (1981) 42 P. & C.R. 19, D.C. As to allotments, see *Crowborough Parish Council v. Secretary of State for the Environment and Wealdon District Council* [1981] J.P.L. 281. D.C.

[4] It seems that "used" must mean "lawfully used". Development of land without planning permission is an unlawful use. *See A.G. v. Smith*, p. 223, post.

[5] S.I. 1972, No. 1385, replacing earlier Orders.

[6] References to a building include land occupied therewith and used for the same purposes. Article 2(3). For a case on the construction of this Article see *Brookes and Burton Limited v. Secretary of State for the Environment and Dorset County Council* [1977] J.P.L. 720, C.A.

[7] Section 22 (2) of the Act and Article 3 of the Order.

Use Class must have the practical effect of enabling a future change of use to be made from that specifically authorised to **any** use within the same class at the time the change is actually made and that any purported condition excluding the application of the Use Classes Order and attempting to limit the use to one particular one within a class was *ultra vires* and void. Such an imposition was not, it was suggested, a **condition** at all, because it did not, in fact relate to the permitted development, *i.e.* the material change of use to the use for which planning permission was sought, but attempted to prevent the future operation of the statute and the Use Classes Order in relation to the land in question.

The interpretation argued for above might be thought to cause difficulty in practice, because, *e.g.* permission for one (known) "general industrial" use would in effect mean **any** (unknown) general industrial use in future (assuming the Use Classes Order provisions remained the same) but in the author's view this argument did not seem to be very strong. The true criterion is the **character** of a proposed use, not the intentions of a particular occupier, and the whole purpose of the relevant provisions seems to accord with the commonsense approach that if, *e.g.* one kind of "general industrial" use is permissible in a particular place another should be. In any event **necessary** exceptions could be made in the Order, as has been done, *e.g.* in the case of fried fish shops in Class I.

The responsible Government Department had always taken the view that it **was** permissible to grant a planning permission limited to a particular use within a Use Class and by means of a condition to exclude other uses within the same Use Class. This view has received the approval of the High Court.

In *City of London Corporation v. Secretary of State for the Environment*[1] the Court (Talbot, J.) in a reserved judgment upheld a decision of the Secretary of State to grant a planning permission for the use of premises for an employment agency subject to a condition that the premises should

---

[1] (1971) 23 P. & C.R. 169.

be used for no other purpose. In the course of his judgment, having posed the question to be decided as "whether the power to impose conditions is limited to conditions which do not impose controls beyond those laid down specifically in the Acts or whether the powers are so widely expressed that in a proper case a local planning authority may add further restrictions to meet local conditions", the learned judge said "Provided a planning authority has regard to the development plan and to material considerations and the conditions are reasonable, and fairly and reasonably relate to the permitted development, then I consider that the conditions may impose further restrictions even if it means a restriction on a use which would not amount to development".

A permission may, in any case, be granted subject to a condition that it is to ensure for the benefit of a particular person only, whose intended use is known and not objected to (this may be done by virtue of section 33 of the Act) or granted for a limited period only, with an express condition requiring cessation of the use at the end of the permitted period.

The case of *Emma Hotels v. Secretary of State for the Environment*[1] provides a recent and interesting example of the application of the Use Classes Order.

E was the owner of a hotel and obtained a full publican's license for a bar. An enforcement notice required E to stop serving non-residents at the bar. On appeal the Secretary of State decided that there was a material change of use of the bar to something like a public house and refused planning permission for the change in use. E appealed on the basis that whether the bar was open to the public or not the hotel was still within Class XI of the Use Classes Order (and therefore he required no permission as there had been no development). The Divisional Court held that the finding of fact that there was a public house use of the bar did not take the hotel outside Class XI and the question was whether that use was one of the incidents of a hotel use.

---

[1] [1979] J.P.L., 390 D.C. and further decision (1980) 41 P. & C.R. 255, D.C.

The Secretary of State then found that as only about 25 per cent of the bar users were hotel guests, there were external advertisements and the bar could be isolated physically from the rest of the hotel, the public bar use was not an incident of the hotel use, but a separate use. A new enforcement notice was served and E again appealed. It was held allowing the appeal, that the Secretary of State had not understood the question he had to consider, a non-residents' bar by its nature had to run as a public house and given this fact, and given the facts the Secretary of State had found, it was impossible for him to decide that the use was not an incident of the hotel use.

THE PLANNING UNIT

In considering whether a particular piece of land has been developed, and especially (but not exclusively) when one is considering a change of use, it is a fairly obvious point that one must be seeking to answer that question by reference to **some** entity. In many cases there is no difficulty, *e.g.* change of use of a house to an office, but in others the question is less simple. In considering a change of use of a barn, for example, is one to consider the building itself as the entity, or the complex of buildings of which it may form part, or the whole farm in which it stands. Or, again, if scrap metal is stored on one field which is part of a farm, is one to judge the question of material change by reference to the one field, or by reference to the farm as a whole.

The concept of the "planning unit" (as the entity to be considered has come to be called), has been examined in a number of cases in the Courts.

The bringing into existence of a new planning unit has important consequences for development control. See the cases discussed *post* pages 31 to 39 under the heading "Abandonment or Loss of Use Rights".

Construction of a new building **may**, but will not *per se*, create a new planning unit. The case of *Jennings Motors Ltd v. Secretary of State for the Environment and the New*

Forest District Council[1] provides the latest illustration of the point. Premises had for some time been used by Jennings Motors Ltd., the appellants, for the conduct of a taxi, car and coach hire business and for vehicle repairs and sales.

In 1975 the appellants had erected a single storey building on part of the site and continued to use it for the same purposes as that for which they used the rest of the site. No planning permission was obtained for this building and the planning authority served an enforcement notice not in respect of the building as such but regarding its **use**. The inspector had taken the view that the planning unit was the whole site, and that there had been no change of use.

The Secretary of State nevertheless upheld the notice. He accepted that the site had established use rights for repair and servicing of vehicles and the other relevant uses and that as the site was a single planning unit the proprietors could rearrange their activities on the site provided the "mix" of uses did not change materially, but he decided that, in view of *Petticoat Lane Rentals Case* (discussed *post* p. 33), when the new building was erected a new planning history began in respect of it and the building had no actual established or permitted use. It could not therefore form part of the planning unit unless and until planning permission was granted for its retention and use for a particular purpose. Therefore (so he found) the continued use of the building for the purposes mentioned involved a material change of use. (It is to be noted that in *Petticoat Lane Rentals* the new building was erected on the **whole** of the site of the planning unit, whereas in this case, the new building occupied only a **part** of the site). Arguing on the basis that the planning unit was the whole site counsel for the appellants contended that there had been no change of use of the site merely by the erection of the building, but counsel for the Secretary of State relied on *Aston's Case* (see *post* p. 37), also in respect of part of the planning unit. The appeal was dismissed on the sole ground that the court was precluded by the authority of the *Aston Case* from

[1] [1980] J.P.L. 521, D.C.

deciding differently, although Donaldson, L.J. expressed himself as by no means certain that the *Aston case* was rightly decided. He gave no reason for his doubts. Leave to appeal was granted.

On appeal to the Court of Appeal[1] the appeal was allowed and the matter remitted to the Secretary of State. Lord Denning M.R. thought that *Aston's Case* had been wrongly decided and the theory of a "new planning unit" should be discarded. He considered there had been no change in the planning history of the site in the Case before the Court. Oliver L.J. considered that the expression "planning unit" had been hallowed by usage and was a convenient phrase for identifying, where the question was whether there had been a material change of use, both the area whose planning history required to be studied and the starting point of that history. *Burdle's Case* (*post*, p. 15) provided an extremely useful general test. The Authorities showed, said his Lordship, not that a new building *per se* had to be equated with a new planning unit, but that it was one of the factors (it might in many cases be a conclusive factor) to be taken into account in considering whether there had taken place in relation to the particular piece of land a change of use of so radical a nature as to constitute a "break in the planning history" or a "new planning unit" (the expressions were used interchangeably). The Secretary of State had misdirected himself in considering himself bound by the *Petticoat Lane* decision to hold that the erection of the new building *per se* constituted a new planning unit. Watkins, L.J. agreed with the judgment of Oliver L.J.

As the cases show, it is clearly established that the question of whether there has or has not been development **must** be determined by reference to the correct planning unit. However, it is not necessary for an enforcement notice to identify the planning unit or even to refer to it, as such, although clearly the notice must identify the actual land which is the subject of the notice. Nor is it necessary for the enforcement notice to be directed to the planning unit. On

---

[1] [1982] 2 W.L.R., 131, C.A.

the contrary an enforcement notice will normally be directed towards the activity complained of.[1]

If an error is made in determining the correct planning unit in a particular case this is an error of law and so the point may be taken to the High Court (*see post*).

In *Vickers-Armstrong v. Central Land Board*[2] the Court was concerned with a claim for development value under the 1947 Act, and the question was whether an administrative block forming part of the appellants' works could have been used on the appointed day under that Act (1st July 1948) for general industrial purposes without planning permission. The value of the land depended on the answer to this question, the parties being agreed that if planning permission was required the development value was £15,000, but if no permission was required such value was nil. The Court of Appeal affirmed the decision of the Lands Tribunal that the use of the administrative block was a use incidental to the industrial use of the works as a whole and no planning permission was therefore required. Parker, L.J., said "It seems to me to produce a wholly unreal result if you confine your attention merely to one part and do not look at the building or works as a whole".

In the more recent case of *Frank Vyner & Son v. Secretary of State for the Environment*[3] the plaintiff company sought to claim that a flat in property adjoining a factory had been in industrial use prior to 1964 and used for a purpose ancillary to the factory, because the occupant of the flat was required to answer the telephone and take messages in connection with the industrial use of the adjoining premises. The Court held that there was no evidence that the flat and the factory comprised a single planning unit and accordingly when the flat was after 1964[4] converted to office use there had been a material change of use.

---

[1] *See Hawkey v. Secretary of State for the Environment* (1971) 22 P. & C.R. 610, D.C.

[2] (1957) 9 P. & C.R. 33, C.A.

[3] (1977) 243 E.G. 597, D.C.

[4] As to the significance of this date see *post*, p. 130.

G. Percy Trentham Ltd. v. Gloucestershire County Council[1] concerned an enforcement notice requiring discontinuance of use of buildings for storage of plant and materials of building and civil engineering contractors. Those contractors, the appellants, had bought a farm, and proceeded, without planning permission, to use some of the farm buildings (previously used for storage of farm machinery and equipment), to store building materials in connection with their contractors' business. They argued that the buildings were a "repository" within Class X of the Town and Country Planning (Use Classes) Order 1963[2] and so by virtue of section 12 (2) (*f*) of the Town and Country Planning Act 1962,[2] then in force, no planning permission was required for a change from use for storage of farm machinery to a use for the storage of contractors' plant and materials. Their argument failed. The Court decided that one must consider the whole of the unit being used. Diplock. L.J., said "What is the unit which the local authority are entitled to look at and deal with . . . for the purpose of determining whether or not there has been 'a material change in the use of any buildings or other land?' . . . what the local authority are entitled to look at is the whole of the area which is used for a particular purpose including any part of that area whose use was incidental to or ancillary to the achievement of that purpose. I think, therefore, that they were entitled here to select as the unit the whole of the hereditament acquired by the appellants and, looking at that, ask themselves, was there any material change in the use of it? It is, I should have thought, as plain as a pikestaff that there was a change of use from an agricultural use as farm buildings to a storehouse for other purposes".[3]

Brazil Concrete Ltd. v. Amersham R.D.C.[4] was another case concerning the Use Classes Order, where the Court Appeal followed *Trentham's Case*. A building company had acquired a building contractor's yard with ancillary buildings

---

[1] [1966] 1 All E.R. 701.

[2] As to the Use Classes Order and its effect *see ante*, p. 5.

[3] For a later case concerning use of a building on a farm see *Hilliard v. Secretary of State for the Environment* (1979) 37 P. & C.R. 129, C.A.

[4] (1967) 18 P. & C.R. 396.

used for storing timber and making breeze-blocks. Planning permission had been obtained to convert a shed on the land to "builder's offices, carpenter's shed, etc." for the purpose of a builder's yard. A concrete mixing plant was installed and a concrete mixing business introduced. An enforcement notice alleged a material change of use. The occupiers contended that they were entitled to use the building and the yard for any purposes within Class IV of the Use Classes Order (use as a general industrial building for any purpose). The Court of Appeal again held that in order to see whether a use was permitted under the Order the land must be looked at as a whole and that it was the primary purpose for which the land as a whole was used which determined the character of the use. The unit in that case was a builder's yard (which did not fall within any of the Classes in the Use Classes Order), and there had accordingly been a material change of use.

Thomas David Ltd. v. Penybont R.D.C.[1] was a rather different type of case from the earlier ones, being concerned with mining operations. Sand and gravel had been extracted from two small areas of land coloured pink on a plan attached to the enforcement notice. The notice required discontinuance of working of sand and gravel over another (much wider) area, most of which had never been worked, shown by a red line on the plan. The Divisional Court rejected a contention of the occupiers that it was not open to the authority to make their enforcement notice relate to the wider area.

The Court held that so far as mining operations were concerned it was not necessary for the notice to relate to the precise area which had been cut by the shovel or bulldozer. It was quite proper for the council to look at the larger area which comprised the planning unit and they had been right in considering that unit to be the area bounded by the red line. Lord Widgery, C.J., delivering the judgment of the Court, referred to the judgments of Lord Denning, M.R., and Diplock, L.J., in *Trentham's Case* and went on

[1] [1972] 3 All E.R. 1092.

to say that he agreed with the contention of counsel for the Secretary of State that a similar approach must be made where the development in question was operational development, such as mining. He said "I think it is permissible and indeed right in mining operations cases to ask whether the land on which the actual cut is taken is not in truth and in fact part of a wider area which is being started in development by the particular immediate activity referred to. If as a matter of fact and commonsense it is clear that the first cut is a cut relative to a larger area, then it is right for the tribunal of fact to determine if it thinks fit that the larger area is a planning unit for present purposes".

In *Brooks v. Gloucestershire County Council*[1] parts of a house were used for shop purposes and from a date in 1965 two rooms previously used concurrently for shop and residential purposes became exclusively used for shop and restaurant purposes, in addition to another room which had been exclusively used since 1962 for shop purposes. The Divisional Court dismissed an appeal against a decision of the Minister that the 1965 changes had involved development, stating that the proper unit for consideration was the whole house.

The *Trentham* and *Brazil Concrete* cases noted *ante* were applied in *Re St. Winifred, Welcomes Road, Kenley, Surrey; British Paper and Board Industry Research Association v. Croydon Borough Council.*[2] In that case the plaintiff association became a company in 1945, its purpose being collection of information by laboratory experiment, the editing of that information and its dissemination to members. In 1946 it acquired premises at which both the experiments and the collation and editing of information were done. In 1956 a two-storey building was erected and used almost entirely as laboratories. In the valuation list for rating purposes the premises were described as laboratory and premises comprising one hereditament. The association asked for a declaration that the use of the premises as offices did not constitute development for the purposes of the Planning

[1] (1967) 19 P. & C.R. 90.
[2] (1969) 20 P. & C.R. 583.

Act. It was held that the two buildings together were used for industrial research development, both as laboratories and offices (and that planning permission was required for any other use).

This question of the **planning unit** was carried a stage further in the important case of *Burdle v. Secretary of State for the Environment*.[1] In this case Bridge, J. (as he then was) set out criteria for determining the planning unit.

The case concerned an area of land on part of which there was a lean-to building, which had been renovated and was used on a large scale for the sale of car spares. The land also contained a house and other buildings and the business of a scrap yard and incidental sales of spare parts had been carried on on the site. The planning authority served an enforcement notice alleging use of the building as a shop. The Secretary of State had dismissed an appeal, on the basis that the notice could only relate to the lean-to building. The appellant in appealing to the Divisional Court contended that the Secretary of State had had regard to the wrong planning unit and thus had not considered the right question—whether the change of activities had been a material change of use of the whole site. The Court held that on the available evidence it was impossible for the Secretary of State to have reached the conclusion he had done that the lean-to building was the correct planning unit, if he had considered the correct criteria. The appeal was allowed and the case sent back to the Secretary of State for reconsideration in the light of the criteria of Bridge, J.

Bridge, J., suggested that it might be a useful working rule "to assume that the unit of occupation is the appropriate planning unit, unless and until some smaller unit can be recognised as the site of activities which amount in substance to a separate use both physically and functionally". He propounded three criteria.

(1) Wherever it is possible to recognise a single main purpose of the occupier's use of his land to which sec-

---

[1] [1972] 3 All E.R. 240.

ondary activities are incidental or ancillary, the whole unit of occupation should be considered.

(2) It may be equally apt to consider the entire unit of occupation even though the occupier carries on a variety of activities and it is not possible to say that one is incidental or ancillary to another. This is well settled in the case of a composite use where the component activities fluctuate in their intensity from time to time but the different activities are not confined within separate and physically distinct areas of land.

(3) It may frequently occur that within a single unit of occupation two or more physically separate and distinct areas are occupied for substantially different and unrelated purposes. In such a case each area used for a different main purposes (together with its incidental and ancillary activities) ought to be considered as a separate planning unit.

These criteria are of very considerable assistance to those concerned with enforcement but, as Bridge, J., himself said [1] "to decide which of these three categories apply to the circumstances of any particular case at any given time may be difficult. Like the question of material change of use, it must be a question of fact and degree. There may indeed be an almost imperceptible change from one category to another".

It will rarely, if ever, be right to dissect a single dwelling and regard one room as a separate planning unit. In *Wood v. Secretary of State for the Environment*[2] buildings on a smallholding including a house had for many years been used for retail sale of farm produce both grown on the holding and bought in. The house was reconstructed and later on a conservatory was added to the house under the permission conferred by the General Development Order.[3] After that this conservatory was used for retail sales more intensively than the rest of the holding. An enforcement

---

[1] At p. 244.
[2] [1973] 2 All E.R. 404, D.C.
[3] As to General Development Orders, *see post*, p. 45.

notice was served to stop the "shop" use of the land. The inspector found that there had been no material change of use, but the Secretary of State attempted to cover the position by varying the notice so as to relate only to the conservatory.[1] The Court held, quashing the notice that the conservatory had taken on the character of the house itself, if it had been part of the house as originally built it could not properly have been treated as a separate planning unit, and the fact that it had been built later made no difference.

The Divisional Court held in *Kwick Save Discount Group v. Secretary of State for the Environment*[2] that a new planning unit is not to be created simply by dividing an existing planning unit and passing ownership or occupation to a new person different from the person owning or occupying the remainder. The premises comprised a petrol station and garage and a large building used as a workshop. Planning permission was granted to convert the workshop to a retail showroom with no restriction on the kinds of goods to be sold. Later the appellants acquired an interest in the workshop (but not the remainder of the premises) and used it as a retail supermarket. On appeal from the Secretary of State, who had upheld an enforcement notice, they had claimed that their acquisition of the workshop created a new planning unit and as there was no restriction on the use the supermarket use was lawful. This argument failed. The Court also held that there was an implied restriction in the planning permission that sales were restricted to automobile products. However, on appeal to the Court of Appeal[3] it was held, dismissing the appeal, that it was clear from the permission as a whole that it was subject to the implied condition and, so the Court held, it was neither important nor helpful to consider whether the showroom constituted a separate planning unit.

A planning authority cannot arbitrarily divide a site up into smaller areas and serve separate enforcement notices in respect of each so as to impose greater restrictions than

[1] As to the Secretary of State's powers of amendment, *see post*, p. 179.
[2] (1979) 37 P. & C.R. 170, D.C.
[3] (1980) 79 L.G.R. 310, C.A.

might have been included in an enforcement notice directed to the whole unit. This was the decision in *De Mulder v. Secretary of State for the Environment.*[1] A owned a small farm on which was carried on a business dealing in animal products and a general dealer's business including buying, selling and repairing cars. In 1963 planning permission was granted for erection of a factory on the farm. This was built and the volume of business of the animal products business was increased, but later declined. A then built up the general dealer's business and used the whole site extensively for that purpose. Three enforcement notices were served on him, each directed to different parts of the site. He appealed, contending that the whole farm was only one planning unit so that the notices were invalid. His appeal to the Secretary of State was dismissed and the notices upheld so as to restrict the intensity of use of each part to that obtaining in April 1970. On appeal to the Divisional Court his appeal was allowed. The farm was one planning unit and if a single notice had been served in respect of it he could have increased the intensity of use of any one of the three different areas provided that the **overall intensity of use** did not exceed the level at April 1970.

In *Wakelin v. Secretary of State for the Environment*[2] it was held that the division of one house and grounds forming one planning unit constituted a material change of use. A house was set in two acres of land. In 1965 planning permission had been given to build a lodge and garages in the grounds on condition that the lodge should not be occupied by other than a close relative or member of staff. In 1972 planning permission granted to new owners permitted the conversion of the lodge into two self contained flats and garages. The flats were used a guest suites. In 1975 a new purchaser sought permission for separate and unrelated occupancy of the lodge. This was refused and an appeal to the Secretary of State dismissed. The Court of appeal, overruling a decision of the High Court Judge, decided that there was a material change of use if the house and grounds were

[1] [1974] 1 All E.R. 776, D.C.
[2] (1978) 77 L.G.R. 101, C.A.

turned into a number of dwellings, even though buildings were not altered.

The reader is also referred to the cases of *Maddern v. Secretary of State for the Environment and Thurrock Borough Council*[1] and *David W. Barling v. Secretary of State for the Environment and Swayle District Council*[2] the facts of which are set out *post*, p. 23.

It was held by Woolf, J in *William R Winton v. Secretary of State for the Environment and Guildford Borough Council*[3] that whether sub-division of planning unit amounts to a material change of use is a matter of fact and degree for the Secretary of State and if sub-division of a planning unit has no planning consequences then it does not amount to development.

BUILDING OR OTHER OPERATIONS

Some expressions relevant to matters now being considered are defined in section 290 of the 1971 Act, and are set out below:—

"Building operations" includes rebuilding operations, structural alterations of or addition to buildings and other operations normally undertaken by a person carrying on business as a builder.

"Building" includes any structure or erection and any part of a building, structure or erection, but does not include plant or machinery comprised in a building. It is a term wide enough to include many things not ordinarily regarded as such. In *Buckinghamshire County Council v. Callingham*[4] a model village was held to have involved building operations.

Cheshire County Council v. Woodward[5] is authority for the proposition that nothing can be regarded as a building

[1] [1980] J.P.L. 676, D.C.
[2] [1980] J.P.L. 594, D.C.
[3] [1982] 2 C.L. 236
[4] [1952] 2 Q.B. 515.
[5] [1962] 2 Q.B. 126.

unless it is a structure or erection which can be said to form part of the realty and to change the physical characteristics of the land.

In *Barvis v. Secretary of State for the Environment*[1] the Divisional Court considered this matter further in relation to a mobile tower crane 89 feet high usually used on contract work, but at the material time erected at a depot and used there. It was so erected as to run on a steel track fixed in concrete. An enforcement notice had been served requiring its removal and it was contended by the owners that its degree of permanence was slight, that it was not fixed to the land and that it had not changed the physical character of the land within the principle established by *Cheshire County Council v. Woodward*. The Court held that the true test relating to a change in the physical character of land was that provided by section 12 and section 221 of the 1962 Act, containing respectively the definitions of "development" and "building", that the crane was a "structure or erection" and therefore a "building" within section 221 and its erection on the site was a "building or other operation" under section 12 (1). (These sections respectively are now re-enacted in sections 22 and 290 of the 1971 Act.)

It was long thought to be the case that demolition of a building did not **of itself** involve development[2] although it appeared from *London County Council v. Marks and Spencer Ltd.*[3] that when demolition was part of rebuilding operations development *was* involved.

An important case on this question is *Coleshill and District Investment Co. Ltd. v. Minister of Housing and Local Government and Another*,[4] in which the House of Lords, affirming a decision of the Court of Appeal,[5] held that demolition of **part** of a building may be development and that there was no error of law in a conclusion of the Minister that

---

[1] (1971) 22 P. & C.R. 710, D.C.

[2] *See* Ministry of Town and Country Planning Circular 67 dated 15th February 1949.

[3] [1953] A.C. 535.

[4] (1969) 68 L.G.R. 334.

[5] (1969) 66 L.G.R. 337.

embankments and blast walls surrounding disused ammunition magazines were parts of buildings, and that the removal of the embankments and of the blast walls were both operations amounting to development requiring planning permission. The Court of Appeal had left open the question of whether total demolition amounted to development and the House of Lords also refrained from ruling on this point. It was made clear in each of the judgments that the correct test to apply is whether what is involved in the demolition in a particular case amounts to "building, engineering, mining or other operations" within the statutory definition, if so it is development (unless falling within one of the exceptions mentioned, *ante*, page 4) and Lord Guest, Lord Upjohn and Lord Pearson all expressed the view that there was nothing in the relevant definition section (section 12 of the 1962 Act) or elsewhere which necessarily excluded demolition *per se* from being development.

"Engineering operations" includes the formation or laying out of means of access to highways and **means of access** includes any means of access, private or public, for vehicles or for foot passengers and includes a street. ("Highway" includes any land over which the public have a right to pass and repass whether adopted by the highway authority or not.)

As to "mining operations" each cut by a bulldozer is a separate act of development.[1]

CHANGES IN USE OF LAND OR BUILDINGS

A **change of use** of land or buildings is only development if it is a **material** change.

Whether a change of use is material or not is a question of fact and degree.[2]

---

[1] *Thomas David Ltd. v. Penybont R.D.C.* [1972] 1 All E.R. 733.

[2] *East Barnet U.D.C. v. British Transport Commission* [1962] 2 Q.B. 484; *Bendles Motors Ltd. v. Bristol Corporation and Another* [1963] 1 W.L.R. 247; *Devonshire County Council v. Allens Caravans (Estates) Ltd.* [1963] J.P.L. 47.

In three cases a material change of use is expressly declared[1] to be involved. These are:—

(1) Use as two or more separate dwellinghouses of any building previously used as a single dwellinghouse.

(2) Deposit of refuse or waste materials on land, notwithstanding that the land is comprised in a site already used for that purpose if **either** the superficial area of the deposit is thereby extended **or** the height of the deposit is thereby extended and exceeds the level of the adjoining land.

(3) Use for the display of advertisements of any external parts of a building not normally used for that purpose. (This is without prejudice to the Regulations for the control of advertisements.)[2]

"Use" does NOT include the use of land by carrying out any building or other operations thereon[3] but for the purpose of enforcement of planning control it **does** include mining operations.[4]

It is quite possible in planning law for land to have a "nil" use. This may arise *e.g.* if a previous use is abandoned. (See the cases referred to *post* under the heading "Abandonment or Loss of Use Rights".)

If a use is merely a "token" use it may be regarded as not a use at all in planning terms. The Court of Appeal took this view in *Kwik Save Discount Group v. Secretary of State for Wales; Kwik Save Discount Group v. Secretary of State for the Environment.*[5] K had been granted permission to use premises as a car showroom. They granted a licence to a firm of motor dealers who moved 5 cars into the sales area (20,000 sq feet) and they were displayed there for about a month with K undertaking to bear all the other firms losses

---

[1] Section 22 (3) and (4).

[2] *See* the Town and Country Planning (Control of Advertisements) Regulations 1969 (S.I. 1969, No. 1532), as amended by S.I. 1974, No. 185.

[3] Section 290.

[4] *See* the Town and Country Planning (Minerals) Regulations 1971 (S.I. 1971, No. 756, Reg. 3).

[5] (1980) 257 E.G. 169, C.A.

or to pocket any gains. After that the licence was terminated and K began to use the premises as a retail discount store. After an enforcement notice and an unsuccessful appeal K appealed to the Court of Appeal on the basis that the change of user had been from use as a motor showroom. The Court of appeal, dismissing the appeal, held that the use as a car showroom had been token and minimal, therefore that use would be disregarded and there had been no change in fact from showroom to store, but a change from non-use to use as a discount store for which planning permission was needed.

The task of deciding whether in a particular case a "material" change has taken place is often a very difficult one. Various cases in the Courts have given some guidance on the way in which the matter should be approached. Some of these are set out below.

It must be remembered particularly, in cases of change of use, that where a use of part of any premises is changed the question of material change of use must be considered in relation to the premises as a whole. (*See* the cases under the heading "The Planning Unit"—*ante*, page 8.)

In *Johnston v. Secretary of State for the Environment*[1] 44 garages were originally used for garaging the owner's taxis. After that he let some privately either as garages or for repair work. Enforcement notices were served in respect of the latter use. It was held, dismissing his appeal, that there was justification for treating the individual garages as separate planning units, and that where three garages had been treated together as one unit (which was justifiable on the facts) an intensification of user in two of them amounted to a material change of use in the whole unit.

Similarly in *Maddern v. Secretary of State for the Environment and Thurrock Borough Council*[2] the renting and occupying separately of three buildings previously used as part of a mushroom farm, and their use for other unrelated industrial and commercial purposes created new planning

[1] (1974) 28 P. & C.R. 424, D.C.
[2] [1980] J.P.L. 676, D.C.

units[3] with nil uses, the respective changes to industrial and commercial uses constituting material changes of use.

David W. Barling v. Secretary of State for the Environment and Swale District Council[1] concerned land used for the storage of building materials. Storage had been in connection with the building of two houses, but enforcement action was taken when the storage continued in connection with a general building business. The general intensity of use had not altered but the land had been fenced off after completion of the two houses. It was held that the fencing off and independent use for commercial purposes made the land a separate planning unit[2] and there was a material change of use. It is interesting to compare this case with *Snook's Case post* p. 26.

Residential occupation

Occupation of a dwelling by several families using different parts of the dwelling does not necessarily amount to a use of the house "as two or more dwellinghouses"[3] at any rate where some accommodation is shared.[4]

Changes from one kind of residential use to another may be material. There have been several cases on this point, *e.g. Birmingham Corporation v. Minister of Housing and Local Government and Habib Ullah*[5] (a change from single family occupation to letting in parts to several families paying weekly rents), *Clarke v. Caterham and Warlingham U.D.C.*[6] (a change from single family occupation to a hotel staff hostel) and *Mornford Investments v. Minister of Housing and Local Government*[7] (a change from a students' hostel to a residential family hotel).

The Court in *Lake District Special Planning Board v.*

---

[1] [1980] J.P.L. 594, D.C.
[2] As to the term "Planning Unit" see *ante* p. 8 *et seq*.
[3] *See ante*, p. 22, as to the statutory provision about such a use.
[4] *Ealing Corporation v. Ryan* [1965] 2 W.L.R. 223.
[5] [1963] 3 W.L.R. 937.
[6] (1966) 198 E.G. 583, D.C.
[7] [1970] 2 All E.R. 253, D.C.

Secretary of State for the Environment[1] held that where a building is converted from some other purpose to use for residential purposes it is **possible** for there to be a change of use for planning purposes even though no **actual** residential use has been commenced.

There is a sufficient difference between bed-sitting room units and a hotel to constitute a material change of use. *See Mayflower Cambridge v. Secretary of State for the Environment*,[2] referred to *post*, page 121.

In *Blackpool Borough Council v. Secretary of State for the Environment*[3] the Divisional Court held that the Secretary of State was entitled to conclude on the facts that there had been no material change in the use of a house where an owner at a seaside resort allowed use by himself and his family, members of his office staff and "family groups" paying rent. Lettings were for nearly half the four month holiday season. An Enforcement Notice had alleged a change of use to lettings on a commercial scale, the Secretary of State had allowed an appeal and the Planning Authority had appealed to the Divisional Court.

Seasonal uses

Where there are normally two "seasonal" uses, *e.g.* camping in summer and agriculture in winter, the change from one to the other from time to time each season is not a material change of use.[4]

Use and occupation

It is the character of the use of **the land** which has to be considered and not the particular purpose of a particular occupier.[5]

A decision of the Divisional Court highlights this point.

---

[1] [1981] J.P.L. 363, D.C.
[2] (1975) 30 P. & C.R. 28, D.C.
[3] (1980) 40 P. & C.R. 104, D.C.
[4] *See Webber v. Minister of Housing and Local Government* [1967] 3 All E.R. 981, C.A.
[5] *See East Barnet v. British Transport Commission, supra.*

Lewis v. Secretary of State for the Environment and Another[1] concerned an appeal against a decision of the Secretary of State to uphold an enforcement notice. The owner of farm land had, since 1962, used buildings for maintenance of and repairs to vehicles belonging to businesses he owned. Men were permanently employed for this purpose. In 1968 he sold the property to L and the buildings were then used for repair of vehicles belonging to members of the public. An enforcement notice alleging a material change in 1968 was served in 1970. Lord Widgery, C.J., giving the judgment of the Court, said that the change from repair of vehicles from one source connected with the occupier of the land to repair of vehicles of the public was *not* in law a material change. The actual activity was identical and this being so a change in the identity of the occupier could not affect the position. The Secretary of State had erred in law and the matter was remitted for rehearing.

Similarly in *Snook v. Secretary of State for the Environment*[2] the Divisional Court held that it was the character of the use which had to be considered in deciding whether there was a material change and that the purpose of the occupier concerning that use was not relevant. In that case land was used for storage of builders materials from 1951 to 1969. Most of the materials were new. The occupier during that period was a builder who used most of the stored materials elsewhere in the course of his business, but about a quarter of the materials were sold. In 1969 the site was acquired by the appellant, who was a demolition contractor. He used the site for the storage of the same kinds of materials but in his case used only a very small proportion of the materials himself and sold the rest. An enforcement notice alleged a material change of use in 1969. On appeal the Inspector found that there had been no material change, but the Secretary of State took a different view, holding that the change was from a composite use as a builders yard including some storage, some manufacturing and ancilliary sales, to a primarily sales use and that this was material. On

---

[1] (1971) 23 P. & C.R. 125, D.C.
[2] (1977) 33 P. & C.R. 1, D.C.

appeal to the Divisional Court it was held that the Secretary of State was in error and the matter was remitted to him for reconsideration. Reference was made in that case to the *Lewis Case* cited above. Dealing with the question of whether the change in proportions of the different activities on the site amounted to a material change Bridge J. (as he then was) agreed with the view the Inspector had taken that the means of disposal of materials after they had left the site was of little importance (his Lordship thought no importance) in land use terms, and decided that, the off site sales being excluded from consideration, there was no material in the inspectors report which could justify the conclusion reached by the Secretary of State. Eveleigh, J. and Lord Widgery, C.J. agreed.

Part-time uses

A change from part-time to a full-time occupation **may** be a material change, but such a change is not **of itself** a material change.[1]

Business conducted from a house

A type of case met with in practice quite often is illustrated by *Cook v. Secretary of State for Wales*.[2] Here, a taxi business, comprising the running of three taxis, operated from a rank in a town. C, the owner, used his private residence, a typical semi-detached house, to do the firm's paper work and his home address and telephone number were in the telephone directory under the name of the taxi business. There was no other sign of business use of the house. It was held that there was evidence on which the Minister could find a material change of use and an enforcement notice was upheld.

Ancillary uses

If in fact a use is ancillary or incidental to some other use which is the main use, the ancillary or incidental use does

---

[1] *See Peake v. Secretary of State for Wales* (1971) 22 P. & C.R. 889, the facts of which are set out *post*, p. 56.

[2] (1971) 220 E.G. 1433, D.C.

not require planning permission. In practice, however, it may be difficult to determine which is the "ancillary" and which is the "main" use. The cases afford some guidance on questions arising in connection with ancillary uses.

In deciding the question whether a use is incidental to the running of a retail shop, the requirements of particular localities or particular customers is not a factor to be considered. Regard must be had to the retail trade generally. This was decided in *Hussain v. Secretary of State for the Environment.*[1] The appellants bought a greengrocery, meat and poultry shop and in order to cater for the local Muslim community kept there live chickens which were slaughtered there according to the Muslim ritual. An enforcement notice having been served, the appellants contended that the keeping and slaughtering of chickens was ordinarily incidental to the running of the food shop. It was held that the question was whether the use was ordinarily incidental to the retail trade generally, and in this case it was not.

Where a former incidental use of land becomes the main use, this may be a material change of use of the land. In *Alexandra Transport Co. v. Secretary of State for Scotland*[2] (a Scottish case), the appellants owned land in respect of which there was planning permission for quarrying, subject to conditions about back-filling excavated areas with all waste materials. A new planning permission was obtained for the land to be used for tipping refuse brought in from outside and quarrying was to cease. There was an appeal against an assessment to betterment levy, which was dismissed, it being held that the previous tipping was only incidental to the primary use of the land which was quarrying, and accordingly the use of the land had been materially changed.

Where an ancillary use becomes the main use, there may be a material change of use justifying an enforcement notice **which prevents even the previous ancillary use**. This was held to be the case in *Jones v. Secretary of State for the*

---

[1] (1971) 23 P. & C.R. 330, D.C.
[2] (1973) 27 P. & C.R. 352, Ct. of Session (Second Division).

Environment.[1] From 1941 a site was used for a road haulage business. In the 1950s trailers for use in connection with the business were manufactured on the land. By 1966, the road haulage business had ceased and the main use was manufacturing trailers for outside sales. An enforcement notice was upheld on appeal to the Secretary of State. On appeal to the Divisional Court, the appellants contended that the effect of the notice was to prevent the manufacture of trailers even to the limited extent previously undertaken before 1966. Held, dismissing the appeal that as there had been a material change of use the enforcement notice was a valid notice and that the Secretary of State was not required to give any protection to the ancillary use.[2]

More than one use

Where land is used for two separate purposes the mere cessation of one of these uses does not amount to a material change, but if one use then spreads to the whole site in exclusion of the second use the question of whether this is a material change of use of the site is one of fact and degree.[3]

In *Hartley v. Minister of Housing and Local Government*,[4] Ashworth, J. set out four principles:—

(1) If the sole use to which land is put is suspended and thereafter resumed without there having been any intervening different user, *prima facie* the resumption does not constitute development.

(2) There may be cases in which the period of suspension is so long that the original use can properly be described as having been abandoned.

(3) If land is put to more than one use, usually referred to as a composite use, the cessation of one of the uses does not of itself constitute development.

(4) If one of two or more composite uses is dis-

[1] (1974) 28 P. & C.R. 362, D.C.

[2] But see the *Mansi Case* and others referred to *post*, p. 115.

[3] *See Wipperman and Buckingham v. London Borough of Barking* (1965) 130 J.P. 103, D.C.

[4] (1968) 118 New L.J. 1197.

> continued and thereafter resumed, the question of whether such resumption constitutes development is a question of fact to be determined in the light of all the relevant circumstances.

The *Hartley Case* went to the Court of Appeal[1] who affirmed the decision of the Divisional Court, deciding that where there has been a cessation for a considerable period of a previous use of land, with no evidence of an intention that it shall be resumed at any particular time, a tribunal of fact is entitled to find that the previous use has been abandoned.

In that case, from 1961 to 1965, land had been used as a petrol station, although a previous use included display and sale of cars. The property changed hands in 1965, when sale of cars re-started. An enforcement notice had been served in 1967 and upheld by the Minister, on the basis that resumption of the car sale use was a material change of use requiring planning permission, there having been abandonment of that use in 1961. *See also Brooks v. Gloucestershire County Council*, the facts of which are set out *ante*, p. 14.

Intensification

Difficult questions arise when the change is merely one of **degree** of an existing use.

Intensification of an existing use **may** amount to a material change,[2] but whether it is such or not in a particular case will be a question of fact.

In *Glamorgan County Council v. Carter*[3] Salmon, J., doubted whether intensification of use of a caravan site could ever be a material change of use, but the judgments of Lord Denning, M.R. and Davies, L.J. in *James v. Minister of Housing and Local Government*,[4] indicated an opposite view.

---

[1] [1970] 1 Q.B. 413.

[2] *See* dictum of Lord Evershed, M.R., in *Guildford R.D.C. v. Penny* [1959] 2 Q.B. 112. *See also East Barnet U.D.C. v. British Transport Commission, supra.*

[3] [1963] 1 W.L.R. 1.

[4] [1965] 3 All E.R. 602, C.A.

See also Peake v. Secretary of State for Wales, the facts of which are set out *ante*, page 56.

In *Brooks & Burton Ltd. supra*[1] the Court of Appeal had no doubt that intensification of use could be a material change of use. Whether it was or not depended upon the degree of intensification.[2]

The use of the term **Intensification** in planning matters is perhaps unfortunate and can lead to error. This difficulty has been judicially recognised. During the course of his judgment in *Royal Borough of Kensington and Chelsea v. Secretary of State for the Environment and Mia Carla Ltd.*[3] Donaldson, L.J. pointed out that the word intensification in ordinary language meant "more of the same thing or possibly a denser composition of the same thing" but in planning language it "had a wholly different meaning"—"a change to something different". His lordship went on to say that the word intensification had to be used "with very considerable circumspection" and that it had to be clearly understood by all concerned that intensification which did not amount to a material change of use was **merely** intensification and not a breach of planning control. The Learned Judge also expressed the view (*obiter*) that if it was not possible to formulate what was the use after intensification and what was the use before **intensification** (there being a difference between the two) then there had been no material change of use.

Abandonment or loss of Use Rights

There are two types of case where the question arises of whether a use which has previously existed has been abandoned or has ceased to be exercisable, so that to return to it again may amount to a material change of use and so constitute development. The first type consists of a mere **cessation** either for a shorter or longer period. The second consists of the **taking of positive steps** by way of carrying out some fresh development.

---

[1] P. 5 footnote 6 *ante*.
[2] See the judgment of Lawton L.J. delivering the judgment of the Court.
[3] [1981] J.P.L. 50, D.C.

Hartley's Case (*see ante*, page 29) sets out some principles to be observed in certain cases.

Grillo v. Minister of Housing and Local Government[1] affords another illustration of the same point. There had been industrial user of premises up to 1958. For six years from that date the appellant had been unable to use or dispose of the land for that purpose, and meantime he had utilised it for storage. He recommenced industrial use in 1964 and, an enforcement notice having been served and an appeal to the Minister dismissed, he appealed to the Divisional Court. His appeal was dismissed, it being held that a change of use had occurred in 1964 and the appellant could not argue that the industrial use had notionally continued in his mind, when in fact a different use had supervened.

Prossor v. Minister of Housing and Local Government[2] concerned a planning permission for rebuilding of a petrol station, to which had been attached a condition that there should be no retail sales on the site,other than of motor accessories. The permission was exercised and the station accordingly rebuilt. The appellant (who had taken a lease of the premises) displayed second hand cars for sale and was served with an enforcement notice alleging non-compliance with the condition. He appealed, claiming existing use rights for the sale of cars. After the subsequent inquiry the inspector concluded that there were in fact no such existing use rights. The Minister accepted this finding but decided that in any event there had been a breach of the condition, which he considered to be binding, and he upheld the enforcement notice. An appeal to the Divisional Court was dismissed, it being held that even if the appellant could have established that there was an existing use right as he claimed, he was, by reason of having exercised the permission, bound by the condition attached to it, and the enforcement notice was rightly upheld.

Lord Parker, C.J., in the course of his judgment (with which the other Members of the Court agreed) said "As-

---

[1] (1968) 208 E.G. 1201, D.C.
[2] (1968) 67 L.G.R. 109, D.C.

suming therefore, everything in (the appellant's) favour, assuming that there was at all material times prior to April 1964 an existing use right running on this land for the display and sale of motor cars, yet by adopting the permission granted in April 1964, the appellant's predecessor . . . gave up any possible existing use rights in this regard which he may have had. The planning history of the site as it were seems to me to begin afresh on April 4th 1964 with the grant of this permission, a permission which was taken up and used".

The decision in *Prossor's Case* was applied in *Petticoat Lane Rentals v. Minister of Housing and Local Government.*[1] A bombed site was used by stallholders for street trading. Later, pursuant to a planning permission, a building covering the whole site was erected, part of it being supported on pillars. The ground floor, which was hard surfaced and open at the sides, and generally used for car parking and loading of vehicles, could, by the specific terms of the planning consent, be used for market trading on Sundays. After the building was erected it was used for market trading on weekdays as well, and an enforcement notice was served requiring the discontinuance of the weekday trading. The Minister upheld the notice on appeal. On appeal to the Divisional Court the Court held that the original market trading use had been extinguished by the planning permission acted upon. Development of a clear area of land by erection of a building over its whole area amounted to the coming into existence of a new planning unit,[2] with no planning history and a *nil* use. **Any** use of it after completion was a change of use and if that use was not authorised by planning permission it could be restrained by planning control. Lord Parker, C.J., and Bridge, J., reserved for future consideration the question as to what the position would be if part only of a site were redeveloped by being covered by a building.

Prossor's Case had been referred to in the Court of Appeal in *Gray v. Minister of Housing and Local*

---

[1] [1971] 2 All E.R. 793.
[2] As to the "planning unit" see *ante*, p. 8.

Government[1] and in the course of his judgment in the *Petticoat Lane Rentals Case*, Widgery, L.J. (as he then was) referred to this fact and to observations upon *Prossor's Case* made in the Court of Appeal by Lord Denning, M.R., and Winn, L.J. Lord Denning, M.R., had said "The recent case of *Prossor v. Minister of Housing and Local Government* supports that point of view" (that existing use rights would be lost by an inconsistent and later planning permission). The Master of the Rolls continued "I would not throw the slightest doubt on that decision, but it is unnecessary to go into it today". However, although Winn, L.J., in *Gray's Case* adopted the same reasoning as the Master of the Rolls in his conclusion in that case he had expressed doubts as to the correctness of the *Prossor* decision. After referring to these two sets of observations on *Prossor's Case*. Widgery, L.J., went on to say "For my part I also think that it (*Prossor's Case*)was entirely correctly decided, but I think in extending and applying it we should tread warily and allow our experience to guide us as that experience is obtained". As earlier indicated all three Members of the Court had no doubt that the principle of *Prossor's Case* applied where a clear area of land was developed by the erection of a building over the whole of that land.

The facts of *Gray v. Minister of Housing and Local Government*[2] were as follows.

Premises originally used as a cafeteria became by 1957 predominantly used as an amusement arcade. In June 1960 an enforcement notice in respect of the latter use was served and later upheld on appeal to magistrates (to whom the right of appeal at that time lay). In August 1960 the Minister granted temporary permission for the amusement arcade, to expire on 31st December 1963 (later extended to 11th June 1965). Early in 1965, before that temporary permission expired the building was burned down. In March 1967 permission was granted to develop the site by erecting a building to be used as a cafeteria, on condition that the use

[1] (1968) 208 E.G. 1201, D.C.
[2] (1968) 208 E.G. 1201, D.C.

should be confined to Class I of the Use Classes Order (which excluded use as an amusement arcade). After the building was erected it was again used as an amusement arcade. Appeals against enforcement notices based on a material change of use without permission and breach of the condition on the permission were dismissed by the Minister and the Divisional Court. On appeal to the Court of Appeal it was contended that by 1960 existing use rights had been acquired and that they were not lost by the permission or by the destruction of the building. The appeal failed on the ground that the appellants had failed to prove any "four year"[1] use as an amusement arcade prior to 10th June 1960 (the date of the first enforcement notice) or August 1960 (the date of grant of the temporary permission) and so had not established that they had ever in fact acquired any "existing use" rights at all. The Court did not therefore in that case find it necessary to rule on the correctness of the decision in *Prossor's Case*.

The line of cases just mentioned was reviewed by the House of Lords in the *Newbury Case* (for the facts of which see *post*, p. 78). Among the questions the House was considering was whether the implementation of a planning permission estopped the appellants from relying on existing use rights (which the House held it did not). In the Court of Appeal Lord Denning, M.R. had held to the contrary (although not supported by the other Lords Justices), and this was what led to a review of the cases in question.

In the course of his judgment Viscount Dilhorne pointed out that there were a number of cases, of which *Mounsdon v. Weymouth and Melcombe Regis Borough Council*[2] was one, in which it had been decided that a grant of planning permission did not prevent it being subsequently contended that no such permission was necessary on account of existing use rights and he did not think *Prossor* was sustainable on the basis that the obtaining and taking up of planning permission in itself prevented reliance on such rights. However,

[1] As to the "four year" rule see *post*, p. 134.

[2] [1960] 1 Q.B. 645.

he went on to say that if planning permission (whether to build or for a change of use) was of such a character that its implementation led to the **creation of a new planning unit**[1] then he thought that it was right to say that existing use rights attaching to the former planning unit were extinguished. It might be that in the *Prossor case* the erection of a new building created a new planning unit. If it did, (and his Lordship considered it was not very clear from the report) then in his view that case was rightly decided. In the instant case His Lordship decided that the planning permission did not create a new planning unit. All their Lordships in the *Newbury Case*, (Lord Edmund Davies, Lord Fraser of Tullybelton Lord Lane and Lord Scarman) agreed with these propositions. Lord Lane put the matter thus – "The holder of planning permission will not be allowed to rely on any existing use rights if the effect of the permission when acted on has been to bring one phase of the planning history of the site to an end and to start a new one. It may not always be as easy as it was in *Petticoat Lane Rentals*, to say whether that had happened. There will no doubt be borderline cases difficult to decide, but that does not affect the principle. We were asked by counsel for the Secretary of State to say that the principle can only apply where the permission granted is to build or rebuild or the like and can never apply to cases where the permission is simply to change the use. I do not consider that any such limitation would be proper. It is not the reason for the break in planning history which is important. It is the existence of the break itself, whatever the reason for it may have been no doubt it will usually be a case of permission to build which will attract the doctrine but I myself would not altogether rule out the possibility that in some circumstances the permitted change of use might be so radical as to fulfil the criteria of *Prossor's Case*."

In *Fyson v. Bucks County Council*[2] a use for storage, discontinued before 1949 was resumed in 1956, there having

---

[1] As to the term "planning unit" see *ante*, p. 8.
[2] [1958] 1 W.L.R. 634.

been no other use in the meantime. Resumption of the use in 1956 was held not to be a material change of use.[1]

The fact that a use is discontinued and the land offered for sale does not of itself amount to abandonment of the use, the action of offering for sale being equally consistent with an intention possibly to resume the use.[2]

In *Aston v. Secretary of State for the Environment*[3] a barn used for maintenance of lorries from 1956 to 1961 was blown down in the latter year. Another barn was erected on the site in 1968. It was held that where a new building was erected one had a new planning unit with no effective planning use which destroyed existing use rights. (Section 33 (2) of the 1971 Act makes provision about the permitted use of a new building erected with planning permission. *See ante*, page 56.)

See however the judgment of the Court of Appeal in *Jennings Motors Ltd.* (*ante*, p. 10).

Ratcliff v. Secretary of State for the Environment[4] concerned abandonment of use of a quarry.

A quarry site was used as a local authority refuse tip from 1920 to 1961 when their tenancy ended. Trespassers had sporadically dumped waste materials there since 1961. Held, dismissing an appeal that the Secretary of State had correctly decided that use of the quarry as a tip had been abandoned in 1961 and that planning permission was required for further filling of the quarry, which constituted development.

This case and *Hartley* (see *ante*, p. 29) were applied in *W. F. Nicholls v. Secretary of State for the Environment and Bristol City Council*[5] a case concerning use of land for storage

---

[1] For a later case where on the facts it was held that a use for mushroom farming was abandoned after some four years discontinuance followed by letting for a different use see *Maddern v. Secretary of State for the Environment and Thurrock Borough Council* [1980] J.P.L. 676, D.C.

[2] *Grover's Executors v. Rickmansworth U.D.C.* (1959) 10 P. & C.R. 417, Lands Tribunal.

[3] (1973) 227, E.G. 325, D.C.

[4] (1975) 235, E.G. 901, D.C.

[5] The Times April 10 1981. McNeill J.

of scrap and vehicle breaking. The land had been used as a scrapyard since 1959, but this use declined from 1971 onward and by 1973 was such in the circumstances that a reasonable man might conclude that it had been abandoned. The appellant bought the land in 1977 and used the land for the same purpose. An inspector had dismissed his appeal from an enforcement notice. He unsuccessfully appealed to the Divisional Court on the basis that the inspector had failed to consider or to give proper weight to evidence that the former user of the land had no intention to abandon the use established after 1959. It was held that the question of whether or not a use has been abandoned is primarily one of fact, the conclusion reached being one which a reasonable tribunal properly directed on the law could reach, and that the question of abandonment was one of **intention** which was to be established both by direct evidence and inferred from all the surrounding circumstances, including the conduct of the owner or occupier of the land. The test of abandonment was that the circumstances must be such that a reasonable man might conclude that the use had been abandoned.

In a very recent case[1] Forbes J. held that where a material change of use was made without any period of non-use between the former and the latter use, the ordinary concept of abandonment as instanced by the *Hartley Case* (see *ante* p. 29) did not apply (the change back being itself a material change of use required planning permission) and that the concept of abandonment should not be any further extended.

In *Balco Transport Services v. Secretary of State for the Environment*[2] which concerned use as a transport haulage depot and in which on the facts a finding of abandonment was confirmed, the Court observed that generally where there was a change from a lawful to an unlawful use in respect of which an enforcement notice was served the authority could not normally say that the previous use had

[1] *Young v. Secretary of State for the Environment and Another*, The Times 14 April, 1982

[2] *The Times* June 24 1981, D.C.

thereby been abandoned, otherwise Section 23 (9) of the 1971 Act would be nugatory. (As to this section see *post*, p. 42).

In *Iddenden v. Secretary of State for the Environment*[1] Buckley, L.J., expressed (*obiter*) some views about loss of existing use rights by demolition of buildings, indicating that if the applicants had lost an established use attached to the buildings they pulled down and were thereby worse off, they could only blame themselves and not the planning authority.

Where there are two planning permissions for the same land they cannot both be implemented if inconsistent with each other. It is not the duty of the planning authority to relate one application to another. Each must be considered on its merits.[2]

DETERMINATION AS TO DEVELOPMENT

Under section 53 of the 1971 Act, (as amended) any person who **proposes** to carry out any operations on land or to make any change in the use of land wishes to have it determined whether the carrying out of those operations, or the making of that change would constitute or involve development of the land, and, if so, whether an application for planning permission in respect of it is required under the Act, having regard to the provisions of the development order[3] and of any enterprise zone scheme[4] he may, either as part of an application for planning permission, or without any such application, apply to the local planning authority to determine that question. There is a right of appeal to the Secretary of State against any determination of the local planning authority. The application and the determination must be in writing.[5]

---

[1] [1972] 3 All E.R. 883, C.A.

[2] *See Pilkington v. Secretary of State for the Environment* [1973] 1 W.L.R. 1527, D.C.

[3] As to development orders, *see post*, p. 45.

[4] As to enterprise zone schemes and planning permission granted thereby see *post*, p. 55.

[5] *See* the Town and Country Planning General Development Order 1977 (S.I. 1977, No. 289) (as amended).

An application for a determination can only be made in respect of something yet to be done. It can not be made in respect of operations started or uses begun.

There may be an effective determination under section 53 even though an applicant has not expressly requested such a determination.[1]

In *English-Speaking Union of the Commonwealth v. City of Westminster Council*[2] the Council confirmed, in reply to a letter from the plaintiffs, that planning permission was not required for a certain change of use. Subsequently the plaintiffs entered into an agreement with a third party to lease the premises in question. Later, the Council wrote that the position had altered and that planning permission was necessary. The Court held that the council's original letter was a determination under section 53 though no formal application for one had been made.

---

[1] *See Wells v. Minister of Housing and Local Government* [1967] 2 All E.R. 1041, C.A.

[2] (1973) 226 E.G. 1963.

Chapter 2

PLANNING PERMISSION

WHEN IS PLANNING PERMISSION REQUIRED FOR DEVELOPMENT

When required

Subject to what is said below, planning permission is required[1] and is required **only** for the carrying out of any development of land after 1st July 1948.[2]

When not required

In subsections (2) to (10) of section 13 of the 1962 Act, planning permission[3] was expressly stated **not** to be required in certain cases, but these provisions were modified by section 75 of the 1968 Act. The latter section came into force on *6th December* 1968.[4] The effect of the provisions, now contained in section 23 of the 1971 Act, is as follows:—

(1) Where on the 1st July 1948,[5] land was being used temporarily for a purpose other than the normal purpose, planning permission is not required for the resumption of the "normal" use, provided the resumption took place before the *6th December* 1968.

(2) Where on the 1st July 1948[6] land was normally used for a particular purpose but was also used occa-

---

[1] Section 23 (1).
[2] The appointed day under the Act of 1947.
[3] *See post* as to obtaining such permission.
[4] *See* the Town and Country Planning Act 1968 (Commencement No. 1) Order 1968 (S.I. 1968, No. 1908 (C. 25)).
[5] The appointed day under the Act of 1947.
[6] The appointed day under the Act of 1947.

sionally (whether or not at regular intervals) for some other purpose, planning permission is not required for the future occasional use of the land for the same purposes, but the resumption of any such occasional use on or after the *6th December* 1968 is exempt from the requirement of planning permission only if the land was since the 1st July 1948 used for the "occasional" purpose on at least one similar occasion before the beginning of 1968.

(3) Where land was unoccupied on the 1st July 1948, but had before then been occupied at some time on or after the 7th January 1937, planning permission is not required in respect of its use for the purpose for which it was last used before the 1st July, 1948, provided that that use was begun before the *6th December* 1968.

(4) Where planning permission to develop land has been granted for a limited period[1] planning permission is not required for the resumption at the end of that period of the normal use before the permission was granted.

(5) Where by a development order[2] planning permission to develop land has been granted subject to limitations, planning permission is not required for the "normal" use of the land.

(6) Where an enforcement notice has been served in respect of any development of land, planning permission is not required for the resumption of any **lawful use** to which the land was put before the unauthorised development was carried out.

Where land is used in a manner requiring planning permission and no planning permission is obtained (unless the use began before 1948) that use remains **unlawful** for the purpose of this provision even though it is continued for a sufficient time to acquire immunity from enforcement pro-

---

[1] *See post* page 48.
[2] *See post* page 45.

ceedings. *LTSS Print and Supply Services v. Hackney London Borough Council.*[1]

In cases (4) and (5) above, in determining the "normal" use of land no account is to be taken of any use begun in contravention of Part III of the 1971 Act (which relates to planning control), or in contravention of previous planning control (*i.e.* of Part III of the 1947 Act or Part III of the 1962 Act).

In cases (1), (2) and (3) use of land as a caravan site[2] is not to be treated as a use for which planning permission is not required unless the land was so used on one occasion at least during the two years ending with the 9th March 1960.[3]

Determination whether required

It is possible to make an application to the Local Planning Authority for a formal determination as to whether planning permission is required for proposed works or uses (see *ante*, p. 39).

HOW PLANNING PERMISSION IS GRANTED

Planning permission under Part III of the Act of 1971 may be granted:—

(i) By the Planning Acts themselves.

(ii) By a Development Order.

(iii) By a Local Planning Authority.[4]

(iv) By the Secretary of State otherwise than by a Development Order.

---

[1] [1976] 1 All E.R. 311, C.A., reversing [1975] 1 All E.R. 374, D.C., and overruling *W. T. Lamb & Sons v. Secretary of State for the Environment* [1975] 2 All E.R. 1117, D.C. As to immunity from enforcement, *see post*, page 130.

[2] *I.e.*, land on which a caravan is stationed for the purpose of human habitation and land which is used in conjunction with land on which a caravan is so stationed. *See* s. 290, 1971 Act, and s. 1 (4) of the Caravan Sites and Control of Development Act 1960.

[3] Section 23 (7). This provision was formerly contained in s. 21 of the Caravan Sites and Control of Development Act 1960.

[4] Or by someone to whom they have delegated power. *See* p. 47, *post*.

(v) By a person appointed by the Secretary of State.

(vi) By an Enterprise Zone Scheme.

Permission by the Planning Acts

The 1971 Act provides that permission is **deemed to be granted** in respect of the following development:—

(1) the display of advertisements which comply with the regulations made under section 63 of the Act[1];

(2) certain development by local authorities and statutory undertakers under the authorisation of a Government Department[2];

(3) development authorised between 22nd July 1943 and 30th June 1948, on an application under an interim development order[3];

(4) completion of works for the erection or alteration of a building which were begun, but not completed, before 1st July 1948, provided that such completion could have been effected in conformity with the provisions of any planning scheme or permission granted thereunder, or with permission granted by or under an interim development order.[4]

The provision does not apply in cases (3) and (4) unless any consent which was before 1st July 1948, required under the Restriction of Ribbon Development Act 1935, was in fact granted.

The 1981 Act provides for a deemed grant of planning permission in certain limited cases where an Enforcement Notice is complied with (see *post*, p. 113).

---

[1] Section 64. *See* the Town and Country Planning (Control of Advertisements) Regulations 1969 (S.I. 1969, No. 1532). See also Chapter 10 *post*.

[2] Section 40.

[3] Schedule 24, para. 90.

[4] Schedule 24, para. 91.

Permission by Development Order

The Secretary of State has power under section 24 of the Act to grant planning permission for development by means of a Development Order applying generally to all land or specially to land specified therein.[1] An amendment of section 24 effected by section 90 and schedule of the Local Government Planning and Land Act, 1980 extends this to allow areas of land to be dealt with as a class rather than by precise identification. By the Town and Country Planning General Development Order 1977[2] (replacing earlier Orders), permission is granted for many classes of development. In this respect the key provisions of the Order are Article 3 and Schedule 1. Reference should be made in particular to the latter where the full terms of the provisions granted are set out. The order applies to all land in England and Wales, subject to any modifications which may be specified in any special order relating to particular land. The local planning authority may, under Article 4 of the Order, make directions, subject in most cases[3] to confirmation by the Secretary of State excluding the application of the Order in any particular area or in relation to any particular development, but such directions can only apply to development not yet carried out.[4]

Article 3 of the Order provides that the permission granted for the development specified in the Order shall not operate "so as to permit any development contrary to a condition imposed in any permission granted or deemed to be granted under Part III of the Act otherwise than by this Order". An application for, or conditional grant of, planning permission when in fact permission has already been given by the General Development Order does not prejudice the developer.[5]

---

[1] A number of Special Orders have been made applying *e.g.*, to New Towns and certain areas of Special Landscape Value.

[2] S.I. 1977, No. 289. Amended by S.I. 1977 No. 1781, S.I. 1980, No. 1946 and S.I. 1981, No. 245.

[3] See Article 4 (3) for directions not requiring such confirmation.

[4] *Cole v. Somerset County Council* [1957] 1 Q.B. 23.

[5] *East Barnet U.D.C. v. British Transport Commission (supra)* applying *Mounsdon v. Weymouth and Melcombe Regis Corporation* [1960] 1 Q.B. 645. See also *Newbury District Council v. Secretary of State for the Environment* [1980] 2 W.C.R. 379, H.L. and *ante*, p. 35.

Permission by the Local Planning Authority

Meaning of Local Planning Authority

Local Planning Authority is a term which may mean one of several types of authority, but in most cases for the purpose of obtaining planning permission it will be the **District Council** or, in London, the **London Borough Council** for the area concerned.

The Local Government Planning and Land Act 1980 contains powers[1] enabling the Secretary of State, for the purpose of regenerating an urban development area, to establish what is to be called an **urban development corporation** for any area.

He may,[2] if he is of opinion that it is expedient in the national interest to do so, by statutory instrument designate as an **urban development area** any land in England which is in a metropolitan district or in, or partly in, an Inner London Borough. He must then[2] (also by statutory instrument) for the purpose of regenerating such urban development area, establish an **urban development corporation** for that area, and that instrument may, subject to its terms, provide that the corporation shall be the local planning authority for specified purposes including general planning control.

The Secretary of State has power under section 1 (2) of the 1971 Act by order to set up **joint planning boards** for the areas or parts of the areas of two or more county councils, or as the district planning authority for the areas or parts of the areas of two or more district councils. He must not, however, make such an order except after holding a local inquiry unless all the councils concerned have consented.

One of the innovations of the Local Government Planning and Land Act, 1980 was the concept of **Enterprise Zones**, the idea being that areas so designated would provide tem-

---

[1] Section 135.
[2] Section 134.

porary freedom from certain rates and taxes and relative freedom from some of the constraints of the planning system, thus attracting private enterprise to invest, to the economic advantage of the community. The machinery for setting up such zones is contained in Section 179 and Schedule 32 of the 1980 Act. As might be expected, initiation of a scheme is in the hands of the Secretary of State, who may[1] invite preparation of a scheme by a district council, a London borough council, a new town corporation[2] or an urban development corporation.[3] If a scheme is in fact prepared and adopted, the Secretary of State may[4] then by order designate the area to which the scheme relates as an enterprise zone. The order making power is exercisable by statutory instrument subject to annulment by either House of Parliament and only with the consent of the Treasury.[5]

Any order made must[6] specify the date the designation takes effect, define the boundaries of the zone by means of a plan or map and specify the period for which the area is to remain an enterprise zone. The period can be extended by the Secretary of State by order modifying the original order.[7]

The order may provide that the **enterprise zone authority** shall be the planning authority for the zone for such purposes of the 1971 Act and in relation to such kinds of development as the order may prescribe.[8] A modification order may alter these purposes or the kinds of development prescribed in the original order.[3]

Delegation of power

A local planning authority may delegate its functions to a committee, a sub-committee or an officer of the authority

[1] Schedule 32, para. 1.
[2] See the New Towns Act, 1965.
[3] *Supra.*
[4] Schedule 32, para. 5.
[5] *Ibid.* sub-para. (3).
[6] Schedule 32, para. 5 (4).
[7] *Ibid.* sub-para. (15).
[8] *Ibid.* sub-para. (20).

or to any other local authority.[1] It is also expressly provided[2] that unless a local authority otherwise direct, a committee may delegate to a sub-committee or to an officer and unless the authority or the committee otherwise direct, a sub-committee may in turn delegate to an officer.

Quite apart from the statutory power, administrative practice **may**, to a limited extent, amount to effective delegation.[3]

In *Norfolk County Council v. Secretary of State for the Environment*[4] a local planning authority had refused planning permission for a factory extension but by mistake their planning officer had sent a notice to the applicant stating that permission had been granted. The company ordered machinery. Two days later the council informed the applicant of the mistake and sent a refusal notice. The applicant (a company) maintained that it had permission and began work on the foundations of the factory. The council served an enforcement notice. In the meantime the company had been able to cancel its order for machinery without penalty. The Court upheld the enforcement notice, deciding that the notice by the planning officer could not give permission which the authority had refused and the council were not estopped from denying the representation of their officer because although the company had acted on the representation they had not done so to their detriment.[1]

Grant of planning permission

Planning permission may be granted by the local planning authority pursuant to an application[5] submitted by the intending developer. It may be granted subject to conditions.[6]

---

[1] Section 101, Local Government Act 1972.

[2] Section 101 (2).

[3] *See Lever Finance Ltd. v. Westminster (City) London Borough Council* 68 L.G.R. 757, C.A. referred to *post*, p. 94.

[4] [1973] 3 All E.R. 673, D.C.

[5] See the Town and Country Planning General Development Order 1977 (S.I. 1977, No. 289) as amended. A fee is payable. See the Town and Country Planning (Fees for Applications and Deemed Applications) Regulations, 1981 (S.I. 1981, No. 369), as amended by S.I. 1982 No 716 effective 1 June 1982.

[6] As to conditions see *post* p. 75.

If it is refused, or not decided within the prescribed time,[1] or if conditions are objected to there may be an appeal to the Secretary of State.[1]

The authority, in deciding whether or not to grant planning permission, must[2] have regard to the development plan and to all other material considerations.[3]

In a case in 1977[4] the Court quashed a decision of the Secretary of State because he had not acted in accordance with the policy laid down in the development plan, his decision thus being *ultra vires*. The applicant had temporary planning permission to use Mayfair premises for offices. The Council had refused its renewal and the Secretary of State upheld this refusal although evidence before the inspector showed the premises were not then economically converted to residential use and the inspector had recommended extension of permission for five years. The development plan policy permitted such extensions.

The local planning authority has power not only to grant permission for intended development but to grant permission for continuance of a use begun or for the retention of a building or works constructed or carried out before the date of the application, whether the development was without planning permission or in accordance with a limited period permission.[5]

Express power is also given to grant permission for retention of buildings or works or continuance of use of land without complying with some condition subject to which a previous planning permission was granted.[6]

In *Kent County Council v. Secretary of State for the Environment and Burmah-Total Refineries Trust* the Divisional Court held that the Secretary of State was entitled to grant

---

[1] Section 36 as amended by the Local Government Planning and Land Act, 1980, section 90 and schedule 15, para. 4 (2) and (3).

[2] Section 29.

[3] As to "material considerations" see *post*, p. 171.

[4] *Niarchos (London) v. Secretary of State for the Environment. The Times.* December 16 1977, Sir Douglas Frank Q.C.

[5] Section 32.

[6] (1976) 33 P. & C.R. 70, D.C.

permission for **part only** of the development applied for (in that case construction of part of an oil refinery).

A local planning authority cannot contract or otherwise undertake to decide planning applications in a particular way. If it purports to do so and acts accordingly any relevant planning determination is void (as is the agreement). (This will not, however, prevent the Secretary of State from dealing with a subsequent appeal.) It was so held by the High Court (Cooke, J.) in *Stringer v. Minister of Housing and Local Government and Another*,[1] a case which concerned an agreement designed to prevent development interfering with the efficient working of the Jodrell Bank radio telescope.

In the case of development consisting of building operations an intending developer may apply for, and the local planning authority may grant, an **outline planning permission** which deals with the **principle** of development of the land for the purpose in question reserving matters of detail for subsequent consideration.[2]

For an important decision on the effect of an outline planning permission for a large area developed in stages, *see R. v. Secretary of State for the Environment ex parte Percy Bilton Industrial Properties Ltd.*, the facts of which are set out *post*, page 64.

A question which has been the subject of discussion and is clearly of relevance to enforcement, is whether a planning permission is granted when the planning authority **resolve to grant** an application or when **written notice of approval** is given to the applicant. This matter was the subject of a decision of the High Court in *Regina v. Yeovil Corporation Ex parte Trustees of Elim Pentecostal Church Yeovil*[3] on an application for an order of *mandamus*. The applicants had applied to the planning authority for planning permission for a youth centre. On a date in July 1970 the planning committee resolved to authorise the town clerk to approve

[1] 68 L.G.R. 788.

[2] *See* the Town and Country Planning General Development Order 1977 (S.I. 1977, No. 289) as amended.

[3] (1971) 23 P. & C.R. 39, D.C.

the application when he received certain evidence of an agreement about car parking facilities. The applicants were accordingly informed by letter from the town clerk that there had been no final decision by the Committee because of the car parking question but that the application would be dealt with when that question was settled. Some local opposition resulted in the planning committee considering the matter again in August 1970 and they then decided to refuse the application. Notice of refusal was sent tothe applicants, who applied for an order of *mandamus* directing the authority to issue a form of planning consent in accordance with their decision on the matter in July. It was argued that, having resolved on the matter in July the authority were *functus officio* and that only a "ministerial" act by the town clerk remained to be performed when the conditions were met.

Lord Widgery, C.J., said that the proper interpretation of events in July was that there had been a delegation of powers under section 64 of the 1968 Act[1] to the town clerk. As he had not determined the application the committee could change its mind, withdraw the "approval" and refuse the application. He further decided that there was no planning permission unless and until a written notice of approval had been given to the applicants, although the authority would doubtless be *functus officio* when a written notice was sent out. No planning permission had therefore been granted to the applicants and the application for an order of *mandamus* was refused. The other members of the Court (Browne and Bridge, JJ.) agreed. This case was decided on the basis of a delegation to an officer and as the Lord Chief Justice said in the course of his judgment there was specific reference in section 64 (5) of the 1968 Act (repeated in the 1971 Act) to a delegated determination being "notified in writing to the applicant".

The Court of Appeal decided in *Co-operative Retail Services v. Taff-Ely Borough Council*[2] that the interests of the public should not be allowed to be harmed by a mistake by

[1] As to present powers of delegation, *see ante*, p. 47.
[2] (1979) 39 P. & C.R. 223, C.A.

officers of a local authority and to achieve this the Court will, if necessary, go behind a purported grant of planning permission to examine whether it was truly an effective grant.

In 1975 two large concerns, the Co-op and Tesco, had both applied for planning permission for a hypermarket on sites within a mile of each other. Contention arose, in regard to these applications, between the district council and the county council. The Tesco site was preferred by the district authority whose planning officer had recommended that permission should be granted. The county planning officer when consulted had recommended that permission for the Tesco site be refused. The district planning officer had advised his authority that a joint meeting with the county council would be necessary, and he also recommended his authority to refuse the Co-op application. The district council accordingly refused the Co-op application and adopted a recommendation of its appropriate committee that the Tesco application be granted and that the planning officer take the necessary action. The district planning officer therefore wrote to the county planning officer advising him that the district council had "resolved" to approve the Tesco application and enquiring whether his objection stood. The county Clerk informed the district clerk that the objection indeed stood and there must be a joint meeting. X Company had meanwhile contracted to buy the Tesco site subject to planning permission. The owners of that site informed the district clerk that they regarded his authority's resolution to grant permission as itself the grant of planning permission. All this time the Co-op was pressing the council not to grant planning permission for the Tesco site but to refer both applications to the Secretary of State. The Clerk of the district council then took matters into his hands and, without any consultations, sent the Tesco site owners a grant of planning permission to prevent the county council from tying the district council's hands (under para. 19 of Schedule 16 to the Local Government Act, 1972). The Tesco site was sold on the basis of that grant. Later the council purported to ratify the action of their clerk. A Deputy Judge of the

Queen's Bench Division held the grant to be valid. The Co-op appealed. Their appeal was allowed on the basis that there had been no resolution by the council to grant planning permission, only a recommendation that the planning officer take any necessary action. The permission issued by the clerk "off his own head" was a nullity and it could not be ratified. A declaration was granted that the permission was a nullity.

The defendant's further appeal to the House of Lords was dismissed.[1]

Permission by the Secretary of State otherwise than by General Development Order

The Secretary of State has power[2] to require that a particular planning application, or applications of a specified class, shall be referred to him to deal with, instead of being dealt with by the local planning authority.

He has power, also[3] to grant planning permission on appeal from the local planning authority and to grant permission in default of a decision by the local planning authority within the period prescribed for a decision.[4]

It should be noted that when the Secretary of State is deciding an application on appeal from the local planning authority he may allow or dismiss the appeal or may reverse or vary any part of the decision of the authority, whether the appeal relates to that part or not and may deal with the application as if it had been made to him in the first instance.[5]

A case in 1979 illustrates this.[6] After a deemed refusal of planning permission (on a failure of the authority to deter-

---

[1] (1981) 42 P. & C.R. 1, H.L.

[2] Section 35.

[3] Section 36, as amended by the Local Government Planning and Land Act, 1980 Section 90 and Schedule 15, para. 4 (2) and (3).

[4] Section 37. *See* the Town and Country Planning General Development Order 1977 (S.I. 1977) No. 289 (as amended). *See also Stringer v. Minister of Housing and Local Government and Another, supra.*

[5] 1971 Act Section 36 (3).

[6] *Robert Hitchins Builders v. Secretary of State for the Environment; Britannia (Cheltenham) v. Same* (1979) 251 E.G. 467, C.A.

mine the application within the prescribed period) R and B appealed to the Secretary of State. Before he dealt with the matter they had reached agreement with the planning authority that a conditional planning permission was the right decision and the conditions were submitted to the Secretary of State by the authority who invited him to allow the appeals and grant permission. The Secretary of State refused, on the basis that because the proposals did not form part of the applications for planning permission they were not matters which could properly be required by conditions on a permission pursuant to the applications. R and B appealed and won and the Secretary of State then appealed. It was held by the Court of Appeal, dismissing his appeal, that Section 36 (3) gave the Secretary of State power to deal with the planning applications as if they had been made to him in the first instance.

In *Bernard Wheatcroft v. Secretary of State for the Environment*[1] it was held that the correct test where there is an alteration of plans at the appeal stage is whether or not the development permitted is substantially the same as that for which the original application was made. It was not a question of severability. In that case BW applied for permission for 420 dwellings on 35 acres, were refused permission and on appeal put forward an alternative plan for 250 dwellings on 25 acres. The Secretary of State dismissed the appeal, saying he had no power to grant permission to build fewer dwellings at lower density on a smaller site than in the original application. On BW's application the decision was quashed as it was held the Secretary of State had misdirected himself in law. The correct test was as stated above.

Permission by a person appointed by the Secretary of State

Under provisions of the 1971 Act re-enacting those in Part III of the 1968 Act certain prescribed[2] classes of appeals from the local planning authority may be determined by a

---

[1] (1980) 257 E.G. 934, Forbes J.

[2] See the Town and Country Planning (Determination of Appeals by Appointed Persons) (Prescribed Classes) Regulations 1981 (S.I. No. 804) replacing earlier Regulations.

person appointed by the Secretary of State (the Inspector) instead of by the Secretary of State himself and such a person may grant planning permission on an appeal.[1]

Permission by Enterprise Zone Scheme[2]

An order designating an Enterprise Zone[4] under the Local Government Planning and Land Act 1980 has the effect of granting planning permission for any development or class of development specified in the scheme.[3] Similarly approval of a modified enterprise zone scheme grants planning permission for development or any class of development specified in the modified scheme.[5]

The enterprise zone authority may[4] however, provided they have obtained the approval of the Secretary of State,[5] direct that any such planning permission granted shall not apply in relation to a specified development, or class of development or to a specified class of development in a specified area within the zone.

The planning permissions granted by an enterprise zone scheme do not however prevent other planning permissions being granted in the normal way in relation to land in the zone, under the 1971 Act, either on an application or under a development order.[6] Any rights to carry out development by a previous planning permission are also unaffected by an enterprise zone scheme.[7]

OPERATION OF PLANNING PERMISSION

Any grant of planning permission to develop land **except in so far as the permission otherwise provides** operates for the benefit of the land and every person who has an interest

---

[1] See schedule 9 1971 Act.

[2] As to setting up of an Enterprise Zone see *ante*, p. 46.

[3] Local Government Planning and Land Act 1980, Section 179 and Schedule 32 para. 17 (2) and (3).

[4] Schedule 32, para. 17 (4).

[5] *Ibid*. para. 17 (5).

[6] *Ibid*. para. 17 (7). As to such permissions see pp. 45 and 46 *post*.

[7] *Ibid*. para. 17 (8).

in it.[1] It is clear that it is open to the local planning authority to grant permission restricted to a particular individual, although this is done in few cases.

Where planning permission is granted for erection of a building the permission may specify the purposes for which the building may be used, but if it does not, the permission is to be construed as "including permission to use the building for the purpose for which it is designed".[1]

It was decided in *Trinder v. Sevenoaks R.D.C.*[2] that the meaning of these words is that the permission in such a case is **limited** to use for the purpose for which the building is designed.

The "purpose for which the building is designed" includes ancillary or incidental purposes, but if use for such purposes ceases to be truly incidental to the design purpose, *e.g.* by intensification, it may amount to a material change of use, requiring a new planning permission, and this will be so irrespective of whether or not the building has ever in fact been put to the use for which it was designed.

In *Peake v. Secretary of State for Wales*[3] a private garage was built in 1960 and from that time until 1968 was used by the owner in his spare time to repair other people's cars (for payment). The garage was never used to house the owner's car. In 1968, having lost his job, the owner began to use the building for full time repair and maintenance work. An enforcement notice was served and an appeal dismissed on the basis that in 1968 there had been a material change of use, the pre-1968 use being merely incidental to the designed use as a private garage. The owner appealed to the Divisional Court, contending that since he had never used the garage for his car this finding was bad. The Court held that although a change from part-time to full-time use did not of itself amount to a material change, the Secretary of State might properly as a matter of fact and degree reach the conclusion he had done.

---

[1] Section 33.
[2] (1967) 204 E.G. 803.
[3] (1971) 22 P. & C.R. 889, D.C.

Section 30 (3) of the 1971 Act provides that where it is a condition of permission for **building or other operations** that they shall be commenced within a specified period, development after the time specified does not constitute development for which permission was granted, but this subsection does not operate in a case covered by sections 41 or 42 of the 1971 Act, discussed *post.*[1]

Life of Planning Permission

The 1968 Act imposed statutory time limits on most planning permissions for **all** kinds of development, **including material changes of use**.

Section 65 provided that, with certain exceptions, every Planning Permission granted or deemed to have been granted[2] before 1st April 1969[3] was, **if the development to which it related had not been begun before the beginning of 1968** deemed to have been granted subject to a condition that the development in question must be *begun* not later than the expiration of five years beginning with 1st April 1969.[3]

This provision is saved by section 292 and paragraph 19 of Schedule 24 of the 1971 Act. (As to calculation of the period in certain circumstances relating to office development in the metropolitan region, *see* paragraph 20A of Schedule 24, inserted by section 5 (2) of the Town and Country Planning (Amendment) Act 1972.)

The effect of section 41 of the 1971 Act and the saving provisions of Schedule 24 of that Act is as follows:—

Imp * Every Planning Permission granted or deemed to be granted[4] **after** the 1st April 1969[5] must be granted subject to the condition that the development to which it relates must be begun not later than (*a*) the expiration of five years beginning with the date on which the permission is granted

---

[1] *See* s. 43 (7) 1971 Act.
[2] As to deemed permissions, *see* p. 44, *ante*.
[3] The date of commencement of the section. *See* S.I. 1969, No. 275.
[4] As to deemed permissions, *see* p. 44, *ante*.
[5] The date of commencement of the section. *See* S.I. 1969, No. 275.

or deemed to be granted[1] or (*b*) the expiration of such other period beginning with the date of the grant of permission as the authority concerned with the terms of the Planning Permission[1] direct. (This may be longer or shorter than 5 years.) In fixing such a period they must have regard to the provisions of the Development Plan and to any other material considerations. If permission is granted without the required condition it is **deemed** to have been granted subject to a condition in the terms of (*a*) above.

The date on which development is to be taken to have begun is the earliest date on which any specified operation comprised in the development begins to be carried out. "Specified operation" means[2] any of the following:—

(*a*) any work of construction in the course of the erection of a building;

(*b*) the digging of a trench which is to contain the foundations, or part of the foundations, of a building;

(*c*) the laying of any underground main or pipe to the foundations, or part of the foundations, of a building or to any such trench as is mentioned in the last preceding paragraph;

(*d*) any operation in the course of laying out[3] or constructing a road or part of a road;

(*e*) any change in the use of any land, where that change constitutes material development.[4]

As to **commencement** the case of *United Refineries v. Essex County Council*[5] affords a useful guide. On a planning permission for a scheme costing £15,000,000, there was a requirement that work was to start by 1st January 1969. The question arose of whether work of stripping topsoil and

[1] See *ante*, p. 44.
[2] *See* Section 43.
[3] As to 'laying out' see *Malvern Hills District Council v Secretary of State* (1982) 262 E.G., 1190, C.A.
[4] For the meaning of "material development", *see* s. 43 (3) and Schedule 24, para. 22, 1971 Act.
[5] (1976) 241 E.G. 389, Fox, J.

making a temporary access road, costing about £30,000, amounted to "commencement" of the works. The county council argued that it did not, being either de minimis, or by its nature being preliminary in nature and not amounting to commencement of the works which were the subject of the permission. It was held that as permission had been given for these items of work, which were necessary steps in the whole, work **had** been commenced by the required date.

The operation of the period fixed for commencement cannot be postponed or made to depend on a contingency. The Court of Appeal so held in *L. A. H. Ames v. North Bedfordshire Borough Council.*[1] The appellant had entered into an agreement with the local planning authority under Section 52 of the 1971 Act not to begin his development until sewage works which would serve the development were put in contract. His planning permission (issued immediately after the agreement) required development to commence within 3 years from the date of the permission. By the end of that time the sewage works had not been contracted for. The appellant argued that his permission should come into effect only from the date of the sewage works contract. He claimed declarations to that effect, losing at first instance and again losing on appeal

The result of these provisions in a particular case will be that if the development is not begun within the specified period but is carried out thereafter there will be a breach of planning control and those responsible will be liable to enforcement action.

There are certain permissions to which these statutory conditions do **not**[2] apply. These are as follows:

(*a*) An outline Planning Permission[3] (but this is subject to certain other conditions) (*see post*)).

---

[1] (1979) 253 E.G. 55, C.A.

[2] See section 41 (3) as amended by the Local Government Planning and Land Act 1980, section 179 and schedule 32, para. 18 (1) and by the Town and Country Planning (Minerals) Act 1981 effective from 22 February, 1982. See S.I. 1982/86 (C.4). See also schedule 24 of the 1971 Act para. 19 (2).

[3] For definition, *see* p. 63.

(*b*) A Planning Permission granted by a Development Order.[1]

(*c*) A Planning Permission which was granted or deemed to be granted before the 1st April 1969 subject to an express condition that the development to which it relates should be begun or be completed not later than a specified date or within a specified period.

(*d*) A Planning Permission granted for a limited period.

(*e*) A Planning Permission granted on an application relating to a building or works completed or a use instituted before the date of the planning application.[2]

(*f*) A Planning Permission granted by an enterprise zone scheme [3] (but other provisions apply. See *post*, p. 67).

(*g*) A Planning Permission for winning or working minerals granted or deemed to be granted subject to a condition that the development must be begun before the expiration of a specified period after completion of other mining operations already being carried out by the applicant.[4]

Completion Notice

If development which is subject to **the statutory conditions** set out above is begun within the relevant period, but not completed, before the end of that period and the Local Planning Authority are of the opinion that it will not be completed within a reasonable period, it is open to them by a "**Completion Notice**" procedure, now contained in section 44 of the 1971 Act and described hereafter, to bring the permission to an end on a date to be specified, thus rendering any continuation of the activities constituting the development subject to enforcement action.

[1] *See ante* p. 45.
[2] *See ante* p. 49.
[3] As to such planning permissions see *ante*, p. 55.
[4] But see the conditions imposed pursuant to the Act *post*, p. 67.

It should be noted that although in the circumstances set out in (*c*) above the intention of the express condition is the same as the statutory one the completion notice procedure can *not* be used because the condition will not be one imposed by sections 41 or 42.[1]

If the Secretary of State after consultation with the Local Planning Authority considers it expedient that a Completion Notice should be served he may direct the authority to serve such a Notice or may himself serve it.[2]

A Completion Notice should recite the permission and the condition in question, the fact that the development has been begun but not completed before the relevant date, and the opinion of the Local Planning Authority that the development will not be completed within a reasonable period.

It must[3] specify a period (which cannot be less than 28 days after service[4]) within which any person on whom the notice is served may require a hearing by the Secretary of State before the notice is confirmed.

It must also specify a further period (which cannot be less than twelve months after the notice takes effect) and state that the planning permission will cease to have effect at the expiration of that period.

The Notice must be served[2] on the owner[5] and occupier[6] of the land and on any other person who, in the opinion of the Local Planning Authority, will be affected by it.[7]

A Completion Notice does not take effect unless and until it is confirmed by the Secretary of State.

If within the first specified period mentioned above any person on whom the Notice is served so requires, the Secretary of State must, before confirming the Notice, afford

---

[1] *See* s. 44 (1) and Schedule 24, para. 21.
[2] Section 276.
[3] Section 44 (4).
[4] As to service, *see* p. 121, *post*.
[5] For definition, *see* p. 119, *post*.
[6] This means **all** occupiers. *See* p. 119, *post*.
[7] If the land is ecclesiastical property a notice must also be served on the Church Commissioners. *See* s. 274 and p. 118, *post*.

to that person and to the Local Planning Authority an opportunity of appearing before and being heard by, a person appointed by him for that purpose.[1]

If the Secretary of State decides to confirm the Notice he may[2] in doing so, substitute a longer period for that specified in the Notice at the expiration of which the Planning Permission is to lapse.

If any person aggrieved by a decision of the Secretary of State to confirm a Completion Notice wishes to challenge the validity of the decision on the grounds that it is not within the powers of the Act, or that any relevant requirement has not been complied with in relation to it he may within six weeks from the date of the decision make application to the High Court under section 245[3] of the Act. Apart from this the validity of the decision cannot be questioned in any legal proceedings whatsoever.[4] The Local Planning Authority has a similar right.

When a Completion Notice takes effect (*i.e.* when the Secretary of State confirms it) the result is that the Planning Permission to which it relates is, at the expiration of the specified period, **invalid**, except so far as it authorises any development carried out under the permission up to the end of that period.[5] This means of course that any continued development is subject to enforcement action.

The Local Planning Authority may,[6] however, **withdraw** a Completion Notice at any time **before the expiration of the period specified in it as that at the end of which the Planning Permission will lapse** and if they do so, they must forthwith give notice of that fact to every person who was served with the Completion Notice. This means that the development may proceed pursuant to the Planning Permission.

---

[1] Section 44 (4).
[2] Section 44 (3) (*b*).
[3] For a full statement of the provisions of s. 245, *see post*, p. 195.
[4] *See* s. 242.
[5] Section 44 (5).
[6] Section 44 (6).

In certain limited circumstances the rights under a planning permission may be held to have been abandoned.[1]

Life of Outline Planning Permission

Section 42 of the 1971 Act contained provisions similar to those described above, in respect of Planning Permission granted on an **outline application**. Such an application seeks approval in principle to building or other operations leaving details, *e.g.* design and siting of houses or layout of roads to be settled later by a further submission and approval. Subsection (1) defines an **Outline Planning Permission** as "Planning Permission granted in accordance with the provisions of a development order[2] with the reservation for subsequent approval by the Local Planning Authority or the Secretary of State of matters (referred to in this section as 'reserved matters') not particularised in the application".

Once an outline planning permission is obtained a developer is not confined to one application for approval of a reserved matter. He is entitled to make a further alternative submission of a reserved matter under the original permission and if he gets two approvals in respect of the same matter he may implement either at his option.[3]

Where before 1st April 1969[4] Outline Planning Permission has been granted for development consisting in or including the carrying out of building or other operations, and the development has not been begun[5] before the beginning of 1968, the permission is deemed to have been granted subject to the following conditions[6]:—

(1) that in the case of any reserved matter, **application**

---

[1] (See *Slough Estates Ltd v. Slough Borough Council (No 2) (1969) 2 Ch, 305 and Pioneer Aggregates (UK) Ltd v. Secretary of State for the Environment and Peak Park Planning Board*, Glidewell, J.

[2] *See* the Town and Country Planning General Development Order 1977 (S.I. 1977, No. 289) as amended.

[3] See *Heron Corporation v. Manchester City Corporation* [1978] J.P.L. 471, C.A.

[4] Date of commencement of s. 66, 1968 Act. *See* S.I. 1969, No. 275, *supra*.

[5] For the date when development is to be taken as having been begun, *see ante*, p. 58.

[6] Section 292 and Schedule 24, para. 20, 1971 Act.

for approval must be made not later than the expiration of 3 years beginning with 1st April 1969;[3]

and (2) that **the development to which the permission relates must be begun**[4] not later than whichever is the **later** of the following dates:—

(*a*) the expiration of 5 years from 1st April 1969;[3]

or (*b*) the expiration of 2 years from the final approval of the reserved matters, or in the case of approval on different dates the final approval of the last such matter to be approved. For this purpose a reserved matter is to be treated as finally approved when an application for approval is granted, or when there is an appeal to the Secretary of State against a decision of the Local Planning Authority on an application and the Secretary of State grants approval, when he determines the appeal.[1]

(As to calculation of periods in certain circumstances relating to office development in the metropolitan region, *see* paragraph 20A of Schedule 24 of the 1971 Act, inserted by section 5 (2) of the Town and Country Planning (Amendment) Act 1972.)

This does **not** apply to an outline permission subject to an **express** condition that the development is to be begun or completed, or that application for approval of a reserved matter must be made not later than a specified time.[2]

In *R. v. Secretary of State for the Environment ex parte Bilton Industrial Properties*[3] it was decided that where there is an outline planning permission the carrying out of work on **part** of the land covered by that permission does not result in that part requiring to be treated as a separate entity. The whole of the land must be looked at and the

[1] Section 43 (5).
[2] Schedule 24, para. 20 (2).
[3] (1975) P. & C.R. 154, D.C.

permission regarded as one, and not, even where the development is in stages, as a collection of separate permissions. In that case outline permission was granted in 1952 for the development for industrial purposes of 22 acres. From time to time thereafter detailed plans were approved and work done on parts of the site. In 1973 applications were made for approval of details on areas not yet built on. On appeal against a deemed refusal the Secretary of State held that he had no jurisdiction on the ground (*inter alia*) that the appeals were out of time by virtue of Schedule 24, paragraph 20, of the Act.

The Company applied for an order of mandamus directing the Secretary of State to hear and determine the appeals. The orders were granted, the Court holding that development of the 22 acres had begun before 1968 pursuant to the outline planning permission.

R. v. Bromley London Borough ex parte Sievers[1] concerned a case where the expiry of a three year period for applying for approval of reserved matters fell on a Sunday. S delivered his application in person on the Monday. The authority (whose planning policy had been changed) said that they would not accept the application as one for approval of reserved matters as it was out of time. They treated it as a new "full" application, and refused it. The Divisional Court held that with due allowance for the state of affairs at the town hall on Sunday the Monday was effectively "not later than three years" from the grant of outline permission and granted an order of certiorari to quash the notice of refusal and an order of mandamus to consider the application as one duly made within the prescribed time. The planning authority's behaviour was arbitrary and unfair, especially as it did not itself decide the application for a further six months.

The effect of section 42 of the 1971 Act and the saving provisions of Schedule 24 of the 1971 Act is as follows:—

Every Outline Planning Permission granted after 1st April

---

[1] (1980) 255 E.G. 359, D.C.

1969[1] for development consisting in or including the carrying out of building or other operations must be granted (**and if not so granted is deemed to be granted**) subject to the following conditions:—

(1) that in the case of any reserved matter, **application for approval** must be made not later than the expiration of 3 years beginning with the **date of grant of Outline Permission.**

and (2) that **the development to which the permission relates must be begun**[2] not later than whichever is the **later** of the following dates:—

(*a*) the expiration of 5 years from the date of grant of the Outline Permission.

or (*b*) the expiration of 2 years from the final approval of the reserved matters or, in the case of approval on different dates, the final approval of the last such matter to be approved. For this purpose a reserved matter is to be treated as finally approved when an application for approval is granted, or when there is an appeal to the Secretary of State against a decision of the Local Planning Authority on an application and the Secretary of State grants approval, when he determines the appeal.[3]

In the case of Outline Permission granted after 1st April 1969[4] the authority concerned with the terms of the permission[5] may substitute, or direct that there be substituted for the periods of three, five and two years, such other periods respectively (longer or shorter) as they consider appropriate, having regard to the provisions of the Development Plan and to any other material considerations. (Sep-

---

[1] Date of commencement of s. 66, 1968 Act.

[2] For the date when development is to be taken as having been begun, *see ante*, p. 58.

[3] Section 43 (5).

[4] Date of commencement of s. 66, 1968 Act.

[5] Section 42 (5).

arate periods may be specified in relation to separate parts of the development.[4])

If development is carried out without the conditions being complied with there will be a breach of planning control rendering those responsible liable to enforcement action.

When Outline Planning Permission has been granted or deemed to be granted subject to the statutory conditions described, and the development is begun[1] but not completed before the date required by the relevant condition, and the Local Planning Authority is of the opinion that the development will not be completed within a reasonable period they may use the "Completion Notice" procedure set out on pages 60 to 62, *ante*.[2]

Life at Enterprise Zone Scheme Permission

As already noted[3] an order by the Secretary of State designating an enterprise zone under the Local Government Planning and Land Act, 1980 must specify the period for which the area is to remain an enterprise zone. When that period comes to an end the "automatic" planning permission granted by the 1980 Act[4] in respect of development specified in the scheme also comes to an end. No **operations** can lawfully be carried out thereafter, *i.e.* after the termination date of the scheme, even if they started to be carried out before such date in accordance with the scheme.[5] A fresh planning permission must be sought in the normal way for any such uncompleted operations *i.e.* by application to the local planning authority. New **uses** already begun under the scheme are not affected by the ending of it.

Life of permission relating to Mineral Workings

Under section 44 A of the Town and Country Planning Act 1971 inserted by section 7 of the Town and Country

[1] As to when development is begun, *see* p. 137, *post*.
[2] Section 44.
[3] See *ante*, p. 47.
[4] See *ante*, p. 55.
[5] Schedule 32, para. 22.

Planning (Minerals) Act 1981[1] every planning permission for development consisting of the winning and working of minerals is to be subject to a condition as to the duration of the development. Except where a condition is specified under the following provisions the condition, in the case of planning permission granted or deemed to be granted after the date of commencement of section 7 of the 1981 Act is that the development must cease not later than the expiration of 60 years beginning with the date of the permission.

The authority may specify a longer or shorter period. The Secretary of State has power to prescribe a longer or shorter period than 60 years for the above purposes. Where planning permission was granted or deemed to have been granted before the commencement of section 44 A there is a statutory condition that the development must cease not later than the expiration of the period of 60 years beginning with the date of commencement of that section.

A condition to which planning permission for development consisting of the winning and working of minerals is subject by virtue of the above provisions is not to be regarded for the purposes of the Act as a condition such as is mentioned in section 30 (1) (b) of the 1971 Act (as to which see *post*, p. 76).

Conditions may be appealed against to the Secretary of State.

Revocation or Modification of Planning Permission

Section 45 of the 1971 Act enables a local planning authority, or a mineral[2] authority subject to certain conditions, and subject to confirmation by the Secretary of State, to make an Order to revoke or modify a planning permission granted on an application. Where such an order is submitted to the Secretary of State for confirmation notice has to be served on the owner and occupier of the land affected and on other persons who in the opinion of the authority, are

[1] Effective from 22 February, 1982. See S.I. 1982/86 (C.4).

[2] See section 45 (5) inserted by the Town and Country Planning (Minerals) Act 1981 and effective from a date to be appointed.

affected by the order, and such persons have a right to be heard by a person appointed by the Secretary of State.

This power of revocation or modification may be exercised:—

(*a*) Where the permission relates to building or other operations, at any time before the operations are **completed** (it cannot, however, affect so much of the operations as has been previously carried out).[1]

(*b*) Where the permission relates to a change of use, at any time before the change has taken place.

There is a right to compensation.[2]

Section 46 of the 1971 Act provides that, with some exceptions, and subject to certain safeguards, revocation and modification orders of local planning authorities which are unopposed and which are unlikely to give rise to claims for compensation do not require confirmation by the Secretary of State.

For default powers of the Secretary of State, *see post*, page 140.

CONDITIONS OR LIMITATIONS IMPOSED ON PLANNING PERMISSION

Conditions or limitations may be imposed and planning permission:—

(i) by statute;

(ii) by a Local Planning Authority;

(iii) by a Development Order;

(iv) by the Secretary of State other than by a Development Order;

(v) by a person appointed by the Secretary of State.

(vi) by an Enterprise Zone Scheme

---

[1] See the proviso to Section 45 (4).

[2] See Section 164 and Section 164A.

Conditions imposed by Statute

Since the 1962 Act certain conditions have been imposed by Statute. These relate to:—

(*a*) Office and Industrial Development.

(*b*) Duration of planning permissions.

The position regarding the duration of planning permissions is set out on pages 57 to 68, *ante*.

The position regarding (*a*) above is as follows:—

Control of Office and Industrial Development

The effect of provisions formerly contained in the 1962 Act, the Control of Office and Industrial Development Act 1965 and the Industrial Development Act 1966, and later re-enacted in the 1971 Act (sections 66 to 86), was that certain conditions were directed to be imposed, and if not expressly imposed were deemed to be imposed, on planning permissions relating to office and industrial development of various kinds.

As hereafter noted, the provisions relating to offices have ceased to have effect and those relating to industrial development have been suspended (though the legislation relating to industrial development remains in force and could be re-activated).

The provisions are somewhat complicated and a full discussion of them would be out of place here, but a brief summary is as follows:—

An application for planning permission to develop by erecting an industrial building[1] of prescribed classes[2] or to change the use of premises which are not at present such a building in such a way that they become industrial buildings of the prescribed class, must be accompanied by an **Industrial Development Certificate** issued by the Department of

[1] For definition, *see* s. 66, 1971 Act.

[2] *See* the Town and Country Planning (Erection of Industrial Buildings) Regulations 1966 (S.I. 1966, No. 1034), which prescribed all classes of industrial buildings, as amended.

Trade and Industry, certifying that the development in question can be carried out consistently with the proper distribution of industry. An application under section 32[1] to retain buildings or to continue a use is also subject to this requirement.[2] An application **not** accompanied by a copy of the appropriate certificate is **of no effect**.

Certain classes of development were exempted from the above requirement.[3]

The Government eventually concluded that the Industrial Development Certificate procedure had outlived its usefulness but it did not legislate to abolish the controls, and instead made an Order[4] revoking all the regulations which prescribed the kinds of industrial buildings in relation to which Industrial Development Certificates were then currently required. The effect was to remove from the requirements about Industrial Development Certificates all buildings previously subject to them.

Similar provisions relating to erection of new offices, extension of existing offices, conversions into offices and changes of use to offices were intended to be of a temporary nature. In the original enactment (and in the consolidating measure of 1971) they were "unless Parliament otherwise determines" to cease to have effect at the end of seven years beginning with 5th August 1965 i.e. after 4th August 1972. Parliament however otherwise determined by section 5 (1) of the Town and Country Planning (Amendment) Act 1972 which provided for the extension of the powers of control for a further five years so that they then ceased to operate after 4th August 1977. The Control of Office Development

---

[1] *See* p. 49, *ante*.

[2] *See* s. 67 (2) and (5).

[3] *See* ss. 68 and 69 and The Town and Country Planning (Industrial Development Certificates: Exemption) Order 1979 (No. 839) replacing earlier Orders and see the Town and Country Planning (Industrial Development Certificates) Regulations 1979 (No. 838) amended by S.I. 1979 (No. 1643) and S.I. 1981 No. 867. See also the Town and Country Planning (Industrial Development Certificates) Regulations 1981 (No. 867) operative 11th July 1981 exempting from the requirement of a certificate erection of a building or change of use of a building in an enterprise zone. As to enterprise zones see *ante*, p. 46.

[4] The Town and Country Planning (Industrial Development Certificates) (Prescribed Classes of Building) Regulations, 1981 (S.I. 1981 No. 1826).

Act 1977 continued the controls until 4th August 1982 but there was provision that Her Majesty might by Order in Council specify an earlier date and the Control of Office Development (Cessation) Order 1979[1] provides that the statutory provisions shall cease to have effect. It became operative on 6th August 1979.

The provisions applied in any case only to certain specified[2] areas of the country.

Applications of the kind mentioned were **of no effect unless** accompanied by a copy of an **Office Development Permit** issued by the Department of Trade and Industry who, in deciding whether or not to issue such a Permit had to have particular regard to the need for promoting the better distribution of employment in Great Britain.

Certain classes of development were exempted by reference to floor space.

There were provisions about mixed industrial and office development, the effect of which was that, in the case of certain industrial development involving offices as well, no Office Development Permit was required, but conditions restricting office floor space might be imposed on the Industrial Development Certificate.

The Department of Trade and Industry might attach restrictions (*e.g.* as to the period within which an application for planning permission was to be made) on the grant either of an Industrial Development Certificate or an Office Development Permit[3] and where they did so and the restrictions were not complied with, the planning application was a nullity.

The Department might also in either case impose conditions.[1] Where this power was exercised the requisite condi-

---

[1] S.I. 1979, No. 908.

[2] *See* s. 74 (4) and the Control of Office Development (Designation of Areas) Order 1966 (S.I. 1966, No. 888), as amended by the Control of Office Development (Designation of Areas) (Variation) Order 1969 (S.I. 1969, No. 173), and the Control of Office Development (Designation of Areas) (Variation) Order 1970 (S.I. 1970, No. 1823).

[3] *See* ss. 70 and 77.

tion had to be imposed by the Local Planning Authority if and when they granted planning permission. (Other conditions might of course be imposed by the authority, but if these conflicted with those imposed by the Department of Trade, the **latter** prevailed.[1]) If planning permission was granted without complying with these requirements the permission was **deemed to have been granted subject to the conditions imposed on the Industrial Development Certificate or the Office Development Permit** as the case might be.[2]

In the case of **Office** development the statutory conditions had a limited life, **unless** the planning authority had, as they might under section 82 (3) (formerly under section 8 (3) of the 1965 Act), included in the permission a certificate that the condition could, and would, have been imposed apart from the provisions of the Control of Office and Industrial Development Act 1965, or those provisions as re-enacted in the 1971 Act.

Section 6 (1) of the Town and Country Planning (Amendment) Act 1972, amended section 82 of the 1971 Act, so as to provide that, unless such a certificate was included in the permission, where by virtue of an order made by the Secretary of State under the relevant provisions of the 1971 Act[1] any land ceased to be within an area to which office development control applied, any conditions attached to a planning permission as a result of office development control, would lapse. Section 6 came into force on the 27th July 1972, but subsection (2) made similar provision for land which ceased to be within a controlled area for office development purposes by virtue of an order made **before** the passing of the 1972 Act (under the 1965 Act). In such a case, unless such a certificate as previously mentioned was included in the planning permission, any conditions attached to the permission as a result of office development control lapsed on the passing of the 1972 Act, *i.e.* on 27th July 1972.

Apart from the above, conditions attached to planning permissions as a result of office development control ceased

---

[1] Sections 71 (3) and 82 (4).
[2] Section 74.

to have effect when the control provisions lapsed[1] (*see* page 71, *ante*), unless the permission contained such a certificate as mentioned earlier.

In the case of **Office** development also, the Act of 1965 contained a further provision (section 7) restricting the use for office purposes of buildings erected pursuant to planning permission in such circumstances that no Office Development Permit was required. It provided that in such cases, in areas to which the Act applied at the time when the relevant planning permission **was granted**, a condition **must** be imposed, and if not expressly imposed was **deemed** to be imposed, on the grant of planning permission to the effect that the building should not at any time contain office floor space which was more than the prescribed exemption limit[2] (*i.e.* the prescribed limit **at the time when the planning permission was granted**[3]).

These provisions were altered by the 1968 Act, which provided[4] that section 7 should not apply to a planning permission granted after 1st April 1969[5] unless the building was in an area to which the Act applied at the time when the **application** for planning permission **was made**. The 1968 Act also provided[6] that section 7 was not to apply at all to the following:—

(*a*) A planning permission granted after 1st April 1969[4] for a building with a floor space less than twice the prescribed exemption limit.

(*b*) A planning permission granted after 1st April 1969[4] for the erection of a building (of whatever floor space) which has wholly residential.

(*c*) A planning permission which was subject to conditions as a result of a conditional Industrial Development Certificate which restricted the office

---

[1] *See* s. 86 (2) and (3).
[2] *See* s. 2, Control of Office and Industrial Development Act 1965.
[3] Section 7 (5).
[4] Section 84.
[5] Date of commencement of section. *See* S.I. 1969, No. 275.
[5] Section 84 (2) and (3).

floor space which the building may contain or precluded it from containing any office floor space.

The 1968 Act also by sections 85 and 86 imposed in respect of planning permission granted after 1st April 1969[4] restrictions similar to those of section 7 (as amended) regarding the creation of office premises in buildings altered or extended and also regarding each building comprised in development involving the erection of two or more buildings.

These provisions as they stood immediately before the coming into force of the 1971 Act[1] were all re-enacted in that Act. (*See* sections 78, 79, 80 and 81.)

Conditions imposed pursuant to these provisions came to an end in the circumstances described on page 71, *ante*, in relation to other statutory conditions relating to office development.

The Control of Office and Industrial Development Act 1965 contained retrospective provisions relating to the metropolitan region and therefore contained special enforcement provisions[2] to meet this situation.

Conditions imposed by Local Planning Authority

Section 29 (1) of the Act authorises local planning authorities to grant planning permission "**either unconditionally or subject to such conditions as they think fit**" (or of course to refuse permission).

Section 30 of the Act provides that, without prejudice to the generality of the words in section 29, conditions may be imposed[3]:—

(1) for regulating the development or use of **any land under the control of the applicant** (whether or not it is the land in respect of which the application is made), or requiring the carrying out of works on any such land, so far as appears to the local plan-

[1] 1st April 1972.
[2] Sections 9 and 18 (4). *See* now s. 83 and Schedule 12 and s. 86 (4), 1971 Act.
[3] *See* pp. 57 to 68, *ante*, as to conditions about duration of planning permissions.

ning authority to be expedient **for the purposes of or in connection with the development authorised by the permission**. Whether an applicant has a sufficient degree of "control" for this purpose is a question of fact and degree.[1]

(2) for requiring the removal of any buildings or works authorised by the permission or the discontinuance of any use of land authorised, at the end of a specified period and the carrying out of any works required for the reinstatement of the land at the end of that period (*i.e.* permission for a limited period).

Under the Town and Country Planning (Minerals) Act 1981 a mineral authority (normally the county planning authority) have additional powers, when granting planning permission for winning and working of minerals subject to a restoration condition,[2] to impose an "aftercare condition" requiring that the land be specially treated for up to five years after restoration to make it suitable for agriculture, forestry or amenity.[3]

There is no such difference between development consisting of operations and development consisting of a material change of use as to affect the type of conditions which may be imposed. In *Roberts v. Vale Royal District Council*[4] there had been a planning permission for tipping of waste materials in a quarry, conditional upon materials tipped being approved the authority before tipping began. An enforcement notice alleged tipping of materials not approved. The appellants argued that there was a difference between the two types of development affecting the type of conditions permissible. Unlike operations in respect of which there might be an outline permission with reservation of approval of details later[5] there was no provision for matters to be reserved and dealt with later. The argument failed.

---

[1] *George Wimpey & Co. v. New Forest District Council* (1979) 250 E.G. 249, Sir Douglas Frank, Q.C.

[5] See *ante*, p. 50.

[2] For details see section 5 of the Act effective from 22 February, 1982. See S.I. 1982/86 (C.4).

[3] [1977] J.P.L. 369, D.C.

The power given to local planning authorities to impose conditions is expressed in wide terms, but it is clearly not an unlimited power.

When an authority is given a discretion in such terms it must act reasonably, but the Court will not interfere with the exercise of the discretion unless it is shown that the authority disregarded something they should have taken into account, or had regard to something which they should not have taken into account.[1]

They are, in this case, expressly directed[2] to **have regard to the provisions of the development plan so far as material to the application and to any other material[3] considerations**.

Conditions imposed must "fairly and reasonably relate to the permitted development".[4]

They must relate to local **planning** considerations.

A condition may be void for unreasonableness. Two cases concerning such a point were *Hall and Co. Ltd. v. Shoreham-on-Sea U.D.C.* and *Allnatt London Properties v. Middlesex County Council* (*see post*, p. 85).

In *R. v. Hillingdon London Borough Council ex parte Royco Homes*[5] a local authority imposed a condition on planning permission for residential development that the houses must be occupied by people on the council's housing list who would have security for ten years. On application for a writ of certiorari to quash the terms, the Divisional Court held that despite the availability of the procedure for appeal against a condition under the Town and Country Planning Act, certiorari could still be used to control the acts of a local planning authority where there was an error of law or an excess of jurisdiction and that the conditions

---

[1] *Associated Provincial Picture Houses Ltd. v. Wednesbury Corporation* [1948] 1 K.B. 223.

[2] Section 29 (1). *See also* s. 29 (2), (3) and (4).

[3] *I.e.*, material from a planning point of view. As to such considerations see *post*, p. 171.

[4] *Per* Lord Denning, M.R. in *Pyx Granite Co. Ltd. v. Minister Housing and Local Government* [1958] 1 All E.R. 625, at p. 633.

[5] [1974] 2 All E.R. 643, D.C.

imposed were so fundamental an interference with the rights of ownership that no local authority could properly impose them. The authority's acts were *ultra vires* and the application for certiorari was granted.

In *Newbury District Council v. Secretary of State for the Environment*[1] the Divisional Court considered an enforcement notice served on owners of two hangars used for rubber storage. Planning permission had been granted conditional upon removal of the hangars at the end of a specified period. The planning permission applied for had been for a **change of use** of substantial buildings which had existed for many years before the grant of the permission in question. The Secretary of State quashed the enforcement notice on the ground that the condition for removal of the buildings was *ultra vires* as unreasonable, in doing so giving as his reasons that the local planning authority had imposed the condition to remove the hangars as a safeguard for a long term policy for industrial deployment in rural areas and secure improvement of amenity and the Secretary of State considered that as the application had merely been for a change of use of existing and substantial buildings the requirement for the removal of the buildings was not sufficiently related to the use in question and was unreasonable and invalid. The council applied to quash the Secretary of State's decision and the Divisional Court held that removal of the buildings would prevent reversion to previous use[2] and might cause injustice to the freeholder. The condition had been imposed for ulterior motives and was *ultra vires*. This decision was reversed by the Court of Appeal[3] and the condition held valid.

On appeal to the House of Lords[4] it was held, allowing the appeal, that there had in fact been no need for the initial permission as there had been no material change of use. Conditions must be for a **planning** purpose and not an ul-

---

[1] [1977] J.P.L. 373, D.C.

[2] Permitted under Section 23 (9) of the 1971 Act – see *ante*, p. 42.

[3] *Newbury District Council v. Secretary of State for the Environment; Newbury District Council v. International Synthetic Rubber Company* [1980] 2 W.L.R. 379.

[4] [1981] A.C. 578, H.L.

terior purpose and they must fairly and reasonably **relate to the permitted development**. This condition did not fulfil the latter requirement and was void.

One matter which has been the subject of some controversy is whether an authority can impose a condition which restricts existing activities otherwise lawful, without compensation.

City of London Corporation v. Secretary of State for the Environment (see *ante*, p. 6) was one case where such a condition was held to be lawful.

There was a clear and emphatic statement of the law on this point in the later case of *Kingston-upon-Thames Royal London Borough Council v. Secretary of State for the Environment.*[1]

In that case the British Railways Board had applied for permission to rebuild a station. To the south of the station was a piece of land in the Board's ownership, with no buildings on it, but with the main electric traction cable running across its southern boundary. The plan attached to the application showed that land as having parking spaces for seven cars. Planning permission was granted but a condition imposed that the land shown allocated for car parking on the plan should be made available for such purposes at all times and should be used for no other purpose. The condition not having been complied with, an enforcement notice was served, and on appeal to the Secretary of State the condition was discharged, it being stated in the decision that "... the land is used operationally for the purposes of the undertaking ... This is a lawful use of the land which if it is strictly complied with the condition seeks to prevent without the payment of compensation. For these reasons it is considered that the condition as drafted is *ultra vires* and should be discharged". The planning authority appealed to the Divisional Court.[2] The Court, which consisted of Lord

---

[1] [1974] 1 All E.R. 193. See also *Peak Park Joint Planning Board v. Secretary of State for the Environment and Imperial Chemical Industries* [1980] J.P.L. 114, Sir Douglas Frank Q.C.

[2] Under s. 246 of the 1971 Act as to which *see post*, p. 156.

Widgery, C.J., Bridge, J. (as he then was) and May, J., held that the power to impose conditions on the grant of planning permission was subject to only two restrictions:—

(1) the condition had to be reasonably related to the development for which the permission had been granted, and

(2) a condition which was so clearly unreasonable that no reasonable planning authority could have imposed it was *ultra vires*.

The proposition that there was a further restriction to the effect that a condition could not restrict existing activities which otherwise would be lawful unless compensation was paid was untenable.

The Secretary of State's decision was wrong and the case was sent back to him for re-consideration.

In the course of his judgement Lord Widgery, C.J., said that "there never has been any general principle requiring a local planning authority when granting planning permission to refrain from attaching a condition affecting existing use rights without financial compensation. It has never been any part of the planning law". Bridge, J., said "the effect on existing rights in no way affects its (the condition's) validity".

The Divisional Court again held in *Penwith District Council v. Secretary of State for the Environment*[1] that a condition can restrict existing use rights without compensation provided the condition relates to the permitted development. The second respondents owned a factory built with unconditional planning permission. Later they applied for permission for an extension of the factory, and got permission subject to conditions about noise and emissions. The Secretary upheld an appeal against the conditions, regarding them as ultra vires as they were to remedy existing deficiencies at the existing premises. The council applied to have this decision quashed and the court as stated above upheld

[1] [1977] J.P.L. 371 D.C.

the validity of the condition, considering that it properly related to the development for which permission was granted.

It is clear that a condition may properly be imposed as to the classes of persons who may use or occupy a building as well as a condition related to the actual use of the building.[1]

This must be done however, by means of a condition to this effect, and to grant planning permission for a dwelling "for the purpose of dwelling accommodation for an agricultural worker" is not an effective means of achieving the desired objective. This is because a change of occupier to someone not engaged in agriculture would not amount to a material change of use of the dwelling and therefore would not be development, so that enforcement action would not be possible.[2]

A condition may be void for uncertainty, but will only be so if it can be given no meaning or no sensible or ascertainable meaning, and not merely because it is ambiguous or may lead to absurd results.[3]

A common condition is one requiring that materials to be used on the exterior of a building shall be approved by the council. In *Sutton London Borough Council v. Secretary of State for the Environment*[4] it was held that such a condition does not imply any requirement that the work should be done to any particular standard, so that the authority does not have control over the quality of the work.

Where an applicant for planning permission undertakes to fulfil a condition to be imposed and is then granted planning permission conditional upon that undertaking he

---

[1] *Fawcett Properties Ltd. v. Buckinghamshire County Council* [1961] A.C. 636. *See* the Rent (Agriculture) Act 1976 for suspension of an "agricultural" occupancy condition in certain circumstances.

[2] *East Suffolk County Council v. Secretary of State for the Environment* (1972) 70, L.G.R. 595, D.C.

[3] *Per* Lord Denning, in *Fawcett Properties Ltd. v. Buckinghamshire County Council, supra.*

[4] (1975) 29 P. & C.R. 350, D.C.

is estopped from thereafter challenging the power to enforce compliance with it.[1]

As previously noted[2] the implementation of a planning permission does not estop an owner from relying on any existing use rights he may have. Where, however, there are no existing use rights, a person who implements a planning permission, though contravening the terms on which it was granted will not be able to ignore the permission so as to free himself of other conditions which can operate (at any rate where the development he has carried out amounts to the substantial implementation of the planning permission.) This appears to be the effect of the judgment of the Divisional Court in *Kerrier District Council v. Secretary of State for the Environment and Brewer.*[3] In that case planning permission for a bungalow was conditional upon occupation being restricted to an agricultural employee. The bungalow was constructed contrary to the approval plans, although the Council purported retrospectively to approve the variation (no formal application for planning permission was in fact made). Thereafter the authority served an enforcement notice alleging breach of the condition. On appeal, the Secretary of State decided that the council had no power to give the retrospective approval, that the bungalow had been built without permission (on the basis of the *Copeland Case*[4]) and so there could be no breach of the condition attached to the permission. On appeal to the Divisional Court the Secretary of State's reasoning was held to be defective and the appeal was allowed, on the basis that the fact that development did not comply with a planning permission did not make the permission a nullity and therefore conditions attached to such a permission which had been implemented were enforceable. Leave was given to take the case to the Court of Appeal.[5]

---

[1] *Augier v. Secretary of State for the Environment* (1979) 38 P. & C.R. 219, D.C.
[2] See *ante*, p. 35.
[3] (1981) 41 P. & C.R. 284, D.C.
[4] As to the facts of this case see *post*, p. 109.
[5] See also *J. Toomey Motors Limited v. Secretary of State for the Environment and Basildon District Council* [1981] J.P.L. 418.

Conditions or limitations imposed by General Development Order

Section 24 (4) of the Act authorises the Secretary of State in granting planning permission by General Development Order to grant it either unconditionally or "*subject to such conditions or limitations as may be specified in the order*". Without prejudice to this provision, where planning permission is granted for erection, extension or alteration of buildings the order may require the approval of the local planning authority to be obtained to design or external appearance and where a development order grants permission for development of a specified class it may enable the Minister or a local planning authority to direct that the permission shall not apply in relation to development in a particular area or in relation to any particular development.[1]

Where by development order permission is granted for use of land for any purpose on a limited number of days in a specified period, the permission has effect as being subject to a limitation that the land shall not be used for any one purpose pursuant to the permission on more than that number of days in that period.[2]

Conditions imposed by the Secretary of State other than by a Development Order

The Secretary of State's powers to impose conditions when dealing with applications referred to him, or coming before him on appeal, or in default of decision by the Local Planning Authority[3] are the same as those of the Authority.[4]

Conditions imposed by a person appointed by the Secretary of State

As earlier noted[5] an Inspector of the Department of the Environment may grant planning permission on appeal. When this happens he may impose conditions.[6]

---

[1] Section 24 (5) (*a*) and (*b*).
[2] Section 24 (6).
[3] *See* p. 53, *ante*.
[4] Sections 35, 36 and 37.
[5] Page 54, *ante*.
[6] *See* Schedule 9, para. 2.

Conditions imposed by Enterprise Zone Scheme

As already noted,[1] the effect of an Enterprise Zone Scheme (or a Modification of such Scheme) specifying development or a class of development is that planning permission is automatically granted therefor.[2] An Enterprise Zone Scheme or a Modification Scheme may also specify conditions or limitations subject to which the development or class of development may be carried out[3] and it may[4] also specify matters in relation to any development it permits for which its further approval is required.

Pre-1948 Conditions

By virtue of paragraphs 89 and 90 of Schedule 24 of the Act the provisions as to enforcement of planning conditions are effective against conditions imposed:—

(*a*) On permission granted before 1st July 1948, under a planning scheme or Interim Development Order for works or uses existing on that date.

(*b*) On a determination as to deemed compliance with planning control under the Building Restrictions (Wartime Contraventions) Act 1946.

(*c*) On a planning permission granted after 21st July 1943, and before 1st July 1948, on application under an Interim Development Order if and so far as the development was not carried out on the latter date and the permission was in force immediately before that date. (Development for which permission was required under the Restriction of Ribbon Development Act is excluded unless that permission was obtained and any conditions on such a consent will also apply.)

Paragraph 89 (2) of the Schedule also provides that in cases (*a*) and (*b*) where a condition imposed a time limit

---

[1] *Ante*, p. 55.
[2] Although the authority may direct that it shall not apply in certain case. See *ante*, p. 55.
[3] Local Government Planning and Land Act, 1980 Schedule 32, para. 17 (3).
[4] Schedule 32, para. 17 (6).

expiring after 1st July 1948, if the works are not removed or the use discontinued in accordance therewith the enforcement provisions apply as if the development had been carried out at the expiration of the limited period without planning permission.

Implied Conditions

For a case in which both the Divisional Court and the Court of Appeal decided in favour of the validity of an **implied** condition see *Kwik Save Discount Group v. Secretary of State for the Environment*, the facts of which are set out *ante*, p. 17.

Effect of Invalid Conditions

The effect on a planning permission of the invalidity of a condition attached to it is important to enforcement. There are two possibilities:—

(1) That the invalidity of a condition renders the permission itself void.

(2) That the invalid condition is severable and that the permission is effective without it.

There have been several cases concerning this question.

In the Court of Appeal in *Pyx Granite Co. v. Minister of Housing and Local Government*,[1] Hodson, L.J. speaking *obiter* expressed the view that an invalid condition would render a permission void, but in *Fawcett Properties Ltd. v. Bucks County Council*,[2] Roxburgh, J. expressed doubt as to the correctness of this view, instancing the case where there might be a large number of conditions, some of them important but some of them trivial.

In *Hall and Co. Ltd. v. Shoreham-on-Sea U.D.C and Another*,[3] the Court of Appeal, reversing the decision of Glyn-Jones, J., decided that where, as in that case, the void

---

[1] [1958] 1 Q.B. 554. The decision was reversed by the House of Lords on another ground.

[2] [1958] 1 W.L.R. 1161. The decision was reversed by the Court of Appeal, and the reversal affirmed by the House of Lords on another ground.

[3] [1964] 1 All E.R. 1.

condition is fundamental to the grant of planning permission the permission itself is rendered void. In this case the conditions in question required the plaintiffs to construct a road on their own land and to allow a public right of way over it. These conditions were held to be *ultra vires* and void for unreasonableness.

Allnatt London Properties v. Middlesex County Council,[1] heard after *Hall's Case*, concerned a planning permission for the erection of a factory extension in place of existing outbuildings of premises having industrial use rights and the conditions imposed required (*inter alia*) that the extensions should be used only in conjunction with the main building and that until a specified date they should be used only by a person or firm who at the date of the permission occupied an industrial building in the county. The Court (Glyn-Jones, J.) decided that these conditions were unreasonable and void and that as the authority had gone outside the matters which they could properly take into consideration the permission stood free of the conditions. (This decision was explained and distinguished in *Kingston-upon-Thames Royal London Borough Council v. Secretary of State for the Environment and Another, supra.*)

In *Kingsway Investments (Kent) Ltd. v. Kent County Council*,[2] a condition on an outline planning permission required that approval of details had to be obtained within 3 years.[3] The plaintiffs sought declarations that the condition was void and that the outline planning permission subsisted. The Divisional Court held that as there was no provision in the condition to cover the time for an appeal to the Minister of Housing and Local Government the condition was void, and that as the condition was not severable the outline permission was void *in toto*.

In the Court of Appeal[4] the decision of Lyell, J. on the

[1] (1964) 62 L.G.R. 304.
[2] [1968] 3 All E.R. 197.
[3] As to this sort of condition, *see* now the statutory provisions described, *ante*, p. 57.
[4] *Kingsway Investments (Kent) Ltd. v. Kent County Council; Kenworthy v. Kent C.C.* (1968) 112 S.J. 1008, C.A.

question of the effect of the void condition was reversed. The Court held, Lord Denning, M.R., dissenting, that the condition **could** be severed from the permission which accordingly remained in existence and could be acted on by the developer.

The case eventually reached the House of Lords[1] who by a majority (Lord Reid and Lord Upjohn dissenting) held that the condition in question was **valid**, so reversing the decision of the Court of Appeal. The time condition was thought also by the majority to be fundamental and, so, if it had been void, **not** to be severable. The whole permission would therefore have been invalid.

In *R. v. Hillingdon London Borough Council ex parte Royco Homes*,[2] *supra*, where fundamental conditions were held to be void, the view was again taken by the Court that this rendered the whole planning permission invalid.

It seems clear that a planning permission is generally to be regarded as entire and that void conditions are severable only if they are relatively unimportant. It appears that the importance or otherwise of a condition is likely to be tested by the subjective method of trying to assess the intentions of the planning authority. If they would not have granted planning permission without the condition in question it will usually be regarded as fundamental and therefore **not** severable.

If a permission is rendered void because of a void condition, development carried out will be without permission and therefore subject to enforcement action (provided that the period for taking such action has not expired).[3]

In *Kent County Council v. Secretary of State for the Environment and Burmah-Total Refineries Trust*[4] the Secretary of State, in granting permission for part only of an oil re-

---

[1] *Kent County Council v. Kingsway Investments (Kent) Ltd.* [1970] 1 All E.R. 70, H.L.

[2] [1974] 2 All E.R. 643, D.C.

[3] *See post*, Chapter 3.

[4] (1976) 33 P. & C.R. 70, D.C.

finery had imposed a condition that there be no access by road. The Divisional Court held that it was a question of fact whether conditions imposed nullified the permission and the condition was upheld.

CHAPTER 3

CIRCUMSTANCES IN WHICH AN ENFORCEMENT NOTICE MAY BE SERVED

INTRODUCTORY

The enforcement of planning control is dealt with in Part V of the Town and Country Planning Act 1971, a consolidating measure incorporating the Town and Country Planning Act 1962 and other enactments passed between that Act and 1971, including the Town and Country Planning Act 1968. By virtue of section 294 most of its provisions, including those relating to enforcement, became operative from the 1st April 1972. The 1971 Act provisions have been substantially amended by the Local Government and Planning (Amendment) Act, 1981 with effect from 27th August 1981. Enforcement generally[1] concerns two classes of case, namely:—

(*a*) where development has been carried out without the grant of planning permission required in that behalf in accordance with Part III of the 1962 Act or Part III of the 1971 Act.

(*b*) where any conditions or limitations subject to which planning permission was granted have not been complied with.

The initial step is the service of an "enforcement notice".

[1] *See* Chapters 8 to 11, *post*, as to enforcement in certain special types of case.

POWER TO SERVE AN ENFORCEMENT NOTICE

On whom conferred

The power to serve an enforcement notice is conferred on a **local planning authority**.

By changes effected under the Local Government Act 1972[1] the council of a county is the local planning authority for a county and the council of a district is the district planning authority for the district.

Section 1 (2A) of the Town and Country Planning Act 1971 provides that references in that Act to a **local planning authority** shall, except as respects Greater London[2] and the National Parks,[3] be construed as references to **both** county and district authorities, but subject (*inter alia*) to Part I of Schedule 16 of the Local Government Act 1972.

Under Schedule 16, paragraph 24, it is the **district council** who are given the power to serve an enforcement notice. However, where it appears to them that it relates to a "county matter" they must first consult the county council.[4] Where a county planning authority consider that there is in question a matter which should properly be considered a county matter, they may themselves serve an enforcement notice.[5]

The phrase "county matter" is defined in Schedule 16 paragraph 32, as amended by the Local Government, Planning and Land Act 1980 section 86 (4) to which reference must be made for the detailed provisions. Briefly, they cover mineral extraction and related matters, cement works and waste disposal[6] and development partly in and partly outside a national park. The 1980 Act provisions (effective from

---

[1] Section 182, effective from 1 April 1974.

[2] As to London see Schedule 3 of the 1971 Act. See also S.I. 1981 No. 1081.

[3] As to which *see* s. 182 (4), (5) and (6) and Schedule 17 of the Local Government Act 1972 as amended.

[4] Schedule 16, para. 24 (2).

[5] *Ibid*., para. 24 (3).

[6] See the Town and Country Planning (Prescription of County Matters) Regulations 1980. Effective from 13th January 1981, made under sections 266 and 270 and paragraph 32 (f) of schedule 16 to the Local Government Act 1972.

13th January 1981) removed earlier provisions under which "county matters" included cases where development would conflict with a county council's basic planning policy. From the 22nd February, 1982, under the Town and Country Planning (Minerals) Act 1981 section 2[1] the **county** planning authority as the mineral planning authority will have exclusive power in relation to all enforcement matters relating to minerals.

An enforcement notice may, therefore, emanate from either the county council or the district council.

The effect of paragraph 51 (2) of Schedule 16 is that, for the purposes of an enforcement notice, whether the matter dealt with is a "county matter" or not is of little concern, except perhaps to the authorities themselves.

In the Merseyside urban development area the development corporation have exclusive enforcement powers (excepting the power residing in the Secretary of State).[2]

Extent of power

Subject to the provisions enumerated hereafter an enforcement notice may be served by a local planning authority **if it appears to them that a breach of planning control has occurred after the end of 1963**[3] and "**if they consider it expedient to do so, having regard to the provisions of the development plan** (for their District) **and to any other material considerations**".[4] "Material" means material for the purposes of town and country planning. Section 87 (3) provides that there is a breach of planning control "if development has been carried out (whether before or after the commencement of this Act) without the grant of the planning permission required in that behalf in accordance with Part III of the Act of 1962 or Part III of this Act (*i.e.* the 1971 Act), or if any conditions or limitations subject to

---

[1] Date of coming into force of Section 2. See S.I. 1982/86 (C.4.).

[2] See the Merseyside Development Corporation (Planning Functions) Order 1981 (No. 561).

[3] For the significance of this date, *see post*, p. 130.

[4] As to "material considerations" see *post*, p. 171.

which planning permission was granted have not been complied with".

It should be noted that the Act confers a **power** on the local planning authority. It does not impose a duty. Consequently, the authority is not bound to serve an enforcement notice in any particular case. In circular 109/77 (in Wales circular 164/77) the Secretary of State has reminded local planning authorities of this fact and has said (para. 3) that in the case of unauthorised changes of use it "would clearly be right to concentrate enforcement action on those uses which are causing particular harm to the environment or which, if allowed to continue, would substantially prejudice the provisions for the development plan". Further ministerial guidance on the exercise of the discretionary power is given in circular 22/80 dated 28th November 1980 (Welsh Office circular 40/80).

Estoppel

As has already been stated (see *ante*, p. 39) it is possible for someone who proposes to carry out development to apply to the planning authority for a formal determination under section 53 of the 1971 Act as to whether what he proposes to do involves development and if it does whether he requires planning permission for it, but not all those who run the risk of enforcement action may be aware of this provision, and even where its existence is known it may often happen that enquiries are made of a local planning authority by developers and others in a much less formal way. So it may come about that, perhaps in an endeavour to be helpful, perhaps in answer to a precise enquiry, an officer of a local planning authority may make statements as to whether a course of action intended to be followed by an individual does or does not need planning permission with the enquirer acting upon the statement. It was perhaps inevitable that the courts should have had to consider suggestions that in these circumstances an estoppel should operate against a local planning authority, preventing them from proceeding to take enforcement action contrary to a representation earlier made on their behalf.

There have been a number of cases, and as a result it is now possible to state the position with some confidence. The general principle is that no estoppel can be raised to hinder the exercise of a statutory discretion and as also noted elsewhere (see *ante*, p. 50) a local authority cannot **contract** not to exercise its statutory powers (but see *Royal Borough of Windsor and Maidenhead v. Brandrose Investments Limited* referred to *post*, p. 244).

It was decided in *Southend-on-Sea Corporation v. Hodgson (Wickford) Limited*[1] that estoppel did not operate to prevent enforcement action, where a developer had relied on a statement of an officer that planning permission was unnecessary for what he proposed to do and he had afterwards been served with an enforcement notice.

In *Brooks and Burton Limited v. Secretary of State for the Environment*[2] Lord Wigery C.J. had said " . . . local government officers should feel free to help applicants who come and ask them questions without all the time having the shadow of estoppel hanging over them and without the possibility of their immobilising their authorities by reason of some careless remark which produces such an estoppel".

In the *Newbury Case*[3] Lord Scarman in the course of his judgment said that he agreed with a view consistently expressed by Lord Parker C.J. that it was wrong to introduce into public administrative law concepts such as equitable estoppel which were essentially aids to the doing of justice in private law. Equitable estoppel had no place in the law of planning control.

The principal case on estoppel is *Western Fish Products Limited v. Penwith District Council and Another*.[4]

The Court of Appeal in a reserved judgment dismissed an appeal by Western Fish products Limited from dismissal of an action against Penwith Council claiming declarations and other relief. In 1976 the company had bought a site at

---

[1] [1961] 2 All E.R. 46.
[2] [1978] 1 All E.R. 733.
[3] For the facts of this case see *ante*, p. 78.
[4] (1978) 38 P. & C.R. 7.

Newlyn in Cornwall with the intention of establishing a fish processing factory. They had been refused planning permission and the council had issued stop[1] and enforcement notices. The company contended that as a result of conversations and correspondence between itself and the council's planning officers prior to refusals of permission the council were estopped from denying that they had existing use rights entitling them to use the site as proposed and from refusing it the permissions which it sought. It further claimed that what the council officers had said amounted to determinations under section 53[2] and 94[3] of the 1971 Act and that the council had abused their statutory powers, or had acted negligently with a result that they had a right to damages (their potential claim had been mentioned as running into millions of pounds). The Court of Appeal held that there was no case on which any estoppel could be founded whether "proprietary" or otherwise because there had been no relevant representation but if there had been it had not been acted on by the company to its detriment to the knowledge of the council. Even if there had been a case sufficient to found an estoppel the company's claim would still have failed first because it did not have the equitable right which had come to be known as proprietary estoppel and secondly because in law the council could not be estopped from performing their statutory duties.

The Court of Appeal expressly endorsed the *dicta* of Lord Widgery C.J. in *Brooks and Burton Limited* (see above). Megaw L.J. said that there seemed to be two kinds of exception to the general principle that a statutory body could not be estopped from performing its statutory duties the first being that if a planning authority delegated to its officers the power to determine specific questions (such as applications under sections 53 and 94 of the 1971 Act) any decisions they made could not be revoked. *Lever Finance Limited v. Westminster London Borough Council*[4] could be considered as an application of that exception, but it was

[1] As to stop notices see *post*, p. 142.
[2] As to such a determination see *ante*, p. 39.
[3] This section relates to established use certificates, as to which see *post*, p. 130.
[4] [1970] 3 All E.R. 496.

not an authority for the proposition that every representation made by a planning officer within his ostensible authority bound the authority which employed him. For an estoppel, if there were an estoppel at all, to arise there had to be some evidence justifying the person dealing with the officer in thinking that what the officer said would bind the authority, and holding an office, however senior, could not be enough by itself. In the *Lever Finance Case*[1] there had been evidence of a widespread practice among planning authorities of allowing planning officers to make immaterial modifications to plans produced when planning permission had been given. Lever Finance's architect had presumably known of that practice and had been entitled to assume that the practice had been authorised by the authorities in whose area it was followed.

The second apparent exception (so said His Lordship) was that if a planning authority waived a procedural requirement relating to an application made to it for the exercise of its statutory powers it might be estopped from relying on lack of formality. Much would however turn on the construction of any statutory provisions setting out what the procedure was to be.

In the *Western Fish Case* the court rejected all the company's arguments and dismissed the appeal.

If there is a planning application submitted for development and a written statement of the authority makes a representation that planning permission is not required this may amount to a determination under section 53 and so in fact estop the authority from acting contrary to its terms (see *Wells v. Minister of Housing and Local Government*[1] as interpreted by the Court of Appeal in *Western Fish*. For a further case after *Western Fish* see *Bedfordia Plant Limited and Others v. Secretary of State for the Environment and North Bedfordshire District Council.*[2]

---

[1] [1967] 2 All E.R. 1041.
[2] [1981] J.P.L. 122.

PRELIMINARY MATTERS

Initial considerations

If the allegation is to be that land has been **developed without planning permission** three factors have to be considered:—

(1) Is there development?

(2) If there is development is it of a kind for which planning permission is required?

(3) Did an effective grant of planning permission exist at the time the development was carried out? In this connection the provisions imposing time limits on planning permission should be carefully noted.

On the first question the reader is referred to chapter 1 and on the second and third to chapter 2.

If the allegation is to be a **breach of a condition** it must be borne in mind that an Enforcement Notice can only properly be served in respect of this kind of breach of planning control if the conditions (or limitations) have been lawfully imposed. As to this matter the reader is referred to chapter 2.

Obtaining information prior to enforcement action

To enable local authorities to carry out their functions under the Act, including the taking of enforcement action, powers are given to them—

(*a*) to enter upon private property,

and (*b*) to require information to be supplied as to ownership and occupation of property.

An exercise of the first power will usually be necessary before the question of taking enforcement action can be properly considered and the second power will be exercised by a prudent authority to ensure, as far as can reasonably be done, that any notice is in due course properly served upon the correct persons.

Rights of entry

Subject to certain provisions (referred to hereafter) for the protection of owners and occupiers, any person duly authorised **in writing** by the Secretary of State or by a local planning authority may at any reasonable time enter upon any land[1] for the purpose of surveying it in connection with (*inter alia*) any proposal of the local planning authority or the Secretary of State to issue or serve any notice under Part V of the 1971 Act (which deals with enforcement of planning control) or under any order or regulations made thereunder, or under section 115 of the Act.[2]

This will include:—

(*a*) an enforcement notice;

(*b*) a stop notice;[3]

(*c*) a listed building enforcement notice;[4]

(*d*) a Notice of intention to do urgent works for preservation of an unoccupied listed building;[5]

(*e*) a notice to enforce the duty of replacing certain trees;[6]

(*f*) an enforcement notice relating to advertisements (if the current advertisement regulations contain the power to serve such a notice);[7]

(*g*) (Under section 115) a Repairs Notice as a preliminary to compulsory acquisition of a listed building in need of repair.[8]

Section 280 also confers the same powers of entry, in precisely the same terms, in respect of a proposal to serve any notice under Part IV of the 1971 Act and this includes

---

[1] This includes a building. *See* s. 290.
[2] Section 280.
[3] *See post*, p. 142.
[4] *See post*, p. 263.
[5] *See post*, p. 286.
[6] *See post*, p. 298.
[7] *See post*, p. 318.
[8] *See post*, p. 273.

a notice under section 65 requiring the proper maintenance of waste land (as to which, *see post*, page 320).

It is to be noted that the right of entry conferred is "in connection with any proposal . . ." to serve a notice. There must, therefore, be a "proposal" in existence **before** entry can lawfully be made as of right.

There can it seems be a **proposal** of the authority only if and when they have resolved to serve a notice and the question then arises as to the way in which such a resolution can properly be passed where entry is not yet obtained. In many cases entry will be possible simply by obtaining the permission of the occupier to enter and inspect and no difficulty is found in practice, but what is the position when permission is denied or there is no-one from whom permission can be obtained? It must be remembered that the decision to serve an enforcement notice is authorised if "it **appears** to the local planning authority that there has been a breach of planning control" and the authority must "consider it expedient" to serve the notice. How can the first requirement be satisfied before entry to the land is gained to see precisely what is going on? The answer appears to be that a *prima facie* case will be sufficient for this purpose and the judgments in the Court of Appeal in the *Miller Mead Case*[1] particularly that of Upjohn, L.J., seem to make this clear. In practice it should rarely be the case that the development of land can take place without there being some "external" evidence sufficient to raise a *prima facie* case.[2]

By section 280 (9) the power to **survey** includes power to search and bore for the purpose of ascertaining the nature of the subsoil or the presence of minerals therein.

It appears that the extensive powers of delegation given to local authorities by the Local Government Act 1972[3] mean that authority to enter may be conferred by a committee or even an officer of a local planning authority (if such a power

---

[1] [1963] 2 Q.B. 196.

[2] *See also Tidswell v. Secretary of State for the Environment* and *Thurrock Borough Council* [1977] J.P.L. 104, D.C.

[3] Sections 101 and 101 (2). *See ante*, p. 47.

has been delegated to them). Section 101 (12) of the 1972 Act provides that references to "functions" capable of delegation includes "the doing of anything which is calculated to facilitate, or is conducive or incidental to, the discharge of any of those functions".

Any person similarly authorised may at any reasonable time enter upon any land in respect of which any of the above-mentioned notices has been served, for the purpose of ascertaining whether the notice has been complied with.[1]

In relation to control over buildings of architectural or historic interest **the Secretary of State** may under section 280 (2) **in writing** authorise any person to enter at any reasonable time upon any land for the purpose of surveying any building thereon in connection with a proposal to include the building in, or exclude it from, a list[2] compiled or approved under section 54 of the Act.

Under section 280 (3) any person duly authorised in writing by the Secretary of State or a local planning authority may at any reasonable time enter any land[3] for the purpose of ascertaining whether, with respect to any building on the land, an offence[4] has been, or is being, committed under section 55 or 98 of, or Schedule 11 to the 1971 Act, or whether the building is being maintained in a proper state of repair.[4]

Under section 280 (4) any person duly authorised in writing by the Secretary of State or a **Local authority**[5] may at any reasonable time enter upon any land for the purpose of ascertaining whether (*inter alia*) an offence under section 57 of the Act (which relates to damage to listed buildings)[6] appears to have been committed on the land, or any of the functions conferred by sections 101 or 103 of the Act (which relate respectively to the preservation of unoccupied listed

---

[1] Section 280 (8).
[2] As to such a list, *see post*, p. 252.
[3] This includes a building. *See* s. 290.
[4] *See post*, Chapter 8.
[5] For definition, *see* s. 290. The term will include anyone acting under delegated powers.
[6] *See post*, p. 272.

buildings and the enforcement of the duties of replacing certain trees[1]) should or may be exercised in connection with the land or for the purpose of exercising these functions in connection with the land.

Protection of owners and occupiers

The following provisions exist for the protection of persons whose land is entered upon[2]:—

1. If so required a person authorised to enter land must produce evidence of his authority before entering.[3] This does not mean that the right of entry is restricted to occasions when there is someone to whom the evidence can be produced.[4]

2. Admission cannot be demanded as of right to land **which is occupied** unless 24 hours notice[5] of the intended entry has been given to the occupier. Where works are to be carried out to ascertain the nature of the subsoil or the presence of minerals the notice must state the intention to carry out such works.[6]

3. If land is held by **statutory undertakers**[7] and they object to proposed works to ascertain the nature of the subsoil or the presence of minerals on the grounds that their carrying out would be **seriously detrimental** to the carrying out of their undertaking the works cannot be carried out except with the authority of the appropriate Minister.[8] Objection cannot it seems be taken on any other grounds.

4. If any authorised person is admitted to a factory, workshop or workplace and discloses to any person any information obtained by him while on the premises, as to say manufacturing process or trade secret

[1] *See post*, p. 298.
[2] Section 281.
[3] Section 281 (1).
[4] *Grove v. Eastern Gas Board* [1951] 2 All E.R. 1051, C.A.
[5] Section 281 (1). As to service of notice, *see* s. 283, and see *post*, p. 118.
[6] Section 281 (6) (*a*).
[7] *See* p. 102 *post*.
[8] *See* p. 102 *post*.

he is, unless the disclosure is made in the course of performing his duty in connection with the survey for which he was authorised to enter, liable on summary conviction to a fine of up to £1000[1] or, on conviction on indictment to imprisonment for a term not exceeding two years or a fine of unlimited amount or to both imprisonment and fine.[2]

5. Where land is damaged in exercise of a right of entry or in the making of an authorised survey, any person interested in the land may recover compensation from the Secretary of State or authority on whose behalf the entry was effected.[3] Any question of disputed compensation is to be referred to and determined by the Lands Tribunal,[4] and in relation to the determination of any such question the provisions of sections 2 and 4 of the Land Compensation Act 1961 (as amended)[5] (as to certain aspects of procedure and as to costs), apply, subject to any necessary modifications and to the provisions of any Regulations under the Act.[6]

6. In addition to the above statutory provisions the exercise of the rights of entry must be strictly confined to the minimum necessary for the purposes prescribed by the Act. If the statutory right of entry is exceeded the authority and their servants will be trespassers *ab initio* and accordingly liable in damages.[7]

---

[1] Maximum fine increased from £400 to £1000 by the Criminal Law Act 1977, section 28.

[2] Section 281 (3).

[3] Section 281 (4).

[4] Section 281 (5) and s. 179. The Lands Tribunal was established by s. 1 of the Lands Tribunal Act 1949. As to procedure, *see* that Act and the Lands Tribunal Rules 1975 (S.I. 1975, No. 299) consolidating and amending earlier Rules, as amended by S.I. 1977, No. 1820.

[5] An amendment originally contained in the Community Land Act 1975 was saved by the Local Government Planning and Land Act 1980 section 193 and schedule 33, para. 5 notwithstanding the repeal by that Act of the relevant part of the 1975 Act.

[6] No regulations have so far been made.

[7] *Six Carpenters Case* (1610) 1 Sm. L.C. 134.

By virtue of section 290 and section 224 the "appropriate Minister" in relation to paragraph 3 above, relating to objections by statutory undertakers, is as follows:—

(*a*) in relation to statutory undertakers carrying on any railway, light railway, tramway, road transport, dock, harbour or pier undertaking, the Secretary of State for Transport;

(*b*) in relation to statutory undertakers carrying on an undertaking for the supply of electricity, gas or hydraulic power, the Secretary of State for Energy;

(*c*) in relation to the British Airports Authority or the Civil Aviation Authority or statutory undertakers carrying on any lighthouse undertaking, the Secretary of State for Trade;

(*d*) in relation to the Post Office, the Secretary of State for Industry;

(*dd*) in relation to statutory undertakers carrying on an undertaking for the supply of water, in the application of this Act to England, the Secretary of State for the Environment;"

(*e*) in relation to statutory undertakers carrying on an undertaking for the supply of water, in the application of this Act to Wales, the Secretary of State for Wales; and

(*f*) in relation to any other statutory undertakers, the Secretary of State for the Environment."

"Statutory undertakers "means[1] persons authorised by any enactment to carry on any railway, light railway, tramway, road transport, water transport, canal, inland navigation, dock, harbour, pier or lighthouse undertaking or any undertaking for the supply of electricity, gas, hydraulic power or water.

---

[1] *See* s. 290.

Obstruction

Any person who wilfully[1] obstructs[2] a person acting in the exercise of the powers of entry is liable on summary conviction to a find of up to £20.[3]

Power to require information

To enable the Secretary of State or a local authority[4] to serve any notice or other document relative to the enforcement of planning control the Secretary of State or a local authority may by a notice in writing under section 284 of the Act as amended by the Town and Country Planning (Amendment) Act 1977 section 3 and the 1981 Act require the occupier of any premises and any person who, either directly or indirectly, receives rent in respect of any premises to give in writing within twenty-one days after the date of service of the notice or such longer time as specified in the notice, or as the Secretary of State or local authority may allow, such information as the notice specifies as to the following matters:—

(1) The nature of the interest in the premises of the person served with the notice.

(2) The name and address of any other person known to the recipient of the notice as having an interest in the premises.

(3) The purpose for which the premises are being used.

(4) The time when that use began.

(5) The name and address of any person known to the recipient of the notice as having used the premises for that purpose.

---

[1] This expression "means that the act is done deliberately and intentionally, not by accident or inadvertence, but so that the mind of the person who does the act goes with it" *per* Lord Russell, C.J. in *R. v. Senior* [1899] 1 Q.B. 283.

[2] Anything which makes it more difficult for a person to carry out his duty may it seems amount to an obstruction, and physical violence is not necessary. *See, e.g., Hinchcliffe v. Sheldon* [1955] 1 W.L.R. 1207.

[3] Section 281 (2).

[4] For definition, *see* s. 290. The term will include anyone exercising delegated powers.

(6) The time when any activities being carried on on the premises began.

A person served with such a requisition for information will need to exercise great care in answering it, particularly as to questions (3) (4) and (6) and would be well advised to take professional advice before doing so. It goes without saying that **accurate** information must be given, but the risk is rather in an incomplete, ambiguous or careless answer which could later prove a substantial difficulty in conducting an appellant's case at an appeal Inquiry.

Failure without reasonable excuse to give information so required renders the person responsible liable on summary conviction to a fine not exceeding £100.[1]

Any person who, in giving information so required, **knowingly** makes any **misstatement** in respect of it, is liable on summary conviction to a fine of up to £1000[2] or, on conviction on indictment, to imprisonment for a term not exceeding two years or to a fine of unlimited amount, or to both imprisonment and fine.[3]

FORM OF AN ENFORCEMENT NOTICE

There has been much litigation on the question of what form an Enforcement Notice must take, so that this is a matter which has always required the greatest care on the part of the draftsman. The law before the coming into force of the Local Government and Planning (Amendment) Act 1981 was contained in sub-Section (6) (7) and (8) of Section 87 of the 1971 Act. The 1981 Act came into force for this purpose on the 27th August 1981 and its provisions made significant amendments to the law by substituting a substantially amended Section 87 which attempts to overcome certain problems arising out of decided cases under the old provisions.

---

[1] Section 284 (2) as amended.

[2] The maximum fine was increased from £400 to £1000 by the Criminal Law Act 1977 section 28 (2) as from July 17th 1978.

[3] Section 284 (3) as amended.

In particular the new Section 87 (1) provides for a Planning Authority to **issue** an Enforcement Notice and then to serve copies of it on interested parties in accordance with the statutory provisions, whereas the earlier law had merely required a Notice to be served on interested parties. As will be clear from the cases referred to subsequently, the matter of service of an Enforcement Notice had given rise to a number of practical difficulties and the revised procedure for issuing an Enforcement Notice is intended to overcome these difficulties. The intention is that in future there will be no mistake that there is only one Notice issued (which takes effect on a date specified in it), for a particular alleged breach of planning control, and of course as hitherto each of the parties with an interest in the land will have to be served with it. In the annex to Circular 26/81 issued by the Department of the Environment and the Welsh Office on the 18th August 1981 it is stated that the new requirement to **issue** a Notice is interpreted as meaning that the Local Planning Authority should prepare a properly authorised document and retain it in their records.

The statutory amendments brought about by the 1981 Act are also intended to give Local Planning Authorities better powers to formulate the requirements of an Enforcement Notice so as, in the words of paragraph 6 of the Circular, "to bring about precisely the effect they consider appropriate to remedy a breach of planning control instead of being limited (as at present under sub-Section 6 (b)) to requiring steps which will restore the land to its prior condition or will secure compliance with planning conditions or limitations which have been breached". There are other amendments including a provision to enable authorities to specify that different steps for compliance with the Notice should be taken within different periods of time. All these matters are dealt with subsequently.

It still remains the law that an effective Enforcement Notice must deal with four matters as follows namely:

(1) The contravention

(2) The steps required for compliance

(3) The period for compliance

(4) The date the Notice takes effect.

The courses which may be open to the recipient of a Notice if it fails adequately to deal with these matters are discussed in Chapter 4 post.

The Town and Country Planning (Enforcement Notices and Appeals) Regulations[1] made by the Secretary of State under the 1981 Act, effective from 11th January 1982 now require (regulation 3) that every enforcement notice issued must specify:—

(1) The reasons why the local planning authority consider it "expedient" to issue the notice.

(2) The precise boundaries of the land to which the notice relates, whether by reference to a plan or otherwise.

In a circular[2] dealing with the regulations the Secretary of State suggests that the first mentioned information be given in a separate annex to the enforcement notice. He further suggests that the second requirement is "always best done by means of a plan (preferably on an Ordnance Survey base with a scale not less than 1/2500)."

The four requirements mentioned above will now be examined in more detail.

(1) The contravention

The Notice must specify the matters alleged to constitute a breach of planning control. As to what is such a breach see *ante*, page 91.

The rule derived from the early decisions of the Courts was that strict and rigid adherence to the formalities prescribed by the Act was required for a valid enforcement notice.

In the Court of Appeal in *East Riding County Council v.*

---

[1] S.I. 1981, No. 1742.
[2] Circular 38/81 (Circular 57/81 for Wales).

Park Estates (Bridlington) Ltd.,[1] Denning, L.J., said "in my judgment an enforcement notice, in order to be valid, ought to **specify the particular development which is complained of** It could be one of three things: First, development carried out after 1st July 1948, without permission; secondly, breach of conditions after 1st July 1948; thirdly, development before 1st July 1948, in contravention of previous planning control.[2] These three complaints raise such different considerations that it seems to me to be necessary to the validity of the notice that it should specify clearly and distinctly which of them is charged against the owner in question".

In *Francis v. Yiewsley and West Drayton U.D.C.*[3] a notice was held invalid because it lacked any true factual basis. The notice had in that case alleged a use begun without planning permission when in fact a specific (temporary) permission then expired, had been granted in respect of the use in question.

In *Cater v. Essex County Council*[4] this principle was applied to invalidate an enforcement notice which alleged a use without planning permission when in fact a limited permission was available to the landowner by virtue of Article 3 and Class IV of the First Schedule to the 1950 General Development Order[5] which granted permission for the use of the land for any purpose on not more than 28 days in total in any calendar year.

This latter decision was followed by the Divisional Court in *Miller-Mead v. Minister of Housing and Local Government*[6] but the Court of Appeal, after considering these earlier decisions at length, reversed the Divisional Court's decision and held that *Cater's Case* was wrongly decided. The basis of this decision appears to be that if in fact a use is a **permanent** use, the **limited** permission by the

---

[1] [1957] A.C. 223.
[2] An enforcement notice in respect of such development cannot now be served.
[3] [1958] 1 Q.B. 478.
[4] [1960] 1 Q.B. 424.
[5] S.I. 1950, No. 728. The current General Development Order is S.I. 1977, No. 289 (as amended).
[6] [1963] 2 Q.B. 196.

General Development Order is not available and an allegation of use without permission is accurate. *Tidswell v. Secretary of State for the Environment and Thurrock Borough Council*[1] appears to support this approach.

In *Garland v. Minister of Housing and Local Government*[2] the Court of Appeal held that an enlargement of a house substantially exceeding the limits permitted under the General Development Order was correctly referred to in an enforcement notice as development **without planning permission**.

In the *Miller-Mead Case*,[1] Upjohn, L.J., postulated as the test for a valid enforcement notice the following "does the notice tell (the person on whom it is served) fairly what he has done wrong and what he must do to remedy it". This test was approved by the Court of Appeal in *Munnich v. Godstone R.D.C.*[3] It was also held in the *Miller-Mead Case*[1] that an inaccurate statement in an enforcement notice which could be the subject of appeal to the Minister did not invalidate an enforcement notice, since other methods of challenge on these grounds were excluded by section 177 of the 1962 Act, now section 243 of the 1971 Act (as to which, *see post*, page 197).

In the case of *Mansi v. Elstree R.D.C.*[4] the Divisional Court upheld a decision of the Minister not to quash an enforcement notice although there had been a misdescription of the pre-existing use, because there was no discrepancy between the facts alleged and the facts proved, such that the owner concerned could complain of injustice or say that the notice had not given him a fair picture of the case against him or such that doubt was cast on the *bona fides* of the local planning authority.

That an enforcement notice must correctly allege **either** development without permission **or** non-compliance with a condition or limitation, is still the law, as stated in the

---

[1] [1977] J.P.L. 104, D.C.
[2] (1968) 20 P. & C.R. 93, C.A.
[3] [1966] 1 W.L.R. 427, C.A.
[4] (1964) 108 S.J. 178, D.C.

Miller-Mead Case, and accepted by the Court of Appeal in the *Garland Case* (although Lord Denning, M.R., in the latter case, said the position might one day require reconsideration).

The Court in *Eldon Garages v. Kingston-upon-Hull County Borough Council*,[1] applying *East Riding County Council v. Park Estates (Bridlington)* and *Miller-Mead v. Minister of Housing and Local Government, supra*, reiterated that an enforcement notice must make it clear whether the alleged breach of planning control is development without planning permission or failure to comply with a condition of planning permission, although it was not necessary to use the precise words of the Act. In that case it was held that the notice did in fact make it clear on its true constructions that it alleged development without permission.

The concept of a "breach of planning control" had been introduced by section 15 (2) of the Town and Country Planning Act 1968 and it was intended[2] by this to get away from the necessity of stipulating whether the breach arose from development without permission or from failure to comply with a condition. This intention has not been fulfilled, however. In the *Eldon Garages Case* it was stated that the difference in wording between the earlier statutory provision (section 45 of the 1962 Act) and section 15 of the 1968 Act (now section 87 of the 1971 Act) was not sufficient, there being no clear indication in the Act that this was the intention, to make any change in the law. The 1981 Act has not altered the position.

If development has been carried out without permission the notice must say so, describing the development in question.

It is important to describe an authorised operation correctly. This is illustrated by the case of *Copeland Borough Council v. Secretary of State for the Environment and Ross*.[3]

---

[1] [1974] 1 All E.R. 358, Templeman, J.

[2] *See* Department of the Environment publication "*Selected Enforcement and Allied Appeals*", October 1974, p. 23.

[3] (1976) 31 P. & C.R. 403, D.C.

In that case there was planning permission for erection of a house with grey roofing slates. The house was built with buff coloured tiles. An enforcement notice described the alleged contravention as building operations consisting of the construction of the roof of the dwelling in buff coloured tiles and it required the removal of the tiles. The Secretary of State allowed an appeal on the ground that the notice wrongly stated the breach of planning control. This decision was upheld by the Divisional Court, Lord Widgery, C.J., posing the question of whether the breach consisted of building a **house** not in accordance with the plans or building a **roof** not in accordance with the plans and answering that question by ruling that the former was the case. The mistake was held to be too fundamental for the Secretary of State to correct[1] without causing injustice.

It should be noted that although in circular 26/81 the Secretary of State (dealing with the 1981 Act) refers to that Act as overcoming problems caused by (*inter alia*) the *Copeland Borough Council Case* the Act does nothing to disturb the principle here discussed; that the breach of planning control must be correctly identified.

In *Clarke v. the Minister of Housing and Local Government*[2] the Divisional Court discussed the question of whether in the case of a material change of use an enforcement notice ought to recite the use before the change took place. It appears from this case that although there may be cases where it is desirable to do so, there is no **general** requirement disregard of which will invalidate a notice.

It is not necessary for an enforcement notice to identify the **planning unit**[3] in question and it will not be invalid because it does not do so.[4]

A notice may be directed to the whole planning unit or to a part of it.[5] However, an authority must not arbitrarily

[1] As to the Secretary of State's power of correction, *see post*, p. 179.
[2] (1966) 64 L.G.R. 346.
[3] As to the *planning unit*, *see* p. 8, *ante*.
[4] *Hawkey v. Secretary of State for the Environment* (1971) 22 P. & C.R. 610. As to the *planning unit*, *see ante*, p. 8.
[5] *See Morris v. Thurrock Borough Council* (1976) 237 E.G. 649.

divide a unit up and serve separate enforcement notices for different parts so as to impose on the owner greater restrictions than those to which he would be subject under a single notice for the whole planning unit.[2] This principle was enunciated in *De Mulder v. Secretary of State for the Environment*,[1] the facts of which are set out *ante*, page 18.

Where there is a failure to comply with any conditions or limitations imposed on a permission the notice should recite the permission and the conditions or limitations in question and give particulars of the acts or omissions which constitute the contravention.

As described previously (pages 57 to 67, *ante*) the result of sections 41 and 42 of the 1971 Act is that there will be conditions imposing time limits on most permissions, requiring the development to be begun within a specified period. It is not of course a breach of planning control merely to refrain from carrying out development but it **is** a breach to begin the development after the date in question. In effect a permission subject to a section 41 or section 42 condition lapses if the development is not begun within the specified period, and development thereafter is development without permission.

It is suggested that in such a case the notice should recite the permission and the condition (stating whether deemed or expressly imposed) and that the development the subject of the permission was not begun within the period in question and should then state expressly that the development was begun on a date after the expiration of the period without planning permission.

As also earlier described (page 60, *ante*), even where development the subject of conditions under sections 41 or 42 has been **begun** (but not completed) within the specified period, it may be affected by a **completion notice** under section 44 of the 1971 Act. Where a completion notice takes effect, the planning permission to which it refers will, at the end of the period specified in the completion notice (or

---

[1] [1974] 1 All E.R. 776, D.C.

substituted by the Secretary of State in confirming the notice), become invalid, except so far as it authorised development, carried out under the permission up to the end of the period.

In such a case the enforcement notice should, it is suggested, recite the permission and the condition (stating whether deemed or expressly imposed), that the development the subject of the permission was begun within the specified period, and that the period has elapsed without the development having been completed. It should then further recite the completion notice, that by virtue of that notice the planning permission ceased to have effect on a certain date (stating it), and that development (specifying it) has been carried out after that date without planning permission.

(2) The steps required for compliance

The notice must specify any steps required to be taken to remedy the breach of planning control complained of.

These may require restoration of the land to its condition before the development took place,[1] or, according to the circumstances of the case, compliance with the conditions or limitations subject to which permission was granted. In cases arising out of requirements of sections 41 or 42 of the 1971 Act followed by completion notices the developer can only be required to restore the land to its condition **at the expiry of the relevant period** prescribed in a completion notice, since earlier development is not unlawful.[2] The steps may include demolition or alteration of any building or works, the discontinuance of any use or the carrying out on the land of building or other operations.

Even before the 1981 Act it was apparent from *Iddenden and Others v. Secretary of State for the Environemnt*[3] that a notice need not require complete restoration of the earlier

---

[1] Where there is development beyond the limits of the General Development Order the requirement need not be confined to the "excess" development. *See Garland v. Minister of Housing and Local Government, supra.*

[2] *See ante*, pp. 60 to 63.

[3] [1972] 1 W.L.R. 1433.

situation, but might require less than that. The 1981 Act has however introduced a greater flexibility into the authority's powers. They may under the substituted section 87 (10) of the 1971 Act require steps to be taken to **make the development comply with the terms of any planning permission** which has been granted in respect of the land or for **removing or alleviating any injury to amenity** which has been caused by the development. So, they may insist on complete restoration to the original state of affairs, or something less than that (to the extent necessary to comply with a planning permission, a permission under a development order[1] or a deemed permission,[1] or to remove or alleviate injury to amenity. Moreover, they need not require **any** restoration as such but may confine the requirement as to steps to be taken to steps directed solely to removing or alleviating injury to amenity with the development itself remaining e.g. they may require landscaping works or erection of a screen fence, or hours of work at a factory to be restricted to those specified. In any case where the enforcement notice relates to development by the erection of a building or the carrying out of works (as distinct from a change of use) and steps are required to be taken for the purpose of removing or alleviating injury to amenity caused by that development the taking of those steps will automatically result in planning permission for retention of the building or works in question as they are as a result of compliance with the notice, being deemed to be granted on an application.[2] Under the new section 87 (11) where the alleged unauthorised development the subject of an enforcement notice includes development which has involved the making of a deposit of refuse or waste materials, the steps to be taken may be that the contour of the deposit may be modified by altering the gradient or gradients of its sides as specified in the notice.

Where a developer has partly completed development for which he has permission, it will not be possible to require him to complete it, unless there was a specific condition attached to his permission which required him to do so.

---

[1] As to such permission see *ante*, pp. 44 and 45.
[2] Section 87 (16).

It is true that in *Copeland Borough Council v. Secretary of State for the Environment and Ross (see ante*, page 109) it was decided that a planning permission was for the building of a house as an entirety and not for the numerous separate operations comprising the erection of the total building, and it might be argued from that that where a part only of a building is put up an enforcement notice could require its completion, on the basis that what had been done was development without permission. It is submitted that this is not sound. In the *Copeland Case* the house was erected in whole but with a part (the roof) not in accordance with the planning permission. It was clear that there was no planning permission for the house as erected.

Lord Widgery, C.J., in the course of his judgment referred to the possibility of an eccentric developer leaving holes in walls or leaving the roof off, if a planning permission was regarded as approving a number of separate operations comprising the construction of a house. He said this would be very unsatisfactory, as of course it would but with respect to the learned Lord Chief Justice it seems difficult to say that if a person simply starts, but does not finish, a building operation authorised by a planning permission (and does not depart from the approved plans as the owner did in the Copeland case) he is carrying out development without permission. The Completion Notice procedure described earlier (page 60) which is of almost universal application appears in any case to provide **some** machinery to facilitate completion of buildings.

In *Ormston v. Horsham R.D.C.*[1] the Court of Appeal refused to declare invalid an enforcement notice which required discontinuance of a use and removal of buildings and the **restoration of the land to its condition before the development** without specifying the actual steps required, the owner in that case well knowing what the previous condition of the land was.

Where there is an established use followed by development, any enforcement notice served in respect of that de-

[1] (1965) 63 L.G.R. 452.

velopment must be in such terms that the established use is safeguarded.

The leading case is *Mansi v. Elstree Rural District Council*[1] which concerned a notice requiring discontinuance of sales of any goods from certain premises, whereas there was evidence of an established use for retailing of garden nursery products which should have been, but initially was not, safeguarded. The notice was remitted to the Minister for variation accordingly. Later cases[2] have extended the principle to protect ancillary uses properly established and Use Class Order rights arising out of a revision to a formal lawful use. (For a case where the Divisional Court held that it was **unnecessary** to provide for a lawful ancillary use because in that case it would be to "specify the obvious" see *Cord v. Secretary of State for the Environment*.)

(3) The period for compliance

The notice must specify a period for compliance with its terms. The time allowed must be reasonable and will not begin to run until the notice has become effective (*see post*).

The 1981 Act now provides (in the substituted section 87 (8) that the notice may specify different periods for the taking of different steps. This provision is a consequence of the amended provisions described earlier which widened the scope of what steps may be required to be taken. The reasonableness of the period given was, prior to the 1981 Act, a matter which could be raised before Justices on a prosecution (see *Smith v. King post*, p. 206) but as there stated such a matter can **not** now be raised except by appeal to the Secretary of State (as to such appeals see *post*, p. 152).

The period may be extended at the discretion of the

---

[1] (1964) 16 P. & C.R. 153. See also *Trevors Warehouses v. Secretary of State for the Environment* (1972) 23 P. & C.R. 215, D.C., *Ipswich County Borough Council v. Secretary of State for the Environment* (1972) 225 E.G. 797, D.C. and *Clever v. Secretary of State for the Environment* [1981] J.P.L. 38.

[2] See *e.g. Newport v. Secretary of State for the Environment and Bromley London Borough Council* (1980) 40 P. & C.R. 261, D.C. and *Day v. Secretary of State for the Environment* (1979) 78 L.G.R. 27, D.C.

authority (*see* section 89 (6) and section 91), but it does not appear that the authority has any discretion to vary the time allowed for compliance, once that period has expired. Their rights of subsequent action have accrued and postponements of exercise of these powers will be merely acts of grace which would not prevent action contrary to their terms. This was the view taken in *Joyner v. Guildford Corporation*[1] (a County Court case).

Again in *St. Albans District Council v. Norman Harper Autosales*[2] the Divisional Court took the view that the power to extend time for compliance had to be exercised before the expiry of the initial time specified, although the circumstances of this case were perhaps a little unusual and the purported extension was a unilateral act of the authority to the prejudice of the developer. For the facts of this case see *post*, p. 219.

No estoppel can be raised to hinder the exercise of a statutory discretion[3] and a local authority cannot **contract** not to exercise its statutory powers. Any such purported contract is unenforceable.[4]

(4) The date the notice takes effect

Section 87 (13) now provides that an enforcement notice is to take effect "on a date specified in it". Therefore the notice must specify a calendar date and having regard to provisions about service in sub-section (5) (as to which see *post*) the date so specified must be one more than 28 days following service of the notice.

Before the coming into force of the new provisions the requirements were different in that a notice had to specify

---

[1] (1954) 5 P. & C.R. 30.

[2] (1977) 121 S.J. 851, D.C.

[3] *See Southend-on-Sea Corporation v. Hodgson (Wickford) Ltd.* [1962] 1 Q.B. 416. *See also Lever Finance v. Westminster (City) London Borough Council, supra*, and *Norfolk County Council v. Secretary of State for the Environment* [1973] 3 All E.R. 673, D.C., the facts of which are set out *ante*, p. 48. See also as to estoppel *ante*, p. 92.

[4] *See Triggs v. Staines U.D.C.* (1968) 2 W.L.R. 1433 *sub nom. Re Staines U.D.C.'s Agreement, Triggs v. Staines U.D.C.* [1968] 2 All E.R. 1. *See also Stringer v. Minister of Housing and Local Government, ante*, p. 50.

a period at the expiration of which it was to take effect, which period had to be not less than 28 days after service.

Difficulties which had previously arisen (see *Bambury v. London Borough of Hounslow* discussed *post*, p. 122 and *Stevens v. London Borough of Bromley Post*, p. 120) because of the fixing of time limits by reference to date of service appear to have been overcome by the new provision about "issuing" a notice with a fixed date for coming into effect and a fixed date for compliance, but an authority must still bear carefully in mind, when fixing a date of coming into effect, that all those to be served must receive the notice 28 days before it is to take effect and they must allow sufficient time for this. Defective service is a ground of appeal to the Secretary of State (see *post*, p. 155).

Under the earlier provisions, failure to specify separately and distinctly from the period for compliance, the date when the notice takes effect was held to render the notice a nullity.[1]

An appeal[2] suspends the operation of an enforcement notice pending final determination or withdrawal of the appeal.[3]

An appeal is to be regarded as finally determined when the time limited for a further appeal from a particular tribunal has expired without the institution of any such appeal and disregarding the possibility of obtaining leave to appeal out of time.[4]

Notice of Right of Appeal

Regulation 4 of the Town and Country Planning (Enforcement Notices and Appeals) Regulations 1981[5] made under the 1981 Act now requires an enforcement notice served by a local planning authority to be accompanied by (a) a copy

---

[1] *Burgess v. Jarvis* [1952] 2 Q.B. 41; *Mead v. Chelmsford R.D.C.* [1953] 1 Q.B. 32. In *Godstone v. Brazil*, [1953] 1 W.L.R. 1102, a requirement to remove a caravan "within seven days after the expiry of 28 days from the date of service" of a notice was held by the Divisional Court to be insufficient in that the notice "does not state that the notice will take effect at the expiration of 28 days".

[2] As to appeals, *see post*, Chapter 4.

[3] Section 88 (10). *See also Button v. Jenkins* discussed *post*, p. 164.

[4] *See Garland v. Westminster London Borough Council* (1970) 21 P. & C.R. 555.

[5] S.I. 1981, No. 1742 effective from 11 January 1982.

of sections of 87 to 87 B of the 1971 Act or a summary of those sections which explains that there is a right of appeal to the Secretary of State against the notice and that any appeal must be in writing and give grounds on which an appeal can be made and (b) notification that an appeal must be supported simultaneously (or within time limits imposed by the Secretary of State) by a statement of the grounds and facts on which it is based. The Department of the Environment in circular 38/81 issued on 18th December 1981 suggests that the best method of meeting this requirement is to send with the enforcement notice a copy of the Department's explanatory booklet "Enforcement Notice Appeals – A guide to Procedure" and a copy of the official appeal form.

SERVICE OF MORE THAN ONE NOTICE

Two alternative forms of enforcement notices may be served, though inconsistent with each other, provided that each is precise and unambiguous in itself and the fact that the notices are in the alternative is made clear to the persons served.[1]

SERVICE OF NOTICE

Persons to be served

A copy of the notice **must**[2] be served on the owner and the occupier of the land to which it relates. (Formerly the notice itself had to be so served.)

If the land is ecclesiastical property a copy notice must also be served on the Church Commissioners.[3]

"Ecclesiastical property" means[4] land belonging to an ecclesiastical benefice, or being or forming part of (*a*) a church, (*b*) the site of a church, or (*c*) a burial ground,

---

[1] *See Britt v. Buckinghamshire County Council* (1962) 60 L.G.R. 430.
[2] Section 87 (5).
[3] Section 274 (1).
[4] Section 274 (5).

either of which is subject to the jurisdiction of a bishop of a diocese.

If any other person has an interest in the land and the local planning authority are of opinion that his interest is materially affected by the notice they **must**[1] serve the notice on him also.

"Owner" is defined[2] as "a person other than a mortgagee not in possession who, whether in his own right or as trustee for any other person is entitled to receive the rack rent of the land, or where the land is not let at a rack rent, would be so entitled if it were so let". This definition was considered in *London Corporation v. Cusack-Smith*.[3] The Corporation were the assignees of a lease at a rent less than the rack rent. It was held that the freeholders were not "owners" within the meaning of the definition as the land was not let at a rack rent, and it was the Corporation who would be entitled to let at a rack rent to a new hypothetical tenant.

The 1962 Act definition of "owner" included a person entitled to receive the rack rent **as agent** but the definition was amended by the 1968 Act[4] to exclude such a person. The amendment was effective from 1st April 1969.[5]

"Occupier" is not defined, but it appears that the question of who is the occupier will be one of fact in each case. The question was considered in the case of *Caravans and Automobiles Ltd. v. Southall Borough Council*[6] when it was held that the word "occupier" in the section in question must mean all the occupiers of the land the subject of the enforcement notice.

In the case of *Munnich v. Godstone R.D.C.*[7] the Court of Appeal made some observations on the question of whether Enforcement Notices ought to be served on the occupants

---

[1] Section 87 (5) (*b*).
[2] Section 290.
[3] [1955] A.C. 337.
[4] Section 106 and School, 9, para. 53 (*c*) and Sched. 11 of 1968 Act.
[5] S.I. 1969, No. 275.
[6] [1963] 1 W.L.R. 690.
[7] [1966] 1 W.L.R. 427.

of caravans. In that case T and the Plaintiff were the owners of one and a half-acre field on which they had allowed 4 caravans to be stationed, all of which were occupied. Enforcement Notices were served on the Plaintiff and T in each of which they were described as the owners and one of the caravan dwellers as the occupier, requiring them in each case to remove the caravan concerned from the field. The Court held that the documents to served constituted a valid Enforcement Notice properly served on the Plaintiff and T who were in fact the owners and also the occupiers of the land. The caravan dwellers were merely licensees and the fact that they were served as occupiers was immaterial, it having been unnecessary to have served them at all. In the course of his judgement, Lord Denning, M.R., said "they had the 4 documents with the names of the caravan dwellers on them telling them what ought to be done, namely, remove those caravans from the land. I can see no difficulty whatever in holding that all 4 documents, coupled together and served together, constitute a perfectly valid Enforcement Notice. I know that (the caravan dwellers) were described as 'occupiers'. That was erroneous. They were not occupiers within the meaning of the Act. They were simply caravan dwellers. Caravan dwellers are only licensees and are never to be regarded as occupiers unless they are granted a tenancy. It was unnecessary to serve them at all." He also said that he did not think it was necessary for all the occupiers to be named in one Notice.

However, it was observed by Danckwerts, L.J., and Salmon, L. J., in the same case, that there **might** be cases where caravan dwellers were occupiers for the purpose of service of an Enforcement Notice, and in a later case, that of *Stevens v. Bromley London Borough Council*,[1] the Court of Appeal (Stamp, L.J. dissenting) has held that to be an occupier it is **not** necessary to have a legal or equitable interest in land. In that case an owner had a site for caravans, selling caravans as permanent homes to licensees of his. Enforcement notices were served on the owner and a licensee on different dates and so, on the authority of the

---

[1] [1972] 1 All E.R. 712.

Bambury Case,[1] were not valid if the licensee was an "occupier" for the purpose of the Act. (The question of the correctness of the decision in the *Bambury Case* was expressly left open by the Court.) The licensee in this case **was** an "occupier".

In this case, Salmon, L.J., regarded the question of whether a licensee was or was not an **occupier** as one of fact and degree and Edmund Davies, L.J., had regard to the element of control and duration of enjoyment of the premises by the caravan dweller. It is clearly a wise precaution to serve a Notice on caravan dwellers as well as on the owner and anyone else appearing to be an occupier. Nothing can be lost by so doing.

There may be other cases where it is desirable to serve to several people as 'occupiers', who might possibly be thought at first sight not to be necessary recipients of an enforcement notice—*e.g.* people in bed-sitting room accommodation. In *Mayflower Cambridge Ltd. v. Secretary of State for the Environment and Another*[2] the Divisional Court held that there was a proper distinction between rooms in a hotel and rooms used as bed-sitting room accommodation depending on the stability or transient nature of the occupants and the extent to which they made the rooms their homes.

Failure to serve copies of an enforcement notice as required by the statute will be a ground for appeal to the Secretary of State and in the case of an owner of an interest may be a defence to prosecution under section 89 in certain circumstances (see *post*, p. 199).

Method of service

A notice may be served in any of the following ways[3]:—

1. By delivering it to the person to whom it is addressed.
2. By leaving it at the usual or last known place of

---

[1] *Infra*, p. 122.
[2] (1975) 30 P. & C.R. 28, D.C.
[3] Section 283.

abode[1] of that person or where an address for service has been furnished, at that address. It may be that where a person places a box *e.g.* at the end of a path in which communications can be and are habitually placed he will be taken to have invited, if not requested, use of the box (other than for anything requiring a signed receipt) and so a notice placed in such a box may be sufficiently served by being left at his usual place of abode.[2]

3. By sending it in a prepaid registered letter or by the recorded delivery service, the letter being addressed to the person concerned at his usual or last known place of abode,[3] or where an address for service has been given, at that address.

4. In the case of a corporation by delivery to the secretary or clerk of the corporate body at their registered or principal office, or by sending it in a prepaid registered letter or by the recorded delivery service addressed to the secretary or clerk of the body at that office.

In relation to the service of an enforcement notice before the coming into force of the 1981 Act provisions[3] relating to this matter the case of *Bambury v. London Borough of Hounslow*[4] needs to be borne carefully in mind. (This case was referred to in the Court of Appeal in *Stevens v. Bromley London Borough Council* (*supra*) when the Court expressly refrained from pronouncing upon its correctness.) In that case enforcement notices properly drawn, in exactly the same terms were served on three occupiers of land, on 22nd August 1964. The notices stated that they were to take effect 28 clear days after service. The occupiers were not the owners of the land and on 8th September 1964, similar notices were served on the owners. They were in the same terms and were stated to take effect 28 clear days after

[1] Or perhaps of business. *See Morecambe and Heysham Corporation v. Warwick* (1958), 56 L.G.R. 283.

[2] See *Steeples v. Derbyshire County Council* [1981] J.P.L. 581, Webster, J.

[3] 27 August, 1981.

[4] [1966] 2 Q.B. 204.

service. The occupiers appealed to the Minister, who upheld the notices. There was then an appeal to the Divisional Court under section 180 of the 1962 Act (now section 246 of the 1971 Act).[1]

It was argued for the appellants that there could not be two dates for the coming into force of an enforcement notice, and that if there were, then there were really two notices differing in an essential particular. In this case the notices were, by virtue of their terms to come into effect on two different dates, and so no valid notice had been served on the appellants.

Counsel for the Minister conceded that an enforcement notice could have only one effective date, but argued that since there had been an appeal to the Minister, there was now a common effective date because both would, by virtue of section 46 (3) (now section 88 (3) of the 1971 Act) take effect on final determination of the appeal. He also suggested that the Minister could, by exercising his power of correction,[2] alter the notices to provide for a common effective date, although it was in fact not necessary for him to do so.

The Court rejected the arguments in the preceding paragraph and quashed the notices, holding that the result of the notices being served on the occupiers and owner respectively on different dates was that the notices came into effect at different times, which was a fatal defeat, not cured by the fact that the appeal to the Minister meant that all the notices could not take effect until final determination of the appeal. They further held that the Minister could not cure the defect by exercising his powers of correction, because the materiality of the defect was to be judged at the outset and not at the moment of appeal.

It is clear, therefore, that if an enforcement notice served before the coming into effect of the 1981 Act was specified to take effect from a stated number of days after service, it

---

[1] As to Section 246, *see post*, p. 193.

[2] Formerly under s. 16 (4) (*a*), 1968 Act, now s. 88 (4).

was essential that it be served on all owners and occupiers on the same day.

The decision in the *Bambury Case* appeared to give rise to a dilemma. Before this case it had been the practice to specify the date of taking effect by reference to the date of service, *e.g.* "28 days from service", in order to overcome the difficulty that one might not be sure of the actual date of service in each case, and that accordingly if one stated a **specific** effective date one might find that it turned out to be less than the required[1] 28 days from service, and thus the notice would be invalid on this ground. This practice appeared to be jeopardised by the *Bambury* decision for the same sort of reason as the stating of a **specific** effective date was unsatisfactory, *i.e.* because the actual dates of service on various persons might turn out to be widely different, even if the notices were issued on the same date, through no fault of the authority, perhaps because of postal delays or for other reasons. Whatever form was used it was of course possible to provide for a date of taking effect well in excess of 28 days in the hope that it would turn out, in respect of each recipient, to be in excess of the required 28 days from service, but there was still the element of uncertainty, which might, particularly where the four-year rule[2] applied, be fatal to enforcement action.

In the case of *Moody v. Godstone R.D.C.*,[3] heard by the Divisional Court a short while after the *Banbury Case*, the appellant, who was the owner of a caravan site, had been convicted of not complying with an enforcement notice, which had been served on him by A.R. registered post. The justices had found as a fact that the notice had been posted on 1st June 1965 by registered post. He had denied on oath that it had been served, stating that he was out of the country at the time, and had not been cross-examined on this denial. He appealed against conviction.

The Court held that the adducing of evidence of posting

---

[1] *See ante*, p. 116.
[2] As to the four-year rule, *see post*, p. 134.
[3] [1966] 1 W.L.R. 1085.

of the notice by prepaid registered post was sufficient by virtue of section 214 (1) (*c*)[1] of the 1962 Act and section 26 of the Interpretation Act 1889[2] to prove service of the enforcement notice on the appellant, who had therefore been rightly convicted.

Section 26 of the 1889 Act[3] provided that:—

> "Where an Act passed after the commencement of this Act, authorises or requires any document to be served by post, whether the expression 'serve' or the expression 'give' or 'send' or any other expression is used, then, unless the contrary intention appears the service shall be deemed to be effected by properly addressing, prepaying and posting a letter containing the document and unless the contrary is proved to have been effected at the time at which the letter would be delivered in the ordinary course of post."

In the course of his judgment James, J., referred to the judgment of Parker, L.J., in *R. v. Appeal Committee of County of London Quarter Sessions Ex parte Rossi*[4] in which the latter had dealt with section 26 and referred to it as being in two parts, the first providing that despatch of a document in the manner laid down should be deemed to be service of it, and the second providing that, unless the contrary was proved, service was effected on the day when in the ordinary course of post the document would be delivered. Parker, L.J. had said in that case "This second part . . . comes into play, and only comes into play, in a case where under the legislation to which the section is being applied the document has to be received by a certain time. If in such a case the contrary is proved, *i.e.* that the document was not received by that time or at all, then the position appears to be that, though under the first part of the section the document is deemed to have been served, it has been proved that it was not served in time."

---

[1] The provisions of this sub-subsection are set out on p. 122, *ante*, as the third method of service.

[2] See now Section 7 and Schedule 2, para. 3 of the Interpretation Act, 1978.

[3] See now Section 7 and Schedule 2, para. 3 of the Interpretation Act, 1978.

[4] [1956] 1 All .E.R 670.

James J., went on to say that in the case of an enforcement notice, one has to look at the event of serving the notice and at that point of time, and that at that point of time there is no vital element that the enforcement notice has to be served by or at a particular date in question, and that the second limb of section 26 of the Interpretation Act cannot therefore be invoked in such a case.

Hewitt v. Leicester Corporation[1] in the Court of Appeal concerned the question of service of a notice to treat in respect of land acquisition under the Housing Act 1957. In May 1965 the Corporation sent a notice to treat by recorded delivery to the last known address of a claimant. It was returned to them marked "Gone away". In December 1965 the notice was served on the claimant through agents. On the hearing of the claimant's compensation claim the parties agreed the value of the property as at the "date of service" in May and the "date of service" in December, the latter figure being half as much again as the former. The Corporation contended that under the relevant statutory provisions, including section 26 of the Interpretation Act 1889,[2] the notice had been effectively served in May, but the Lands Tribunal had rejected this argument and against that decision the Corporation appealed.

The Court of Appeal dismissed their appeal, holding that the time of service was important, since the valuation depended upon it. (At that time it was thought to be the law that compensation must be assessed as at the date of the service of notice to treat—a longstanding belief which in *Birmingham Corporation v. West Midland Baptist (Trust) Association (Incorporated)*[3] the House of Lords later held to be erroneous). Accordingly, a notice could not be "deemed" to have been served at a time when in fact it had not been. The Court held that the notice had been served in December and the higher valuation therefore applied. *R. v. London County Quarter Sessions Appeals Committee, Ex*

---

[1] (1969) 67 L.G.R. 436.
[2] See now Section 7 and Schedule 2, para. 3 of the Interpretation Act 1978.
[3] [1970] A.C. 874.

parte Rossi was followed, and Moody v. Godstone R.D.C. distinguished.

It is submitted that the *Hewitt Case* does not disturb the decision in *Moody v. Godstone* for the reason that in the case of service of an enforcement notice the **time** of service is **not** of vital importance, whereas it was (or rather was believed to be) in *Hewitt's Case* and it was in *Rossi's Case*.

Maltglade Ltd. and Others v. St. Albans Rural District Council[1] concerns a **Building Preservation Notice**.[2]

The appellant company owned an empty property called Town Farm. The company had changed its address from 35 to 35A Manchester Street, Luton. The respondent council, having decided to serve a building preservation notice in respect of Town Farm, did so by sending a copy to the company by recorded delivery service addressed "35 Manchester Street" and a further copy to the "occupier" at Town Farm. The recorded delivery letter was never in fact delivered and was returned to the Post Office marked "Gone Away", the postman having been unable to identify the address on the envelope. No part of 35 Manchester Street was marked "35A" and the company's registered office was in fact in a room marked "Private". The letter to the occupier of Town Farm was also returned marked "deceased" to the council, on the 7th May. The letter to the company was returned to the council by the Post Office on the 11th May. Town Farm had meanwhile been demolished on the 8th May. The company were prosecuted and convicted. On the company's appeal against conviction the council contended that service must be deemed to have been effected by section 26 of the Interpretation Act 1889, but the contention was not accepted. The Court held that this was a case where **the time of service was important**, and therefore, although service was **deemed** to have been effected by the proper addressing, prepaying and posting of the letter, it was open to the appellant company to prove that the notice had not in fact been served in time and consequently to

[1] [1972] 3 All E.R. 129.
[2] As to such notices, *see post*, p. 276.

prove it was not served at all. As this notice was not in fact served the company could not be guilty of a breach and the conviction was quashed. Although the notice did not have to be served by a particular date on the calendar its effectiveness depended on its being received before demolition or, as Lord Widgery, C.L., put it in the course of his judgment "its effectiveness depended on its being received before the bulldozers came in and the actual demolition began". The *Rossi Case* was followed and *Moody v. Godstone R.D.C.* distinguished.[1]

Service where information lacking

Where a notice is to be served on a person as having an interest in premises and the **name** of that person cannot be ascertained after reasonable enquiry, or where the notice is to be served on a person as an occupier of premises, it may be addressed to him as "the owner" or "the occupier" of the premises (describing them) and served by method (1), (2) or (3) described at page 121, *ante*, or by method (*a*), (*b*) or (*c*) described in the next paragraph.[2]

Where the **address** of the person to be served cannot be ascertained after reasonable enquiry the notice may be served by addressing it to him by name, or by description as "the owner" or "the occupier" of the premises (describing them) and (*a*) sending it **to the premises** the subject of the notice, in a prepaid registered letter or by the recorded delivery service (provided that the letter is not returned to the authority sending it), (*b*) by delivery to some person on the premises, or (*c*) by affixing it conspicuously to some object on the premises.[1] In either of these cases the notice **and** envelope must be marked "**Important—This communication affects your property**".[3]

The provisions described above were formerly contained

---

[1] For other cases on service and s. 26 of the Interpretation Act *see Saga of Bond Street Ltd. v. Avalon Promotions Ltd.* [1972] 2 All E.R. 545n and *A/S Cathrineholm v. Norequipment Trading Ltd.* [1972] 2 All E.R. 538, C.A.

[2] Section 283 (2).

[3] *See* the Town and Country Planning General Regulations 1976 (S.I. 1419) replacing earlier Regulations and amending Regulation S.I. 1981, No. 558.

in section 105 of the 1947 Act and its effect was the subject of a decision of the Divisional Court in *Hammersmith London Borough Council v. Winner Investments Ltd. and Another.*[1] W. Ltd. were freeholders of a market site which was used with planning permission expiring on 31st March 1960. On 28th March 1960 the then yearly tenants, G.J.W. Ltd., resolved to transfer the stalls, etc., to M. Ltd. as from 1st April 1960 and W. Ltd. resolved to let the site to M. Ltd. On 9th May 1961 the local planning authority served enforcement notices in respect of the continuance of the use after the permitted date. The authority had previously made inquiries as to the parties interested in the site. They had been told that W. Ltd. were freeholders and that G.J.W. Ltd. was the lessee but were told nothing about M. Ltd. They served the enforcement notices on W. Ltd., G.J.W. Ltd., and on the stallholders, and copies of the notices addressed to "the owner" and "the occupier" were also fixed to the letting office on the site. Eventually proceedings were commenced against W. Ltd. and M. Ltd. for contravention of the enforcement notice. The justices found (*inter alia*) that M. Ltd. was the "owner" within the meaning of the relevant section (section 105 (1) (*d*) of the 1947 Act) and that the notice had not been properly served on M. Ltd. They dismissed the informations and the local planning authority appealed. It was held that it was **not** the case that service on a limited company could only be effected under section 105 (1) (*d*) (now section 283 (1) (*d*) of the 1971 Act—*see* method 4, page 122, *ante*) and that the purpose of what are now the provisions set out in the preceding two paragraphs was to provide alternative methods of service where the true identity of the persons with a relevant interest in the land could not be ascertained. The provision of a fictitious or wrong name could not deprive the authority of the right to use these methods. One of the alternatives had been used (*i.e.* fixing of the notices on the site) and there had accordingly been proper service on M. Ltd. as owners and occupiers.

If it appears to the authority serving a notice that any

[1] (1968) 66 L.G.R. 625, D.C.

part of the land in question is **unoccupied**, a notice will be deemed to be duly served on all persons having interest in, and on any occupiers of premises comprised in that part of the land (**other than a person who has given an address for service**) if it is addressed to "the owners and any occupiers" of that part of the land (describing it) and is affixed conspicuously to some object on the land.[1]

Time for service

Prior to the coming into force of Part II of the 1968 Act[2] an enforcement notice had to be served within four years of the carrying out of the development without planning permission or, in the case of a breach of a condition or limitation, within four years of the alleged failure to comply with it. Thus a person whose contravention remained undetected for four years acquired immunity from enforcement action. There is no doubt that this limitation, the "four-year rule", was a serious handicap to local planning authorities.

Part II of the 1968 Act[2] radically changed the position, and the provisions are now re-enacted in Part V of the 1971 Act, as amended by the 1981 Act.

With exceptions noted later (see *post*, p. 135) an enforcement notice may at any time be served in respect of any **material change of use**, or non-compliance with a condition or limitation relating to a material change of use, **which took place after the end of 1963**.[3] The four-year rule is therefore abolished so far as it relates to this kind of breach of planning control. (As to other kinds, *see post*, page 134.)

Established Use Certificate

As time goes on it will become increasingly difficult to establish the facts relating to commencement of the activity in question. In particular an owner will find it less and less

---

[1] Section 283 (3).

[2] Part II came into force on 1st April 1969. *See* the Town and Country Planning Act 1968 (Commencement No. 4) Order 1969 (S.I. 1969, No. 275).

[3] *See* s. 87 (1), 1971 Act.

easy to challenge an enforcement notice on the basis that his use began before the end of 1963.

To meet this difficulty the 1968 Act, by sections 17 and 18[1] and Schedule 2, provided machinery for the issue of an **established use certificate**. These provisions are now re-enacted in sections 94 and 95 and Schedule 14 of the 1971 Act.

If such a certificate is issued it is, as respects any matters stated in it, **conclusive** for the purposes of any appeal to the Secretary of State[2] against an enforcement notice in respect of any land to which the certificate relates, provided that a copy of the enforcement notice or before 27 August 1981,[3] the notice itself is served **after the date of the application** on which the certificate was granted.[4]

For the purpose of the provisions in question a use of land is established if[5]:—

(1) it was begun before the beginning of 1964 without planning permission **and has continued since the end of 1963**.

or (2) it was begun before the beginning of 1964 under a planning permission granted subject to conditions or limitations which either have never been complied with, or have not been complied with since the end of 1963.

or (3) it was begun **after the end of 1963** as the result of a change of use not requiring planning permission and there has been, since the end of 1963, no change of use requiring planning permission.

An application cannot be made in respect of a use not subsisting at the time of the application, nor can it in any case be made in respect of use of land as a single dwelling-house.[6]

---

[1] These sections came into force on 1st April 1969. *See* S.I. 1969, No. 275.

[2] As to such appeals, *see post*, Chapter 4.

[3] The date of coming into effect of amendments of the 1971 Act by the Act of 1981.

[4] Section 94 (7).

[5] Section 94 (1).

[6] Proviso to s. 94 (2).

An application[1] for an established use certificate is made to the local planning authority and may be made by any person having an interest in the land[2] in question.

A certificate must be granted by the local planning authority[3] if and so far as they are satisfied that the applicant's claim is made out, and if and so far as they are not so satisfied they must refuse the application.[4] If the authority do not, within the prescribed period,[5] or within such extended period as is at any time agreed upon in writing between the applicant and the authority, give notice to the applicant of their decision upon his application, the application is deemed to have been refused.[6]

A certificate may be granted either for the whole of the land specified in the application, or for part of it, or, in the case of an application specifying two or more uses, either for all those uses or for one or more of them.[7]

The date at which the use is to be certified as established is **the date on which the application for the certificate was made.**[8]

Great care is needed in drafting an established use certificate and especially to see that the use is not described in wider terms than necessary having regard to the extent of the land used and the intensity of use. Once a certificate is issued the description of use is conclusive and cannot be altered or "explained" by any evidence as to actual user at the material time.[9]

The authority are required to keep a register of decisions

---

[1] As to the manner of making such an application, *see* Sched. 14 of the 1971 Act and the Town and Country Planning General Development Order 1977 (S.I. No. 289) as amended.

[2] This will include, *e.g.* a person who has contracted to buy the land, or to take a lease, or who has an option to purchase.

[3] Or by an officer to whom the power has been delegated. *See ante*, p. 47.

[4] Section 94 (4).

[5] *See* Article 14A, S.I. 1963, No. 709, *supra*.

[6] Section 94 (5).

[7] Section 94 (3).

[8] *See* Sched. 14, para. 4.

[9] See *Broxbourne Borough Council* v. *Secretary of State for the Environment* (1978) 38 P. & C.R. 31, D.C.

on applications for established use certificates and this register is open to public inspection. Where the Secretary of State, under the powers described below, grants a certificate he is required so to notify the authority.[1]

The Secretary of State has power[2] to direct that applications for established use certificates shall be referred to him to be dealt with.

There is also provision[2] for appeal to the Secretary of State against a refusal (whether deemed or express), of a local planning authority to grant a certificate or a refusal in part, and on such an appeal the Minister may grant a certificate, or modify the certificate granted by the authority or dismiss the appeal. His decision on an application referred to him, or on appeal, is final[2] (but subject to section 245 of the Act, as to which, *see* page 195, *post*).

On any application referred to him under the provision mentioned above, or on an appeal, the Secretary of State has power,[3] in respect of any land for which a certificate is *not* granted, to grant planning permission for the use in question or, as the case may be, for continuance of the use without complying with some condition subject to which a previous planning permission was granted. The authority do *not* have this power in dealing with the application in the first instance.

Before determining any application or appeal the Secretary of State must, if either the applicant or the appellant, as the case may be, or the local planning authority so desire, afford each an opportunity of appearing before and being heard by a person appointed by him for that purpose.[4] See *post*, p. 166 as to Rules[5] giving the procedure where a Local Inquiry is held.

If any person, for the purpose of procuring a particular decision on an application (whether by himself or by some-

---

[1] *See* Sched. 14, para. 5, 1971 Act.
[2] Section 95.
[3] Section 95 (3).
[4] Section 95 (4).
[5] S.I. 1981, No. 1743.

one else) for an established use certificate, or on any appeal:—

(*a*) knowingly[1] or recklessly[2] makes a statement which is false[3] in a material particular;

or (*b*) with intent to deceive, produces, furnishes, sends or otherwise makes use of any document which is false in a material particular;

or (*c*) with intent to deceive, withholds any material information;

he is guilty of an offence and liable on summary conviction to a fine of up to £1000[4] or on conviction on indictment to imprisonment for up to 2 years or to a fine of unlimited amount, or to both imprisonment and fine.[5]

Four Year Rule

The exceptions mentioned at page 130, *ante*, in relation to time for service of an enforcement notice have now to be dealt with. In respect of a breach of planning control consisting of the following an enforcement notice may only be served within a period of four years from the date of the breach.[6]

(1) the carrying out without planning permission of building, engineering, mining or other operations in, on, over or under land.

It appears that the four year period does not

[1] Deliberately to refrain from making inquiries because one might not find the results what one would wish *may* constitute actual knowledge, but mere neglect to find out facts ascertainable by making reasonable inquiries is not tantamount to knowledge. *See dicta* of Devlin, J., in *Taylors Central Garages (Exeter) Ltd. v. Roper* (1951) 115 J.P. 445 at pp. 449, 450. *See also Mallon v. Allon* [1963] 3 All E.R. 843 and *Wallworth v. Balmer* [1965] 3 All E.R. 721.

[2] A statement is recklessly made if the maker has no honest belief in its truth. *See Derry v. Peck* (1889) 14 Appl. Cas. 337.

[3] A statement may be false on account of what it omits even though it is literally true. *See dicta* of Denning, L.J., in *Curtis v. Chemical Cleaning and Dyeing Co. Ltd.* [1951] 1 All E.R. 631; 1 K.B. 805, C.A., at pp. 634 and 808, 809.

[4] Minimum fine increased from £400 by the Criminal Law Act 1977, section 28 (2).

[5] Section 94 (8).

[6] *See* s. 87 (4).

begin to run until the substantial completion of the operation in question and that **parts** of the operation, though themselves completed over four years ago, may be caught by an enforcement notice relating to the operations of which they form a part, provided the notice is served within four years of the completion of the whole operation. This was so in *Ewen Developments v. Secretary of State for the Environment and North Norfolk District Council*[1] in which it was held that the whole of an embankment could be required to be demolished, although parts of it had been erected more than four years before the date of the enforcement notice. Where activities are carried out which in themselves are operational in character but in fact are an integral part of a material change of use an enforcement notice in respect of that change of use may properly require land to be restored to its pre-change of use condition and also require the incidental operational development to be removed, irrespective of the period it may of itself have been *in situ*. See *Murfitt v. Secretary of State for the Environment and East Cambridgeshire District Council.*[2] It seems too that the same result may follow even though the operational development was not an integral part of the change of use.[3]

(2) failure to comply with any condition or limitation which relates to the carrying out of such operations and subject to which planning permission was granted for that development.

(3) Making without planning permission of a change of use of any building **to use as a single dwelling house**.

(4) Failure to comply with a condition which prohibits or has the effect of preventing a change of use of a building to use as a single dwelling house.

---

[1] [1980] J.P.L. 404, D.C.

[2] (1980) 40 P. & C.R. 254, D.C.

[3] See *dictum* of Glidewell, J. in *Perkins v. Secretary of State for the Environment and Rother District Council* [1981] J.P.L. 755.

The breach dealt with in (4) above was added by the 1981 Act. *Backer and Aird v. Secretary of State for the Environment*[1] concerned an enforcement notice in respect of an upper storey build in 1969 for which a planning permission had been granted for use as a loft with a condition that the loft should only be used for storage connected with the residential use of the property. The notice was served after the expiry of four years from the breach. The Divisional Court held the breach to be covered by the provisions described in (3) above.

So far as mining operations are concerned every separate act of abstraction is a separate development.[2] It follows therefore that even though mining operations as a whole started more than four years before, any abstraction within the last four years will make it possible for an enforcement notice to be served stopping further workings.

By providing that, where the four-year rule no longer applies, the development must have taken place after the end of 1963 if enforcement action is to be taken, protection is given to development which had already acquired immunity before publication of the Bill[3] which became the 1968 Act.

It is worthy of note that, to some extent, the Act of 1968 (which received the Royal Assent on 25th October 1968), was retrospective in operation. Development which occurred after the end of 1963 would at varying times (depending on when it commented) from 1st January 1968 have acquired immunity from enforcement action under the 1962 Act and could not have been the subject of enforcement action, but despite that, since Part II of the 1968 Act was brought into effect it **can** be dealt with by the service of an enforcement notice under the new provisions.

As to the question of the applicability of limitations of time within which an enforcement notice can be served in

---

[1] [1981], J.P.L. 357.

[2] *Thomas David (Porthcawl) Ltd. v. Penybont R.D.C. and Others* [1972] 1 All E.R. 733.

[3] 19th December 1967.

respect of breaches of conditions, there has been a great deal of discussion as to whether the determining date is that on which there was first a breach or whether continued failure to comply with a condition means that in effect time begins to run afresh each day and any date may be taken as that applicable for deciding whether the breach is inside or outside the limiting period for the purpose of enforcement. Much depends on the particular circumstances in each case. For example, where, on a planning permission for a house, a condition requires a fence to be erected, failure for four years to erect the fence will it seems render enforcement action impossible. On the other hand it is suggested that where a condition requiring that machinery shall not be operated in a building at certain times is broken on several occasions at long intervals it is possible to argue that the latest breach should be taken as the operative occurrence for the purpose of determining whether enforcement action is possible. Here again, however, the length of the intervals between breaches and their regularity or otherwise might affect the result.

In the case of non-compliance with a condition or limitation attached to a planning permission for working minerals the period is four years from the time the breach comes to the knowledge of the local planning authority.[1]

Section 290 (5) of the 1971 Act re-enacting earlier provision states that for the purposes of the Act development of land shall be taken to be initiated

(*a*) if the development consists of the carrying out of operations at the time when those operations are begun;

(*b*) if the development consists of a change in use, at the time when the new use is instituted;

(*c*) if the development consists both of the carrying out of operations and of a change of use, at the earlier of the times mentioned in (*a*) or (*b*) above.

---

[1] *See* Town and Country Planning (Minerals) Regulations 1971 (S.I. 1971, No. 756), Reg. 4.

In the case of a gradual change of use, development begins at the date when the change first becomes **material**, since it is at that point that the **development** which is the essential prerequisite of enforcement action takes place.[1]

CROWN LAND

The enforcement provisions of the Act apply to Crown land to the extent of any interest therein for the time being held otherwise than by or on behalf of the Crown,[2] but the following restrictions apply:—

1. The consent of the appropriate Crown authority as defined below must be obtained before an enforcement notice is served.[3]
2. No enforcement notice can be issued in respect of development carried out by or on behalf of the Crown after 1st July 1948, on land which was Crown land at the time the development was carried out.[4]

Crown land means[5] land in which an interest is owned—

(1) By Her Majesty in right of the Crown or in right of the Duchy of Lancaster.

(2) By the Duchy of Cornwall.

(3) By a Government Department (or held in trust for Her Majesty for the purposes of a Government Department).

Under the Post Office Act 1969 (the object of which was to confer on the Post Office commercial independence) the work of the Post Office was transferred from a Department of State to a new corporation to be known as the Post Office. That Act, by section 6 (5) expressly declared that

---

[1] For a case where the provisions of section 290 (5) (c) were considered and regarded as **not** relevant see *Lake District Special Planning Board v. Secretary of State for the Environment* [1981] J.P.L. 363, D.C.

[2] Section 266.

[3] Section 266 (2) (*a*).

[4] Section 266 (3).

[5] *See* definition in s. 266 (7).

the Post Office is not to be regarded as the servant or agent of the Crown, or as enjoying any immunity of the Crown, and that its property is not to be regarded as property of, or property held on behalf of, the Crown.

The "appropriate Crown authority", whose consent is necessary before an enforcement notice can be served is specified in section 266 (7) of the Act and the same subsection provides that if, in relation to any land, the question arises as to what authority is the appropriate authority, the question is to be referred to the Treasury, whose decision is final. The appropriate authority is:—

(*a*) in the case of land belonging to Her Majesty in right of the Crown and forming part of the Crown Estates, the Crown Estate Commissioners;

(*b*) in relation to other land belonging to Her Majesty in right of the Crown, the Government Department having the management of the land;

(*c*) in relation to land belonging to Her Majesty in right of the Duchy of Lancaster, the Chancellor of the Duchy;

(*d*) in relation to land belonging to the Duchy of Cornwall, such person as the Duke of Cornwall, or the possessor for the time being of the Duchy, appoints;

(*e*) in the case of land belonging to a government department or held in trust for Her Majesty for the purposes of a government department, that department.

(Similar restrictions apply also in the special cases dealt with in Chapters 8 to 11, *post*.)

In *Molton Builders v. Westminster City Council and Another*[1] the plaintiffs attempted to obtain a declaration that an enforcement notice was void on the basis that the consent to service of that notice given by the Crown Estate Com-

---

[1] [1974] J.P.L. 600, Willis, J.

missioners was a derogation from grant. They failed, it being held that the giving of consent in that case did not amount to derogation from grant and that, the commissioners being given by the statute (then the 1962 Act which contained the same provisions as the 1971 Act), a discretion to act in a public capacity, the exercise of that discretion was a matter of public interest. Accordingly they could not by contract fetter that power.

DEFAULT POWERS

The Secretary of State has under section 276 of the Act[1] power to take certain action in relation to enforcement when the local authority has failed to act.

If, **after consulting with the local planning authority**, it appears to the Secretary of State expedient that any of the orders listed below should be made, he may himself make such an order.

Subsection (4) of section 276 requires that if the Secretary of State proposes to exercise his default powers in relation to cases (*a*), (*b*) and (*c*) below, he must give specific notice to the local planning authority, who have a right to appear before and be heard by a person appointed by him for that purpose.

References to the **local planning authority** in both the above paragraphs mean the county planning authority or the district planning authority as the Secretary of State thinks appropriate.[2]

The orders referred to above, are:—

(*a*) An order revoking or modifying a planning permission.[3]

(*b*) An order that an authorised use shall be discontinued, or that conditions shall be imposed on its continuance.[4]

---

[1] As amended by the 1981 Act.
[2] *See* Schedule 16, para. 47 (1) Local Government Act 1972.
[3] *See ante*, p. 68.
[4] *See post*, p. 227.

(*c*) An order that authorised buildings or works shall be altered or removed.[3]

(*d*) Tree preservation orders and orders amending or revoking them.[1]

If after similar consultation with the local planning authority it appears to the Secretary of State expedient that any of the following notices should be served he may himself serve such a notice.

(*a*) An enforcement notice under section 87 of the Act.

(*b*) A stop notice under section 90 of the Act.[2]

(*c*) A listed building enforcement notice.[3]

(*d*) A completion notice under section 44 of the Act.[4]

The section as originally enacted provided for the Secretary of State to serve (in default) an enforcement notice relating to advertisements (as to which see *post*, p. 318) or a notice requiring proper maintenance of waste land (as to which see *post*, p. 320) but the 1981 Act amendment excluded those matters.

Reference to the local planning authority here is, in the case of a listed building enforcement notice, to the district planning authority, and in any other case to the county planning authority or the district planning authority as the Secretary of State thinks appropriate.[5]

WITHDRAWAL OF ENFORCEMENT NOTICE

Section 15 (8) of the 1968 Act, effective from 1st April 1969, placed beyond doubt the power of a local planning authority to withdraw an enforcement notice. That section is now repealed by the 1971 Act and the power of withdrawal of an enforcement notice is contained in section 87

---

[1] *See post*, p. 290.
[2] *See post*. p. 142.
[3] *See post*, p. 263.
[4] *See ante*, p. 60.
[5] *See* Schedule 16, para. 47 (2), Local Government Act 1972 not applicable to Greater London.

(14) of that Act, as amended by the 1981 Act. The local planning authority may withdraw such a notice (without prejudice to their power to serve another) **at any time before the notice takes effect**,[1] and if they do so, must forthwith give notice of the withdrawal to every person who was served with the notice.

As is clear from paragraph 31 of Schedule 24 of the 1971 Act the power of withdrawal may be exercised in relation to enforcement notices under earlier statutory provisions served before the 1st April 1969.

POWER TO STOP FURTHER DEVELOPMENT PENDING PROCEEDINGS ON ENFORCEMENT NOTICE

Before the coming into force of Part II of the Town and Country Planning Act 1968 an authority who had served an enforcement notice could do nothing further until it had taken effect and the period for compliance had expired. Since, as earlier noted,[2] an appeal suspends the operation of an enforcement altogether until the appeal is determined or withdrawn, a contravening developer could if he wished defy the law with impunity for a considerable period, and sometimes be more likely to succeed in an appeal because of so doing. For example, a house begun without planning consent could be proceeded with and perhaps completed, before the determination of an appeal. To insist on the demolition of a newly completed dwelling is a step so drastic that the offending developer was more likely to obtain permission for the retention of his building, whatever the merits of his case. In respect of enforcement notices served on or after 1st April 1969.[3] Section 19 of the 1968 Act gave the Local Planning Authority a new power to stop certain development pending proceedings on an enforcement notice. The power is now contained in section 90 of the Town and Country Planning Act 9171 as amended by the Town and

---

[1] As to the date a notice takes effect, *see ante*, p. 116.

[2] Page 117, *ante*.

[3] The appointed day for the purpose of s. 19 of the 1968 Act.

Country Planning (Amendment) Act 1977 from 22nd August 1977 and also by the Local Government and Planning (Amendment) Act 1981 from 27th August 1981. It is, however, a power which should be exercised with caution because in certain events compensation may be payable (*see post*).

The Minister of Housing and Local Government, then responsible for planning, said in Circular 4 of 1969 dated 17th March 1969 that he expected planning authorities to be "deliberate and restrained" in their use of this procedure, that they should wait to see whether service of a stop notice was necessary to prevent prejudice to enforcement proceedings and that automatic service of a stop notice after every relevant enforcement notice was "quite inappropriate".

Power to serve a Stop Notice

Where **an enforcement notice** (after 27 August 1981 a copy of an enforcement notice)[1] **has been served** in respect of any land the authority may, at any time **before that enforcement notice takes effect**[2] serve a further notice called a **Stop Notice**. They may do this if they consider it expedient to do so to prevent, before the expiry of the period for compliance with the enforcement notice "the carrying out of any activity which is, or is included in, a matter alleged by the notice to constitute the breach". The stop notice may prohibit the carrying out of that activity on the land, or any part of the land specified in the stop notice. This notice must refer to the enforcement notice and have annexed to it a **copy** of the enforcement ntoice. Before the 1977 Act amendment a stop notice could only prohibit the person carrying out or continuing on the land any **operations** specified in the notice. These operations had to be either within those alleged in the enforcement notice to constitute a breach of planning control or be operations so closely associated with them as to constitute substantially the same operations.

The term "operations" was not defined but in view of the general scheme of the Act and the division of development

---

[1] Date of coming into force of the 1981 Act.

into the two distinct classes of operation and material changes of use, it seemed probable that it meant the "building, mining, engineering or other operations" referred to in section 22 (1).

It seemed that the stop notice procedure was not available before the 1977 Act to bring about the discontinuance of a **use**. Moreover, it seemed clear that a stop notice could not deal with "operations" which were mere incidents of an unauthorised use. The new section was therefore designed to widen the scope of a stop notice.

Exceptions

However the Act provides[1] that certain activities can **not** be prevented by a stop notice. These are:—

(1) Use of a building as a dwelling house.

(2) Use of land as a site for a caravan[2] occupied as a sole or main residence.

(3) Any steps specified in the enforcement notice as required to be taken to remedy the breach of planning control.

(4) Any activity which began more than 12 months previously **except** where such an activity is, or **is incidental to**, building, engineering, mining or other operations or the deposit of refuse or waste materials, in which latter cases a stop notice **can** be served.

Where planning permission for a use has been granted for a limited period and thereafter the use has been carried on in breach of planning control the 12 month limitation period for service of a stop notice begins from the **commencement of the use** and not from the commencement of the breach. The 12 month period does not depend on whether the activity during the period is lawful or unlawful. The Court of Appeal (Brandon L.J. dissenting) so held in *Scott Markets*

[1] Section 90 (2).

[2] **Caravan** has the same meaning as it has for the purposes of Part I of the Caravan Sites and Control of Development Act 1960. See section 90 (2) (b).

v. Waltham Forest London Borough Council,[1] reversing Mars-Jones, J. who at first instance had held that the limitation period applied only to a period of unlawful activity.

Service of a Stop Notice

A stop notice may be served[2] on any person who appears to the Local Planning Authority to have an interest in the land in question. This will include, *e.g.* a person who has contracted to buy the land or to take a lease, or who has an option to purchase.

It may also be served on any person who appears to be engaged in any activity prohibited by the notice including, for example, a builder or even a workman on the site. Before the 1977 Act the reference was to a person concerned with the carrying out or continuance of any operations on the land.

In any case where a stop notice has been served the authority may display on the land a notice (referred to as a "site notice") stating that fact and that **any person contravening it** may be prosecuted for an offence under the section, giving the date when the stop notice takes effect (as to which see *post*, p. 146) and indicating its requirements.

Service of a stop notice is **not** prevented because of an appeal against the enforcement notice on which it is founded. Such an appeal will in fact prolong the period during which it is possible for a stop notice to be served, because a stop notice may be served at any time before the enforcement notice **takes effect** and on appeal against the latter notice that notice is not effective until the appeal is withdrawn or determined.

It may be served on different persons on different dates.

Although it is no doubt desirable to serve a stop notice on the owner and occupier of the land, there is no statutory requirement that this shall be done.

---

1 (1979) 77 L.G.R. 565 C.A.

2 For methods of service see *ante*, p. 121.

Date taking effect

A stop notice, like an enforcement notice, must specify the date when it is to take effect.[1] This date cannot be earlier than 3 nor later than 28 (formerly 14) days from the date on which the notice is first served on any person.

Life of a Stop Notice

Unless a stop notice is earlier withdrawn (see *post*) it continues in force until the enforcement notice which gave rise to it is withdrawn or quashed, or the period allowed for compliance[1] with the enforcement notice expires. It also ceases to have effect if, or to the extent that, the activities prohibited by it cease, on a variation[2] of the enforcement notice, to be included in the matters alleged by the enforcement notice to constitute a breach of planning control.

Withdrawal of a Stop Notice

The Local Planning Authority may at any time withdraw a stop notice[3] (without prejudice to their power to serve another), by serving notice to that effect on the persons who were served with the stop notice, and if a site notice (as to which see *ante*, p. 145) was displayed in respect of the stop notice, displaying a notice of withdrawal in place of the site notice.

The stop notice ceases to have effect on the **date of service of the Notice of Withdrawal**. However, if an authority withdraws a stop notice it is liable to pay compensation (*see post*).

Effect of a Stop Notice

If any person contravenes, or causes or permits the contravention of a stop notice

(1) after a site notice has been displayed or

---

[1] As to this period and possible extension of it see section 90 (10) and see *ante*, p. 115.

[2] As to the power of the Secretary of State or an inspector to vary an enforcement notice see *post*, p. 179.

[3] Section 90 (6).

(2) if a site notice has not been displayed, more than two days after service of the stop notice on him

then, subject to the defence mentioned in the following paragraph, he is guilty of an offence and liable on summary conviction of a fine of up to £1000 or on conviction on indictment to a fine of unlimited amount. If the offence continues after conviction he is guilty of a further offence and liable on summary conviction to a fine of up to £100 for each day on which the offence is continued, or on conviction on indictment to a further fine of unlimited amount.

It is a defence for the accused to prove that the stop notice was not served on him and that he did not know, and could not reasonably have been expected to know, of its existence.

Validity of a Stop Notice

The purpose of a stop notice, in cases when it is applicable, is to preserve the status quo until final determination of the real issue. Consequently there is no statutory right of appeal against such a notice. Its invalidity can however be set up as a defence to prosecution under the provisions described in the preceding paragraph. As earlier stated, service of an enforcement notice is an essential prerequisite of a stop notice but it is expressly provided by subsection (9) of section 90 that a stop notice is *not* invalidated by reason that a copy of the enforcement notice to which it relates was not served as required by section 87 (5) of the Act, if it is shown that the local planning authority took all such steps as were reasonably practicable to effect proper service. Whether the steps taken were sufficient will be a matter for the Court to decide if the point is raised on a prosecution.

Where a stop notice incorporates the terms of the enforcement notice on which it is based, a deficiency in the terms of the stop notice as to defining the activities to which it relates may, according to the circumstances, be validated and the defect cured by reliance on the language of the enforcement notice. See *Bristol Stadium v. Brown*.[1]

[1] (1979) 252, E.G. 803, D.C.

Compensation

As earlier stated, a stop notice ceases to have effect when certain events occur and in such case a person who at the time when it was first served **had an interest in**[1] or who **occupied** the land to which it relates and who is able to show that he has suffered loss or damage directly attributable to the prohibition in the notice, may, **in certain circumstances**, set out hereafter, be able to claim compensation from the Local Planning Authority.[2] It is expressly provided by section 177 (5) that this may include a sum payable in respect of a breach of contract caused by complying with the prohibition. It is to be noted that a person who has no interest in the land and who is not an occupier cannot in any event recover compensation from the planning authority. A contractor will have to rely upon the terms of his contract. On the other hand a person who has the requisite interest in the land need not have had the stop notice served on **him** in order to be able to claim compensation.

The method of making a claim is the same as in the case of a claim following an order for termination of authorised development (as to which, *see post*, page 236). A claim has to be made within six months from the date of the decision in respect of which the claim is made,[3] but the Secretary of State may extend this period.

Questions of disputed compensation are to be determined by the Lands Tribunal[4] and the provisions of sections 2 and 4 of the Land Compensation Act 1961 (as amended)[5] (as to certain aspects of procedure and as to costs) will apply.[6]

Sub-section (6) of section 177, inserted by the Town and Country Planning (Amendment) Act 1977, provides that where a claimant has failed to comply with a requisition for

---

[1] This will include, *e.g.* a person who has contracted to purchase the land, or to take a lease of it, or who has an option to purchase.

[2] Section 177 as amended.

[3] *See* the Town and Country Planning General Regulations 1976 (S.I. 1976, No. 1419) and amending Regulations S.I. 1981, No. 558.

[4] *See* note 4, p. 101, *ante*.

[5] See footnote 5, p. 101, *ante*.

[6] Section 179.

information under section 284 of the 1971 Act,[1] or has failed to supply accurate information, his failure is to be taken into account in assessing compensation to the extent that his entitlement is attributable to his failure.

The events which will cause a stop notice to cease to have effect and which in the circumstances described will give rise to a claim for compensation are four in number and are as follows:—

(1) **The stop notice is withdrawn.**[2]

(2) **The enforcement notice on which the stop notice is based is withdrawn**[3] by the Local Planning Authority otherwise than in consequence of their granting Planning Permission regularising the contravening development, *i.e.* permission for the development in question or permission for its retention or continuance without compliance with a condition or limitation subject to which a previous Planning Permission was granted.[4]

(3) **The enforcement notice is quashed** on grounds other than those in section 88 (1) (*a*) of the 1971 Act.[5]

(4) **The enforcement notice is varied**[6] by the Secretary of State on appeal otherwise than on ground (a) of section 88 (1) so that matters alleged to constitute a breach of planning control cease to include one or more of the activities prohibited by the stop notice.

Default powers of the Secretary of State

If after consultation with the Local Planning Authority it appears to the Secretary of State expedient that a stop notice should be served he may or may himself serve it.[7]

---

[1] As to which see *ante*, p. 103.
[2] As to withdrawal of a stop notice, *see ante*, p. 146.
[3] As to withdrawal of an enforcement notice, *see ante*, p. 141.
[4] As to a grant of permission of this kind, *see ante*, p. 49.
[5] *See* p. 152, *post*.
[6] As to the power to vary, *see* p. 179, *post*.
[7] Section 276 (5) as amended.

REGISTER OF ENFORCEMENT NOTICES AND STOP NOTICES

The Local Planning and Planning (Amendment) Act 1981 inserted into the 1971 Act a new section 92 A providing that every district planning authority and council of a London Borough should keep a register of enforcement notices and stop notices relating to land in their area. The section applies to enforcement notices issued and stop notices served on and after 27th November 1981. The register is to be available to inspection by the public at all reasonable hours.[1]

REGISTRATION AS A LAND CHARGE

An enforcement notice which has become effective is registrable as a local land charge in the Local Land Charges Register.[2]

Under section 10 of the Local Land Charges Act 1975 failure to register gives a right to compensation but does **not** affect the enforceability of the charge.

---

[1] See the 1981 Act section 2 and schedule para. 6 and see the Town and Country Planning General Development (Amendment) (No. 2) Order 1981 (S.I. 1981, No. 1569).

[2] Local Land Charges Rules 1977 (S.I. 1977, No. 985).

CHAPTER 4

CHALLENGING AN ENFORCEMENT NOTICE

RIGHT TO CHALLENGE

There may be:—

(1) a right to appeal to the Secretary of State and a subsequent right to take the matter to the High Court.

(2) a right to take the matter to the High Court in the first instance.

(3) a defence to criminal or other proceedings taken by the authority as a result of non-compliance with the notice or an action for trespass and/or an injunction in respect of positive action taken by the authority themselves to carry out the requirements of the notice.

These different means of challenge, the last two of which are subject to limitations, will now be discussed.

It is first necessary to note, however, that, both in regard to rights and to procedures, the Local Government and Planning (Amendment) Act, 1981 has effected important changes in the law. The relevant provisions came into operation on 27th August, 1981[1]. The Act also enables the Secretary of State by regulation[2] to specify certain procedures on issue of an enforcement notice and in connection with the appeal machinery.

---

[1] Section 2 (3).

[2] See the Town and County Planning (Enforcement Notice and Appeals) Regulations 1981 (S.I. 1981, No. 1742) effective from 11 January 1982.

APPEAL TO THE SECRETARY OF STATE

Deemed planning application

Under Section 88B (3) of the 1971 Act,[1] where an appeal is made the appellant is deemed to have made an application for planning permission for the development to which the notice relates.[2]

Grounds of appeal

In respect of an enforcement notice served on or after the 1st April 1969,[3] section 88 of the 1971 Act, re-enacting section 16 of the 1968 Act provided for an appeal to the Secretary of State on seven specified grounds.

The 1981 Act has substituted an amended Section 88 which adds an eighth ground and modifies other grounds to take account of other provisions of the 1981 Act. The grounds of appeal as they now stand after amendment and applying from 27th August, 1981,[4] are as follows:—

(*a*) *That permission ought to be granted for the development to which the enforcement notice relates, or, as the case may be, that a condition or limitation alleged in the notice not to have been complied with ought to be discharged.*

This ground raises the same issues as those raised by an ordinary appeal against a refusal of planning permission.

The local planning authority are required[5] to give reasons for imposing a condition on a planning permission, but failure to do so does not make the condition invalid, nor does

---

[1] Inserted by the 1981 Act and replacing earlier provisions of the same effect.

[2] A fee is payable. See the Town and County Planning (Fees for Applications and Direct Applications) Regulations 1981 S.I. 1981, No. 369, effective 1 April 1981, as amended by S.I. 1982 No. 716 effective 1 June, 1982.

[3] The date of commencement of Part II of the 1968 Act. *See* S.I. 1969, No. 275. For the position regarding appeals against notices served before this date, *see post*.

[4] Date of operation of the relevant provision.

[5] Town and Country Planning General Development Order 1977 (S.I. 1977, No. 289) (as amended).

it invalidate an enforcement notice which alleges non-compliance with the conditions.[1]

It should be noted, that, in the case of industrial development the subject of the statutory conditions described earlier (page 70, *ante*) the Secretary of State can **ignore** the appeal in so far as it claims that planning permission free of those conditions ought to be granted.[2]

(*b*) *That the matters alleged in the notice do not constitute a breach of planning control.*

An appeal will lie under this head if:—

(1) The activities complained of do not constitute or involve development.[3]

or (2) It is accepted that the activites complained of constitute development but Planning Permission is not required[4] or has been granted.[4]

or (3) Any conditions or limitations, breach of which is alleged in the notice, have in fact been complied with.

An interesting illustration of the kind of case sometimes met with in practice is provided by *Prengate Properties v. Secretary of State for the Environment.*[5]

P. Company built a wall round a house in order to extend a terraced area and soil was brought in and dumped behind it. The amount of soil had not yet reached that which would mean that the wall was serving as a retaining wall. The planning authority served an enforcement notice requiring removal of the soil and demolition of the wall. The Secretary of State upheld the notice on appeal on the ground that the wall was not a means of enclosure (which would have been authorised development under the General Development Order) but a structural wall. On appeal it was held, allowing

---

[1] *Brayhead (Ascot) Ltd. v. Berkshire County Council* [1964] 2 W.L.R. 507.
[2] *See* Section 88 B (4) substituted for an earlier similar provision.
[3] *See ante*, Chapter 1, as to the circumstances in which this may be so.
[4] *See ante*, Chapter 2, as to the methods of granting permission.
[5] 71 L.G.R. 373, D.C.

the appeal, that at the relevant time the wall was permitted development and, this being so, the fact that the owner intended at some future time to incorporate it into a larger engineering operation did not affect the position.

This was a case where the enforcement notice was premature and is perhaps a warning to planning authorities not to act too soon.

The fact that an appellant has applied for and obtained Planning Permission does not preclude him from raising this ground on the basis that Planning Permission was not required or that no development was involved.[1]

(*c*) *that the breach of planning control alleged in the notice has not taken place.*

(This is the new added ground).

(*d*) *In the case of a notice which may*[2] *be served only within the period of four years from the date of the breach of planning control in question, that that period had elapsed at the date when the notice was issued.* (This was formerly ground (c) and has been amended only so as to refer to the date of **issue** of the notice instead of the **service** of it.)

(*e*) *In the case of any notice not requiring*[1] *to be served within four years, that the breach of planning control alleged occurred before the beginning of 1964.*

(This was formerly ground (d).)

Establishment of grounds of appeal (d) and (e) calls for clear evidence as to the facts, but clarity is the very thing which is usually lacking on this kind of issue, and particularly where there has been a gradual change of use. The local planning authority is here often at a disadvantage in being unable to produce any direct evidence as to the past history of a site, and the accuracy of any evidence adduced by the

[1] *See East Barnet Urban District Council v. British Transport Commission* [1962] 2 Q.B. 484.

[2] See *ante*, p. 134 as to when this may be so.

appellant needs to be thoroughly tested. (*See ante*, page 130, as to **established use certificates**.)

Whether this ground is established or not is a question of fact and the court will not upset a finding about this on appeal if there was evidence upon which such a decision could properly be reached.[1]

(*f*) *That copies of the enforcement notice were not served as required Section 87 (5) of the Act.*

This is formerly ground (e) with an amendment to take account of the new provisions about issuing and serving an enforcement notice.

Where this ground of appeal is raised the Secretary of State is empowered by Section 88 A (3) to disregard failure to serve the notice on a particular person if neither the appellant nor that person has been substantially prejudiced by the failure to serve him. This provision, which has only been consequentially amended, was originally enacted to prevent a situation such as occurred in *Courtney-Southan v. Crawley U.D.C.*,[2] in which case a husband successfully challenged an enforcement notice on the ground that it had not been served on the owner (his wife) although he himself had applied for planning permission describing himself as the owner and, having been refused permission, had carried out the development.

(*g*) *That the steps required by the enforcement notice to be taken exceed what is necessary to remedy any breach of planning control, or to achieve a purpose specified in Section 87 (10) of the Act.*

(This was formerly ground (f) except that the latter alternative is a consequential addition to take account of the amended provisions now contained in Section 87 (10). (See *ante*, p. 113.)

(*h*) *That the specified period for compliance with the*

---

[1] See *Bromley London Borough v. George Hoeltshi & Son* (1977) 244 E.G.49, D.C.

[2] [1967] 2 Q.B. 930.

notice falls short of what should reasonably be allowed.

(This was formerly ground (g).)

In respect of an enforcement notice served on the 29th August 1960,[1] or after that date and before the 1st April 1969,[2] the appeal provisions of the 1962 Act continued to apply by virtue of the transitional provisions of the 1968 Act and this position is preserved by the 1971 Act. (Section 292 and Schedule 24, paragraph 31.)

In *London Borough of Redbridge v. Perry*[3] a private house had been converted into bed-sitting-rooms without planning permission. An enforcement notice gave 56 days for compliance. The owner was prosecuted for not complying. Magistrates dismissed the information on the ground that she could not lawfully have removed her tenants in less than 112 days, if they had availed themselves of their rights. The prosecutor appealed. The Divisional Court held, allowing the appeal, that since 56 days was a sufficient time for the tenants to leave, the fact that the owner could not obtain possession by law within that period was irrelevant.

Who may appeal

The right of appeal against an enforcement notice is now confined to "a person having an interest in the land" to which the notice relates.[4] Such a person may appeal whether or not a copy of the notice has been served upon him. Conversely, a person who **has** had a copy of the notice served on him, but who has no interest in the land can **not** appeal. The previous section 88 also gave a right of appeal to any person served with the notice. An "interest in land" will cover e.g. a person with an option to purchase, or who has contracted to buy, or a mortgagee.

---

[1] In the case of notices served before that date the former provisions of the 1947 Act apply. *See* 1971 Act, s. 292 and Sched. 24, para. 32.

[2] The date of commencement of Part II of the 1968 Act. *See* S.I. 1969, No. 275.

[3] (1976) 75 L.G.R. 90, D.C.

[4] Section 88 (1) as substituted by the 1981 Act.

Time for appeal

The appeal must be made made before the date when the notice takes effect.[1] This date will be specified in the notice. (If it is not the notice is invalid.[2]) **Neither the Secretary of State nor the authority has any power to extend the time for an appeal**, and in view of the statutory limitations on other forms of challenge (*see* page 197, *post*) it is vital to an appellant to ensure that any appeal to the Secretary of State is in time.

The case of *R. v. Melton and Belvoir Justices ex parte Tynan*[3] illustrates the point. Having been served with an enforcement notice T had appealed to the Secretary of State, his notice of appeal being one day out of time, although the Secretary of State confirmed "acceptance" of the appeal. The local authority prosecuted for breach of the enforcement notice and T was convicted. It was held, dismissing his application to quash the conviction that his appeal being out of time he had lost the protection of Section 88 Sub-section 10 of which provides that where an appeal is lodged the enforcement notice is of no effect pending final determination or withdrawal of the appeal and the Secretary of State's purported acceptance of his appeal was irrelevant.

Method of appeal

The appeal must be of written notice addressed to the Secretary of State.[4]

Under the Town and Country Planning (Fees for Applications and Deemed Applications) Regulation, 1981[5] a fee is payable on the deemed application for planning permission[6] and the notice of appeal must be accompanied by payment of the appropriate fee. The documents and fee have to be sent to the Cashier's Office at Department of the

---

[1] Section 88 (1).
[2] See *ante*, p. 116. If a notice is invalid see *post*, as to challenge.
[3] [1977] J.P.L. 368.
[4] Section 88 (3).
[5] S.I. (1981), No. 369.
[6] See *ante*, p. 152.

Environment, 197, Marlowes, Hemel Hempstead, Herts, HP1N 1BN or in Wales to the Welsh Office, Cathays Park, Cardiff. CF1 3NQ.

There is a form of appeal which at present it is not obligatory to use but which may be obtained from the Department of the Environment or the Welsh Office as the case may be.

The Local Government and Planning (Amendment) Act, 1981 effected substantial changes in the procedures governing the making of appeals, which were effective from the 27th August, 1981, and the Secretary of State has made regulations[1] under the substituted Section 88 (5) effective from 11th January, 1982.

The law before 27th August 1981 provided that the notice of appeal must indicate the grounds on which the appeal is brought and, in an appeal against a notice served after 1st April 1969,[2] state the facts on which it is based.

This latter requirement to state **facts** was, as indicated, first introduced in the Town and Country Planning Act 1968.

The Minister of Housing and Local Government, in a case in 1970[3] declined to entertain an appeal against an enforcement notice on the ground that a notice of appeal had failed to state the facts on which the appeal was based, taking the view that what is then section 88 (2) imposed a mandatory obligation on the appellant, so that if he failed to comply his appeal was ineffective. (In the case referred to the appellants had purported to state facts, but the Minister regarded them as being not more than restatements of the grounds of appeal and so insufficient to satisfy what in his view were the statutory requirements.) In the third edition of this book the point was made that if the Minister's view was correct it appeared that there had been a reversion to the excessive formalism of earlier days, and that a situation has been produced when there could be grave injustice to an appellant. Neither the Secretary of State nor anyone

---

[1] S.I. 1981, No. 1742, dealt with hereafter.
[2] Date of commencement of Part II, 1968 Act. *See* S.I. 1969, No. 275.
[3] (1970) J.P.L. 340.

else has power to extend the time for an appeal, and if the Minister's view was right it mattered not that an appellant had good grounds for an appeal and had stated them, a mere failure (within a limited period) to state facts at that stage would altogether debar him from obtaining so much as a hearing on the merits. The situation was rendered perhaps even more unsatisfactory when one considered the position regarding **grounds** of appeal, as distinct from the facts on which the appeal is based.

In *Chelmsford Rural District Council and Another v. Powell*[1] the Divisional Court considered the meaning of the statutory requirement as to stating grounds, which contained the words "shall indicate the grounds" on which the appeal was brought. There had been an appeal to the Minister against an enforcement notice, lodged in time and giving two grounds of appeal. There was an inquiry, at which notice was given that there was to be a third ground of appeal. The Minister quashed the enforcement notice, taking the view that he was not precluded from considering the additional ground of appeal (which in that case was vital and in fact was the basis of the decision to quash).

The Council appealed (*inter alia*) on the ground that the Minister had no power to allow the introduction of a ground not stated in the notice of appeal. The Court had no difficulty in holding that the statutory provision did **not** imply that an appellant was confined once and for all to the grounds indicated in his notice and the Council's appeal failed. This decision did not seem to have been affected by the later decision of the Court of Appeal in *Miller-Mead v. Minister of Housing and Local Government*[2] that if a ground of appeal is not raised before the Minister it can not be raised before any Court considering an appeal from the Minister's decision. It seemed clear that, as to **grounds**, the Secretary of State had jurisdiction (and must exercise it) provided that there was a written notice of appeal indicating at least **one** ground. Provided that was done he might allow an appellant to amend or add to his grounds at any time

[1] [1963] 1 All E.R. 150.
[2] [1963] 2 W.L.R. 225.

before the appeal was determined, subject it would seem to due notice being given to the local planning authority and if necessary to an adjournment or re-opening of any inquiry to enable the authority to deal with the points raised. Certainly it was the practice of the Secretary of State to deal with grounds not originally pleaded.[1]

One had apparently the anomalous situation that grounds which might be vital could be omitted from the notice of appeal (provided **one** ground was stated) without ill effect to the appellant but the omission of facts was fatal.

The hope was expressed that the Courts might find it possible, if the point came before them, to find that the requirement to state facts was **directory** and not mandatory and it was submitted that there was material on which they could do so. In the course of his judgment in the case of *Chelmsford R.D.C. and Another v. Powell*, Lord Parker, C.J.,[2] expressed himself as deriving assistance from a principle laid down by Lord Penzance[3] in *Howard v. Bodington.*[4] Lord Penzance then quoted Lord Campbell, L.C., in *Liverpool Borough Bank v. Turner*[5] where the latter said "No universal rule can be laid down for the construction of statutes, as to whether mandatory enactments shall be considered directory only or obligatory, with an implied nullification for disobedience. It is the duty of Courts of Justice to try to get at the real intention of the legislation by carefully attending to the whole scope of the statute to be construed", and Lord Penzance went on to say that "in each case you must look to the subject-matter; consider the importance of the provision that has been disregarded and the relation of that provision to the general object intended to be secured by the Act; and upon a review of the case in that respect decide whether the matter is what is called imperative or only directory".

---

[1] *See, e.g.*, a decision reported in the Journal of Planning Law for 1970 at pp. 465–469.

[2] [1963] 1 All E.R. at p. 157.

[3] (1877) 2 P.D. at p. 211.

[4] (1877) 2 P.D. 203.

[5] (1869) 2 De G.F. & J. 502 at p. 507.

The *Chelmsford R.D.C. Case*, the penal nature of an enforcement notice, its permanent effect if there was no successful appeal, and the absence of any power to extend the time for appeal, appeared all to be relevant considerations.

After that, the matter came before the Court of Appeal in *Howard v. Secretary of State for the Environment.*[1]

In that case an enforcement notice had been served on Mr. Howard by Havering London Borough Council, to take effect (subject to any appeal) at the expiration of 42 days (on November 18th). On November 6th his Solicitors wrote to the Department asking that their letter be accepted as a formal notice of intention to appeal. The Department replied saying that grounds and facts must be sent to them before the date of the enforcement notice taking effect. The Solicitors prepared a letter dated November 16th giving notice of appeal and setting out grounds and facts, but by a mischance it was not posted until November 20th (and did not reach the Department until November 24th). It was therefore outside the time limit specified. The question at issue was therefore whether the first letter dated November 6th (which stated neither grounds nor facts, but which was sent within the specified time) was a valid notice of appeal.

Mr. Howard had sought a declaration that the letter constituted a valid notice of appeal. Bristow, J., had refused such a declaration, but his decision was reversed by the Court of Appeal. In the course of his judgment, Lord Denning, M.R., referred to *Chelmsford R.D.C. v. Powell,*[2] expressing the view that the decision in that case was correct, but disapproving the dictum of Lord Parker, C.J., in that case that a notice of appeal "must indicate at any rate one of the grounds". Referring also to *Howard v. Bodington* and the distinction between requirements that were **mandatory** (and went to the jurisdiction) and those which were **directory** (and did not go to the jurisdiction) his Lordship rejected the contention for the Secretary of State that the requirements about grounds and statement of facts was man-

[1] [1974] 1 All E.R. 644, C.A.
[2] *Supra.*

datory. It was sufficient to appeal in writing in the specified time. The statements of grounds and facts were merely a procedural requirement. The letter of November 6th was a valid notice of appeal.

The 1981 Act changes the situation again. It provides[1] that an appeal must be by notice in writing to the Secretary of State. The Department in fact requires an appeal to be made on a form supplied by them, but subject to regulations, (see post) any notice in writing which complies with the Act will suffice. Sub-section (4) requires that a person who gives notice of appeal shall submit to the Secretary of State, either when giving notice or within such time as may be prescribed by regulations under sub-section (5) a statement in writing specifying the grounds on which he is appealing and also give such further information as the regulations prescribe.

The Secretary of State has power by regulation to prescribe the procedure to be followed on appeals and in particular to prescribe the time within which a statement under sub-section (4) is to be given and the matters on which information is to be given. Similarly he may by regulation require a planning authority to submit, within a prescribed time, a statement of the submissions they intend to make on the appeal and specify the matters to be included in that statement. He may also require the authority or the appellant to give such notice of the appeal as prescribed, so as to bring the appeal to the attention of people in the locality of the land in question. Regulations may require an authority to send to the Secretary of State during a prescribed period a copy of the enforcement notice and a list of people served with it.

The provisions have a substantial sanction for non-compliance, which preclude any argument about the mandatory or directory nature of the requirements of regulations. Under Sub-section (6) the Secretary of State may dismiss an appeal if an appellant fails to comply with sub-section (4) within the prescribed time and he may allow an appeal and

[1] Section 88 (3).

quash the enforcement notice if the authority fail to comply with the requirements of regulations as to submission by them of a statement of case, or the supply of copies of the notice and list of people served.

The Secretary of State has made regulations under the powers mentioned above. These are the Town and Country Planning (Enforcement Notices and Appeals) Regulations 1981[1] effective from 11th January 1981. They apply to all enforcement notices issued on or after that date and to all appeals to the Secretary of State against enforcement notices and listed building enforcement notices (as to which see *post*, p. 263) including any appeals brought before 11th January 1982.

Regulation 5 of the regulations empowers the Secretary of State to require time limits to be observed and the circular makes it clear that although an appellant will be given ample opportunity to take the necessary steps to safeguard his position he will not be given unlimited extensions of time and he should be careful to comply with the requirements imposed.

Under Regulation 5 a written statement of the grounds of appeal together with the supporting **facts** must be submitted either when notice of appeal is given, or within 28 days of being required by the Secretary of State to submit such a statement.

Regulation 6 (1) of the regulations requires the local planning authority to serve on the Secretary of State and the appellant a statement of their written submissions on the appeal which is to include a summary of their response to **each** of the appellant's grounds of appeal and a statement whether they would be prepared to grant conditional planning permission (or listed building consent) for the development or works to which the notice relates. This statement must be served in Inquiry cases not later than 28 days before the Inquiry (unless a later date is mutually agreed by the Secretary of State and the parties) and in other cases (*i.e.*

---

[1] S.I. 1981, 1742.

written representations) not later than 28 days than the date when the Secretary of State sends the authority a notice requiring service of the statement.

If the authority does not conform to these requirements the Secretary of State has a discretionary power to quash the enforcement notice in accordance with section 88 (6) (b). The Secretary of State makes it clear in the circular that he will if necessary exercise that power.

The Secretary of State has power under rule 6 (5) of the Rules mentioned below to require an appellant to serve a written statement of the submissions he intends to make at the Inquiry and he has indicated in the circular that he will exericse that power when the appellant has not provided adequate information in his grounds of appeal.

Rule 4 of the Rules requires notification of inquiries into enforcement listed building enforcement and established use certificate appeals to be given to occupiers of property in the neighbourhood of the appeal site who in the opinion of the authority are affected by the breach of planning or listed building control. When giving this notification the authority must include in it a description of the alleged breach, their reasons for serving the enforcement notice, the grounds of appeal and a time limit for comments.

Regulation 8 of the Regulations requires the authority to send the Secretary of State a copy of the enforcement notice not later than 14 days from the date when he notifies them of an appeal together with a list of the names and addresses of the people served with a copy of the notice. If they fail to do this the Secretary of State has power to quash the notice under section 88 (6) (b) (or in listed building cases section 97 (5) (b)).

The Secretary of State has published a model enforcement notice (see the appendix to circular 38/81 mentioned above).

Button v. Jenkins,[1] although stated[2] to be a case falling to be decided on its own particular facts, illustrated that even

[1] [1975] 3 All E.R. 585.
[2] *Ibid.*, p. 589.

before the amendments made by the 1981 Act an appellant might find that his appeal had lapsed through failure on his part to act expeditiously.

In that case an enforcement notice had been served and on 13th September notice of appeal given to the Secretary of State, the notice of appeal stating grounds, but not facts. By letter of 18th September the Secretary of State pointed out that (as he then considered) the notice was defective in that the facts were omitted. The letter said that if a statement of facts was not forthcoming by 26th October (the effective date of the enforcement notice) the Secretary of State "could not" entertain the appeal. The appellant did nothing. On 26th October the Secretary of State wrote reminding him of the failure to state facts and saying that he could not now accept jurisdiction. The appellant could have appealed to the High Court against that decision under section 246 of the 1971 Act,[1] but he did not do so. He failed to comply with the enforcement notice, was prosecuted, and convicted. The matter came before the Divisional Court by way of case stated. (At the time of the hearing by the magistrates *Howard's Case*[2] had been decided only at first instance.)

For the purpose of the decision it was accepted that the letter from the appellant dated 13th September was a valid notice of appeal. The Secretary of State's letter of the 26th October was treated as an intimation that he regarded the appeal as having lapsed. Since the appellant could have appealed to the High Court under section 246 or requested the Secretary of State to state a case but did not do so within the 28 days allowed, the lapse of time converted the decision into a final determination. That meant that the suspension of the enforcement notice under section 88 (3) now section 88 (10)[3] was at an end. The appeal was dismissed.

The case was applied in *Wain v. Secretary of State for the Environment*[4] in which notice of appeal against an enforce-

---

[1] *See post*, p. 193.
[2] [1972] 3 All E.R. 310.
[3] *See ante*, p. 117.
[4] (1978) 39 P. & C.R. 82.

ment notice had been given without grounds or facts. The Department replied that the appeal could not be entertained without these, and when later the appellant supplied grounds and facts the Department said the appeal was then out of time. (This decision was in fact erroneous as shown by the subsequent decision of the Court of Appeal in *Howard* (see *ante*, p. 161)). However when the plaintiffs sought to re-open their appeal, the Court held that the Department's letter saying that the appeal was out of time was a decision in proceedings on appeal for the purpose of section 246 (as to which see *post*, p. 193) and as the plaintiff had not appealed against that decision in accordance with Section 246 the decision stood and could not be questioned.

There have for many years been Inquiries Procedure Rules[1] governing ordinary planning appeals and the Lord Chancellor has now made similar rules for enforcement appeals which are effective from 11th January 1982. They govern the procedure to be followed on all enforcement appeals, listed building enforcement appeals, and established use certificate appeals made on or after 11th January 1982 for which a public local Inquiry is held.

Under Rule 6 of the Town and Country Planning (Enforcement) (Inquiries Procedure) Rules, 1981 the local planning authority are required to serve on the appellant, not-later than 28 days before the Inquiry (if one is to be held) a statement of any expression of view or opinion expressed by a Government Department or Local Authority on which the local planning authority propose to rely and a list of documents (including maps and plans) they propose to refer to or put in evidence at the Inquiry. Rule 11 (5) permits the authority, if the inspector allows, to alter or add to any statement under Rule 6 or in the statement under Regulation 5 so far as is necessary for determining the questions in controversy between the parties and subject to the appellant being allowed an adequate opportunity of considering any fresh evidence or document.

The secretary of State has issued a lengthy circular (38/

---

[1] See S.I.'s 1974, Nos. 419 and 420.

81—in Wales circular 57/81) explaining in detail in part III how the new regulations and rules are intended to operate and the considerations which he will have in mind in exercising the discretionary powers available to him.

Hearing of appeal

Either the appellant or the local authority is entitled to require a hearing before a person appointed by the Secretary of State.[1]

However, by the new Section 88 (8) the Secretary of State is not obliged to give an opportunity of a hearing if he proposes to dismiss, or as the case may be, allow, an appeal because of failure of the appellant or the local authority to comply with the prescribed procedures within the time allowed (See *ante*, p. 162). Further,[2] if the statement supplied by an appellant specified more than one ground of appeal but the prescribed information in respect of each ground is not given within the prescribed time, the Secretary of State can determine the appeal ignoring any ground in respect of which the requisite information has not been given or not been given in time.

The hearing normally takes the form of a local inquiry before an Inspector of the Department, who sometimes sits with a Legal Assessor. It is a public Inquiry.[3]

Appeals under section 88 of the 1971 Act against enforcement notices may if the Secretary of State has so prescribed under Schedule 9 of that Act be **determined** by the Inspector himself (*see post*, page 190, as to general provisions applicable in such cases).

At the Inquiry it is usual for the appellant to begin and to have a right of reply after the local planning authority's case. The onus of proof is on the appellant.[4]

---

[1] Section 88 (7).

[2] Sub-section (9).

[3] Planning Inquiries (Attendance of Public) Act, 1982 in force June 28, 1982.

[4] *See Nelsovil v. Minister of Housing and Local Government* [1962] 1 W.L.R. 404, and *Parker Bros. (Farms) v. Minister of Housing and Local Government* (1969) 210 E.G. 825, D.C. *See also W. J. Simms, Sons and Cooke v. Minister of Housing and Local Government* (1969) 210 E.G. 705.

An Appellant who appears in person must conduct his own case and the Inspector holding the Inquiry is under no duty to formulate questions to witnesses for such a person.[1]

Where a local inquiry is held and there is a dispute as to facts it is usual to hear sworn evidence and the Inspector conducting an Inquiry has power also to issue a summons requiring the attendance of witnesses and the production of documents.[2]

Adjournment

The High Court has decided that it has no jurisdiction to interfere in a decision of the Secretary of State as to whether or not to allow an adjournment of an Inquiry and this decision has been upheld by the Court of Appeal. This decision was in the case of *Co-operative Retail Services v. Secretary of State for the Environment.*[3] In that case (which concerned an Appeal against a refusal of planning permission for a supermarket) a date was fixed for the Inquiry after consultation with the Planning Authority and the Developers. Some two months before the fixed date the Appellants requested an adjournment so that they might have more time to prepare their case but their requests were persistently refused by the Secretary of State. The Appellants then applied to the High Court for Orders quashing the Secretary of State's refusals on the grounds (inter alia) that they constituted a breach of natural justice, the Judge holding that he had no jurisdiction to so act. On Appeal by the Appellants the Court of Appeal held, dismissing the Appeal, that the refusal of an adjournment was not a decision of the Secretary of State on an Appeal under Section 36 (which relates to an Appeal against a planning refusal) within Section 242 (3) (b) since it did not finally dispose of the Appeal so the Judge lacked jurisdiction to hear the application but even if there had been jurisdiction there had been no breach of natural justice.

---

[1] *Snow v. Secretary of State for the Environment.* (1976) 33 P. & C.R. 81.
[2] *See* the Local Government Act 1972, s. 250 (1), (2) and (3).
[3] [1980] 1 All E.R. 449.

Powers of the Secretary of State

In determining an appeal the Secretary of State is required[1] to "give directions for giving effect to his determination, including, where appropriate, directions for quashing the enforcement notice or for varying its terms". In *Miller-Mead v. Minister of Housing and Local Government*[2] the Minister was held to be entitled under this power (with slightly different wording under the then section 85 (5)) to vary an enforcement notice so as to make it relate only to that part of the development in question in respect of which it was valid.

So far as ground (*a*) is concerned the decision will, as in an ordinary planning appeal, be a matter of **policy** and the planning merits of the case will be the deciding factor. Nothing can it seems turn on the fact that the development is in contravention of planning control.

The Secretary of State has power[3] to grant Planning Permission for the development to which the Enforcement Notice relates, or, as the case may be, to discharge any condition or limitation subject to which a Planning Permission was granted. He may also grant planning permission for **part of the development**, or for the development of **part of the land** to which the enforcement notice relates. This power is new and extends the power of the Secretary of State in the granting of permission. He may[3] also determine the purpose for which the land may lawfully be used, having regard to past use and to any Planning Permissions existing. (This is a provision applying to appeals against notices served after the provisions of Part II of the 1968 Act came into operation.[4]) In relation to a grant of Planning Permission or a determination under these provisions the decision of the Secretary of State is final.[5]

---

[1] Section 88 A replacing earlier provisions with a qualification.
[2] [1963] 2 Q.B. 196.
[3] Section 88 B substituted for Section 88 (5) by the Local Government and Planning (Amendment), Act 1981.
[4] *I.e.*, after the 1st April 1969. *See* S.I. 1969, No. 275.
[5] Section 88 B (3) (b).

Any planning permission granted may[1] be for retention or completion of any buildings or works on the land or for such retention or completion without compliance with some condition attached to previous planning permission, and a permission granted by the Secretary of State may itself be subject to conditions. Where a condition or limitation is discharged another may be substituted, whether more or less onerous.

As already noted (*ante*, p. 152) where any appeal is brought against an enforcement notice the appellant is deemed to have made an application for planning permission for the development to which the enforcement notice relates, and in relation to any exercise by the Secretary of State's powers described above a planning permission granted is to be treated as granted on that application and for the purpose of Section 34 of the 1971 Act (which requires a Register of planning decisions to be kept by the planning authority) is to be treated as having been given by the Secretary of State in dealing with a planning application made to the authority.

The case of *Hansford v. Minister of Housing and Local Government*[2] is relevant to this question of a deemed application. In that case a builder who had for a long time extracted gravel by hand but had changed to mechanical excavation was served with an enforcement notice. His appeal to the Minister on the ground that no permission was required was dismissed and the Minister also refused the deemed planning application under section 64 (2). The builder appealed to the Divisional Court on the basis that the Minister should have considered granting a permission with conditions limiting the gravel extraction to hand methods. The Court held that the deemed application was to do what the enforcement notice complained of and the the Minister had no material for imposing a condition; moreover he was not obliged to consider the question of granting such a permission.

---

[1] Section 88 B (2) (a) and (b).
[2] (1969) 114 S.J. 33, D.C.

In considering whether to grant Planning Permission the Secretary of State must[1] have regard to the provisions of the development plan, so far as it is material, and to any other material considerations.[2]

These requirements are the same as those imposed on a local planning authority considering a planning application at first instance,[3] and on the Secretary of State in determining an appeal from the local planning authority,[4] or after failure of the authority to determine the application within the prescribed period.[5]

Although the requirement is (*inter alia*) to "have regard to" the development plan this does not mean that adherence to the plan is mandatory. It is sufficient that the plan is taken into account. It was so held by Melford Stephenson, J., in *Enfield London Borough v. Secretary of State for the Environment*.[6] The Secretary of State had on appeal allowed the development of green belt land. The written representation procedure had been used and many residents had by letter objected to the development. An order to quash the decision (*inter alia*) on the ground that the Secretary of State had not had regard to the provisions of the development plan was refused.

Material considerations

As to the material considerations to which the Secretary of State must have regard, several cases have provided guidance.

A useful starting point is the decision in *Stringer v. Minister of Housing and Local Government*[7] (a case which is referred to elsewhere—see page 50). In that case Cooke J. said "it may be conceded at once that the material consider-

---

[1] Section 88B (2).
[2] As to material considerations see *post*.
[3] Section 29 (1).
[4] Section 29 (1) as applied by s. 36 (5).
[5] Section 29 (1) as applied by ss. 36 and 37. The "prescribed period" is that laid down by S.I. 1977, No. 289.
[6] [1975] J.P.L. 155.
[7] [1970] 1 W.L.R. 1281.

ations to which the Minister is entitled and bound to have regard in deciding the Appeal must be considerations of a planning nature. I find it impossible, however, to accept the view that such considerations are limited to matters relating to amenity. So far as I am aware, there is no authority for such a proposition and it seems to me to be wrong in principle. In principle it seems to me that any consideration which relates to the use and development of land is capable of being a planning consideration. Whether a particular consideration falling within that broad class is material in any given case will depend on the circumstances. However, it seems to me that in considering an Appeal the Minister is entitled to ask himself whether the proposed development is compatible with the proper and desirable use of other land in the area. For example if permission is sought to erect an explosives factory adjacent to a school the Minister must surely be entitled and bound to consider the question of safety", and later the Learned Judge said "I find it equally difficult to accept that the local Planning Authority and the Minister on Appeal must have regard only to public interests as opposed to private interests . . . it seems to me that it would be impossible for the Minister and local Planning Authorities to carry out their duties as custodians of the public interest if they were precluded from considering the effect of a proposed development on a particular piece of land by a particular occupier in the neighbourhood. The public interest, as I see it, may require that the interests of individual occupiers should be considered. The protection of the interests of individual occupiers is one aspect and an important of the public interest as a whole."

In *R.M.C. Management Services v. Secretary of State for the Environment*[1] planning permission for a ready-mix concrete plant had been refused by the Secretary of State. The site was on an industrial estate but the council and the Secretary of State had taken into account the risk of an abnormal level of abrasive dust arising from the use proposed. The applicant appealed to the Court, but failed,

---

[1] (1972) 222 E.G. 1593.

Bristow, J., holding that the risk taken into account was a "material consideration".

Collis Radio v. Secretary of State for the Environment[1] concerned a proposal that a warehouse should be permitted to be used for the carrying on of the business of a "cash and carry store". The planning officer at the inquiry claimed that there was a shortage of industrial land in the area and although the proposed development was not of itself harmful, proliferation would be. No documentary evidence was produced to support the planning officer's contentions. It was held that the contentions of the planning officer were "material considerations". The officer was speaking from his own knowledge and was entitled to have regard to a potential effect on a locality.

Possible consequences on other sites was also held to be a material consideration in *Tempo Discount Warehouse v. Enfield London Borough and the Secretary of State for the Environment*[2] where the matter in issue was the possible effect on established shopping centres of a substantial number of cash and carry warehouses.

In *J. Murphy and Sons v. Secretary of State for the Environment*[3] Ackner, J., decided that in determining whether planning permission should be granted the Secretary of State was not entitled to have any regard to the cost of developing the site in question.

This decision was applied in *Walters v. Secretary of State for the Environment*,[4] Sir Douglas Frank, Q.C. sitting as a Deputy Judge, holding that the financial viability of a scheme was a matter for the developer. It was not for the authority to refuse planning permission where in their view it could only be carried out at a loss.

However, the cost of conversion was held to be a material consideration in determining whether office premises could

---

[1] (1975) 73 L.G.R. 211, D.C.
[2] [1979] J.P.L. 98, Sir Douglas Frank Q.C.
[3] [1973] 1 W.L.R. 560.
[4] *The Times*, November 8 1978, Sir Douglas Frank, Q.C.

reasonably be adapted for residential use in *Niarchos (London) v. Secretary of State for the Environment.*[1]

The existence of a valid planning permission is a material consideration in determining a further planning application.[2]

The planning history, including any expired permission, is a material consideration to be taken into account. It was so held in *South Oxfordshire District Council v. Secretary of State for the Environment and Faherty Brothers*[3] although the decision was in fact quashed since the Secretary of State had wrongly treated an expired permission as a "**vitally material** consideration in this instance".

It is clear that demolition of an existing building does not of itself entitle a developer to put up another building in its place.[4] Where demolition has been effected those considering any application to build a new building are entitled to look at the state of affairs existing after demolition including the use to which the building will be put.[5]

Existing planning rights were held to be capable of being a material consideration in *North Surrey Water Company v. Secretary of State for the Environment* (*supra*).

In *Brighton Borough Council v. Secretary of State for the Environment*,[6] private school Trustees had applied for planning permission to develop part of its playing fields for residential purposes, the main building of the school being elsewhere and being a listed building. On Appeal an Inspector had granted permission (inter alia) on the basis of the special financial factor that the school building would probably benefit from the development profit by way of urgently needed repairs which were estimated to cost £100,000. The Authority applied to quash the decision but failed, the Court deciding that the restoration and mainte-

---

[1] (1978) 76 L.G.R. 480, Sir Douglas Frank, Q.C.
[2] *Spackman v. Secretary of State for the Environment* [1977] 1 All E.R. 257.
[3] [1978] J.P.L. 383, Sir Douglas Frank, Q.C.
[4] See *post*, p. 31 *et seq*.
[5] See *Magoa Services v. Secretary of state for the Environment and Bromley London Borough*, [1978] J.P.L. 383.
[6] (1978) 39 P. & C.R. 46, Sir Douglas Frank, Q.C.

nance of the listed school building was a planning consideration properly taken into account.

The Court of Appeal held in *Clyde and Co. v. Secretary of State for the Environment,*[1] reversing Willis, J., that the desirability of retaining an existing use (residential as against proposed offices) **was** *a material consideration.*

In *Granada Theatres v. Secretary of State for the Environment*[2] the owners of the cinema wanted to change the use to a bingo hall because a cinema was losing money and they would cease such use even if they could not get planning permission for the proposed change. The Appeal of the owners against a refusal of planning permission was dismissed by the Secretary of State who said that although he was satisfied that it was not commercially viable to continue to run the whole building as a cinema he was not satisfied that all the possibilities of allowing part of the building to be so used had been exhausted. The owners applied to quash this decision on the basis that the desirability of preserving the existing use was not a material consideration where there was no possibility that that use would continue if permission were refused. The Court held that the desirability of retaining the existing use was a material consideration and that the sole question was therefore whether it was reasonable for the Secretary of State to have come to the conclusion he had done. They found his decision not to be unreasonable and dismissed the application.

In *Walter Hermans and Sons v. Secretary of State for the Environment*[3] an inspector had recommended that planning permission should not be given for a building to be used for poultry dressing and storage in connection with an established business of neighbouring land, on the basis that there was no likelihood that the business would not continue to expand and existing unsatisfactory working conditions should be alleviated by moving elsewhere. The Secretary of State had agreed. Willis, J., held, allowing an appeal that

---

[1] [1977] 1 W.L.R. 926, C.A.
[2] (1980) 257, E.G. 1154, Forbes, J.
[3] [1975] J.P.L. 351.

the inspector should not have considere the case as if there were no existing business but should have considered the application in the context of ameliorating conditions. It was not relevant that applications to expand might be encouraged if the appeal were allowed.

When the Secretary of State is determining an appeal he is not bound to accept his Inspector's recommendations. On the contrary he must make up his own mind on the matter, giving due weight to the recommendations of his Inspector.[1]

The Divisional Court decided in *Wholesale Mail Order Supplies v. Secretary of State for the Environment*[2] that the Secretary of State was entitled to rely upon experience and opinion rather than on facts and evidence and that the Court could not consider the facts of another allegedly inconsistent appeal decision, especially since the Secretary of State had never been asked to consider that other application.

The case concerned refusal of permission for a cash-and-carry warehouse in view of the possible effects on a central shopping area project.

In exercising his power to grant planning permission the Secretary of State must truly exercise his own discretion and he cannot be said to have done this where he has effectively delegated the decision to someone else, *e.g.* another Minister of the Crown.

The Divisional Court so held in *H. Lavender & Son v. Minister of Housing and Local Government.*[3] The Minister of Agriculture had objected to any planning permission being granted for gravel workings on certain high quality agricultura land and on that basis the local planning authority had refused L's application for planning permission for such workings. The Minister of Housing and Local Gov-

[1] *Nelsovil v. Minister of Housing and Local Government (supra). See also Vale Estates (Acton) v. Secretary of State for the Environment* [1971] 69 L.G.R. 543, *Knight v. Secretary of State for the Environment* (1971) 219 E.G. 586, D.C., *Hodgkinson's (Ringway) v. Bucklow Rural District Council* (1972) 225 E.G. 2105, and *Felton & Sons (Motors) v. Secretary of State for the Environment* (1973) 227 E.G. 1475, D.C.

[2] (1975) 237 E.G. 185, D.C.

[3] [1970] 1 W.L.R. 1231.

ernment (then the responsible Minister for deciding planning appeals) had upheld this decision on the ground that it was his policy not to release land of this kind for development unless the Minister of Agriculture was not opposed to it. The Court held that although the Courts had no authority to interfere with the way in which the Minister carried out planning policy and he was entitled to consult other Ministers, the Minister had in fact by his stated policy improperly delegated the effective decision to the Minister of Agriculture, when there was no real chance that he would waive the objection, and so the Minister of Houseing and Local Government had failed to exercise any real discretion.

Expert evidence

An Inspector is not obliged to accept the evidence of expert witnesses even if there is no contrary evidence and he may use his own knowledge and common sense. This was decided in *Kentucky Fried Chicken (GB) v. Secretary of State for the Environment* in which case an Enforcement Notice had been served concerning a hot-food-take-away shop. The Appellants called expert evidence about remedial measures for noise and smell but the Inspector, upholding the Enforcement Notice, contradicted the opinion of the experts despite there being no contrary evidence. The Appellants applied for the decision to be quashed but failed.[1]

In *Winchester City Council v. Secretary of State for the Environment and Eccles*[2] the council sought to chellenge an inspector's decision on appeal on the basis that there had been a breach of the rules of natural justice[3] because, having taken into account the architectural quality of an existing house in the curtilage of which another house had been appplied for (and he had granted consent) he had declined to hear expert evidence on the matter. It was held, refusing an order that the inspector was entitled to take into account what he himself saw, without reconvening an inquiry if, as

---

[1] [1977] J.P.L. 727, D.C.

[2] (1979) 77, L.G.R., 715, C.A., affirming [1978] J.P.L. 467, Forbes, J.

[3] For a number of cases regarding breach of the rules of natural justice see *post*, p. 183.

in that case, what he saw served merely to emphasise some point canvassed at the inquiry, and he was also entitled to decide that he could judge for himself.

Mistakes

If the Secretary of State or his Inspector make a mistake of fact in deciding an Appeal this **may** be a ground on which to challenge the decision but only if the mistake is one which might reasonably be said to have affected the decision.

In *Hope v. Secretary of State for the Environment*[1] the Inspector had made a factual error as to the location on the site but this was held not to invalidate the decision having regard to all the circumstances.

The Court of Appeal in *East Hampshire District Council v. Secretary of State for the Environment and C. H. Josephi*[2] was considering a case where planning permission to build 226 residential units on 17 acres had been refused, the Local Authority's case being that the amount of land already released for residential development was such that need was insufficient to outweigh objections. Nevertheless the Secretary of State had allowed the Appeal on the recommendation of his Inspector. The Local Authority applied for the decision to be quashed on the basis that the Inspector had not adequately dealt with the question of housing need and at first instance the decision was so quashed but the developer appealed. The Court of Appeal held that there had been a material error of omission in that the Inspector had not reported the evidence of the principal Planning Officer which might well have influenced the Minister's decision and the decision to quash was upheld.

On the other hand even a bad mistake may not in fact result in the decision being quashed. In *Esher Urban District Council v. Minister of Housing and Local Government*[3] the Court decided that no irrelevant considerations had been taken into account in reaching a decision and despite a bad

---

1 [1979] J.P.L. 104.
2 [1979] J.P.L. 533, C.A.
3 *Estates Gazette* July 3, 1965.

miscalculation as to plot areas both by the Inspector and the Minister an application to quash the decision failed.

This point is demonstrated again in the recent case of *Elmbridge Borough Council v. Secretary of State for the Environment.*[1] Bristow J. held that an obvious harmless mistake in reaching a decision provided it produced no doubt as to whether the decision was reached according to law was not an error or law and did not affect the decision. In that case the Inspector had thought that there was a distance of 400 feet between the existing and proposed properties whereas in fact the distance was 170 feet. This error had been brought about by using the wrong scale and the Planning Authority had applied to quash the decision contending that the error vitiated it as a matter of law. The contention failed.

Power of amendment

Section 88 A (2)[2] gives the Secretary of State power, on appeal, to "correct any informality, defect or error in the enforcement notice, or give directions for varying its terms, if he is satisfied that the correction or variation can be made without injustice to the appellant or to the local planning authority.[3] In regard to a similarly worded provision in the 1962 Act, Lord Denning, M.R., said in the *Miller-Mead Case*[4] "This seems to me to be wider than the 'slip rule'. I think that it gives the Minister a power to amend which is similar to the power of the court to amend an indictment. He can correct errors, so long as, having regard to the merits of the case, the correction can be made without injustice. No informality, defect or error is a material one unless it is such as to produce injustice. Applied to misrecitals it means this—that if a misrecital goes to the substance of the matter,

[1] [1980] J.P.L. 463.

[2] Substituted for the earlier Section 88 (4) (a) by the Local Government and Planning (Amendment) Act, 1981.

[3] He should not exercise this power to make the notice cover development which was not put forward at the time of the Inquiry into the appeal. *See Birmingham Corporation v. Minister of Housing and Local Government and Habib Ullah; Birmingham Corporation v. Minister of Housing and Local Government and Khan* [1963] 3 W.L.R. 937.

[4] [1963] 2 Q.B. 196.

then the notice may be quashed, but if the misrecital does not go to the substance of the matter and can be amended without injustice, it should be amended rather than that the notice should be quashed or declared a nullity."

In *Bevan v. Secretary of State for Wales*[1] the Divisional Court held that a defect in an enforcement notice was not "material" and so could be amended, where the notice had alleged a change of use from domestic purposes and a pig farm to a use partly for the business of a plant hire and haulage contractor, and, to accord with facts found by the Inspector, the allegation was amended so as to relate to a change from composite use as a pig farm and plant hire and haulage contractor's business to user for the latter purpose only.

Similarly in *Hammersmith London Borough Council v. Secretary of State for the Environment*[2] it was held that there was no reason why the Secretary of State should not amend an enforcement notice by substituting a more appropriate description of the offending use than the term "guest house" used by the council, but held by the Secretary of State to be an incorrect description of the use in question which consisted of a use for cheap summer lettings to sixteen people at a time wanting temporary accommodation. The Secretary of State had considered the error a material one and had quashed the notice but an appeal by the Council was allowed.

The power of amendment can be, and indeed should be, used to protect established use rights.[3]

Morris v. Secretary of State for the Environment[4] upheld an amendment made by an inspector.[5] The enforcement notice had recited a business of selling, repairing and respray-

---

[1] (1969) 211 E.G. 1245, D.C.

[2] (1975) 73 L.G.R. 288, D.C.

[3] *See Ipswich County Borough Council v. Secretary of State for the Environment* (1972) 225 E.G. 797, D.C., and *Trevor's Warehouses v. Secretary of State for the Environment* (1972) 23 P. & C.R. 215, D.C. See also *Day v. Secretary of State for the Environment* (1979) 251, E.G. 163, D.C.

[4] (1975) 1 P. & C.R. 216, D.C.

[5] As to the powers of inspectors to determine appeals, *see post.*

ing motor vehicles. It required the appellant to remove the vehicles and stop using the premises for repairing or respraying vehicles but by error did not require cessation of sales. The inspector at the hearing allowed the notice to be amended to correct this error. The court held the amendment to be a proper one, since no injustice could result.

The Secretary of State is entitled to correct a description of a use in an Enforcement Notice to one that is more appropriate to the circumstances and if there is a mis-description it is his duty to try to correct it.[1]

T.L.G. Building Materials and Another v. Secretary of State for the Environment and Carrick District Council[2] is an instructive case on the question of amendment. In that case the Appeal site was a meadow abutting onto two other premises, one a house and the other a Builders Merchants premises. An Enforcement Notice referred exclusively to the meadow and required cessation of its use for the storage of builders materials and the removal of building materials from the site. The Notice was upheld by the Inspector who decided that the planning unit was either the meadow itself or the meadow and the house together. The Secretary of State, however, had concluded that on the removal of a boundary fence and the use of the meadow in connection with the Building Merchants use (which on the facts had clearly taken place) the Appeal site became part of the planning unit of the Builders Merchants premises previously referred to with a single use as a Builders Merchants yard to which the storage was ancillary. He considered that the allegation in the Enforcement Notice should have referred to use as a builders Merchants Yard and he took the view that the error could be corrected without injustice since the Appellants knew all along that the Notice was in connection with the Builders Merchants business. He amended the Notice accordingly and the Appellant applied for the decision to be quashed. The Divisional Court in fact remitted the matter to the Secretary of State to reconsider it. Donaldson

[1] *Hammersmith London Borough Council v. Secretary of State for the Environment.* (1975), 30 P. & C.R. 19.

[2] (1980) 41 P. & C.R. 243, D.C.

L. J. said that he considered it was beyond a mere formality to call upon somebody to stop using land for the storage of building materials and to amend it to the much wider concept of prohibiting use as a Builders yard and it seemed to him that any "wider condemnation—if that is the right word" in an Enforcement Notice must be material except in somewhat exceptional circumstances. But he considered that there was another ground for complaint which was that the deemed planning application (as to which see page 152) required the matter to be looked at from the proper perspective and here the real objection was that the Secretary of State had changed the planning unit, or recognised the correct planning unit after the Inquiry had taken place. The Learned Judge considered that natural justice required that the Secretary of State should go back to the Appellant and give her an opportunity of dealing with the different approach. Hodgson J. agreed adding that he would have thought that it was only in the most unusual circumstances that one could say that the correction of an Enforcement Notice which altered the planning use to which the Notice was directed was not material.

In*Murfitt v. Secretary of State for the Environment*[1] the Secretary of State was held entitled to vary an Enforcement Notice which had required land to be restored to its condition before a material change of use had taken place to a requirement that the land should be restored in accordance with the scheme to be agreed between the owner and the Authority or in default to be determined by the Secretary of State.

In *Dudley Borough Council v. Secretary of State for the Environment*[2] it was held by the Divisional Court that a planning permission might be granted which had the effect of permitting something contrary to conditions previously in force. This is really an application of the Rule (see page 169) that on Appeal the whole question is at large. In the Case an Enforcement Notice had required demolition of

[1] [1980] J.P.L. 598.
[2] [1980] J.P.L. 181, D.C.

two existing buildings to comply with a condition subject to which the erection of another building had been granted. On Appeal the Enforcement Notice had been altered so that it related to only one of the buildings by (*inter alia*) imposition of a new condition. The condition was held to be valid.

In *Cleaver v. Secretary of State for the Environment and Warwick District Council*[1] the Appellant conducted the business of a scrap metal dealer, mainly dealing with motor cycles and cars. Parts from these were sold. An Enforcement Notice alleged a material change of use by use for the reception, storing and breaking up of materials and required this use to cease and required also that the business of sale and exchange should cease. The owner challenged this on the basis that the Notice was bad in law because it required discontinuance of an activity not referred to in the description of the alleged breach. The Divisional Court held that the Notice could have been amended on Appeal so that the selling or exchanging referred to in the Notice was limited to the use alleged to be in breach of planning control. There was an error of law and the matter was remitted to the Secretary of State so that the Notice could be amended.

Natural Justice

It is clear that the Secretary of State in determining an Appeal is the master of his own procedure but even so he must observe the rules of natural justice and if he does not the Courts will interfere. There are a number of cases on the point.

In *T. A. Miller v. Minister of Housing and Local Government*[2] the High Court decided that the technical rules of evidence are not part of the rules of natural justice and the Secretary of State is entitled to act on any evidence which is logically probative including hearsay provided the other party is given an opportunity to comment upon and

---

[1] [1981] J.P.L. 38, D.C.
[2] [1968] 1 W.L.R. 992.

to contradict such evidence. The other party need not necessarily be given an opportunity of cross examining on such evidence. An Appeal must not be decided on an issue which the Appellants have had no opportunity to give evidence because it has not been raised as an issue in the Appeal.[1]

However, this does not mean that an Inspector's Report must refrain from any comment or expression of view unless it is a matter which the Appellant has been able to consider and deal with. The substance of the matter has to be looked at to see "whether something really has been produced which might have affected the Secretary of State's mind and which the Applicants have not had a chance to deal with".[2]

Hyndburn Borough Council v. Secretary of State for the Environment[3] was a case which concerned an Appeal against an Enforcement Notice which was allowed by the Secretary of State following written representations. In his decision letter the Secretary of State had referred to a departmental circular and said that although he accepted that the developments in question were open to objection "bearing in mind the policies outlined" (in the circular) he took the view that the objections did not provide sufficiently strong reasons for withholding a planning consent. As the policies had not been referred to in the written representations it was contended for the Appellants that there was a breach of the rules of natural justice but this contention failed, the Judge (Sir Douglas Frank, Q.C. sitting as a Deputy Judge of the Queen's Bench Division) remarking that it was well settled that a Minister was entitled to have a policy and to apply it without giving parties to an Appeal the opportunity of commenting on it and deciding that the Secretary of State in this case had been under no duty to give the Applicants

---

[1] See for example the decisions in *H. Sabey and Co. Limited v. Secretary of State for the Environment* [1978] 1 All E.R. 586, Willis, J. *and Wontner-Smith v. Secretary of State for the Environment* [1977] J.P.L. 103 and *Ellinas v. Secretary of State for the Environment* [1977] J.P.L. 249.

[2] Per Slynn J. in *General Accident Fire and Life Assurance Corporation Limited v. Secretary of State for the Environment* (1977) 241, E.G. 842.

[3] [1979] J.P.L. 536.

the opportunity of commenting on his reasons for his decision.[1]

Where a Planning Authority refuses to supply documents requested by an Appellant and he is not given an adequate opportunity to consider such documents a decision based on the Inspector's Report may be quashed for breach of the rules of natural justice. In *Performance Cars v. Secretary of State for the Environment*[2] the Appellant Company had prior to an Inquiry asked to be supplied with copies of documents relating among other things to the Authority having canvassed opposition to its proposals from local residents. The copies were not supplied until the day of the Inquiry and the Inspector refused an adjournment to allow the documents to be studied taking the view that an extended lunch break gave the Appellants sufficient opportunity for this purpose. The Appeal was dismissed relying on the Inspector's Report. An application to have the decision quashed was unsuccessful but on Appeal the Court of Appeal allowed the Appellants' Appeal on the basis that natural justice demanded the quashing of the decision since the Appellant had not had full opportunity to study the documents even though the outcome might not in fact have been different. (This was in fact a case where the Authority were in breach of the Rules concerning Local Inquiries into Planning Appeals other than Enforcement Appeals—the Town and Country Planning (Inquiries Procedure) Rules 1974 S.I. 1974 No. 419—and at that time there were no Rules applying to enforcement appeals.).

It often happens that at the end of an Appellant's case the Inspector himself puts questions and this is a point of an Inquiry where care is needed if there is not to be a breach of the rules of natural justice. One such case was *H. Sabey and Co. v. Secretary of State for the Environment.*[3] This Company who were gravel extractors were applying for

[1] For other cases concerning allegations of breach of the rules of natural justice see *Lewis Thirkell Limited v. Secretary of State for the Environment* (1978) 248 E.G. 685, Willis, J. and *Behrman v. Secretary of State for the Environment and East Devon District Council* [1979] J.P.L. 677, Forbes, J.

[2] (1977) 34 P. & C.R. 92, C.A.

[3] [1978] 1 All E.R. 586, Willis, J.

planning permission to extract gravel from agricultural land and were appealing against a refusal which was based on the alleged serious affect on agricultural quality and productivity of the land. At the Inquiry they were careful to show that they could restore the land satisfactorily but at the end of his re-examination, in answer to a question from the Inspector, a Ministry witness raised for the first time a new point namely that gravel was necessary to supply water through capillary attraction to the topsoil and if it was removed the land could not be restored. No questions about this had been put to the Appellants' witnesses and it formed no part of the Planning Authority's case or the case of the Ministry. However, the Inspector decided against the Appellants on this point and the Secretary of State accepted a recommendation to dismiss the Appeal. The Company's Appeal for an Order to quash the decision was successful since there had been nothing to put them on notice that the question might be an important one and there was a breach of the rules of natural justice in the Secretary of State acting of this point without giving the Company an opportunity of dealing with it.

Reasons for decisions

The question of what weight could be given to any particular matter is for the Secretary of State and the Courts will not interfere with a decision of his merely on the ground that he has given too great or too little weight to any matter but where the Secretary of State disagrees with the conclusions of an Inspector he should say why he disagrees and if he does not the decision may be quashed.[1]

In deciding an Appeal the Secretary of State must give reasons for his decision which are capable of being understood by a reasonably intelligent recipient and the decision must deal with the substantial points raised at the Inquiry.[2]

A decision of the Secretary of State on Appeal against

---

[1] See *French Kier Developments Limited v. Secretary of State for the Environment*. No. 2. [1977] J.P.L. 311.

[2] See *Tempo Discount Warehouses Limited v. London Borough of Enfield. [1979] J.P.L. 97.*

Enforcement Notice will be liable to challenge not only for failure to give proper reasons for a decision but if the decision is based on the conclusion that no reasonable person who took into account all the relevant facts would have reached.

In *Preston Borough Council v. Secretary of State for the Environment and E.L.S. Wholesale (Wolverhampton)*[1] a decision of the Secretary of State to allow an enforcement notice appeal was quashed on the ground that in it he had failed to give reasons relating to an important matter. The decision letter had said that "planning permission with conditions will therefore be granted for the retail trading. . . ." In another part of the letter of decision there was no reference to conditions. The Secretary of State explained that the inclusion of the words (about the consent being conditional) was an error. The council applied to quash his decision and the Court (Slynn, J.) decided that the appeal decision did not deal with the essential question of why retail trading should be allowed unconditionally and quashed that decision accordingly.

An Inspector is not under any duty to record legal submissions except where it is necessary to make the case presented intelligible to the Secretary of State (*North Surrey Water Company v. Secretary of State for the Environment*).[2]

Costs

The Secretary of State has power[3] to order either party to pay the costs of any appeal proceedings before him. The Council on Tribunals have issued a Report on the Award of Costs at Statutory Inquiries.[4] In Circular No. 73/65 the Minister of Housing and Local Government, then the responsible Minister, indicated (*inter alia*) that where it is alleged that a party has acted unreasonably, he would have regard to the considerations set out in paragraphs 23 to 29 of the Council's Report before deciding whether to make an award

[1] [1978] J.P.L. 548.
[2] (1976) 34 P. & C.R. 140, Slynn, J.
[3] Section 250 of the Local Government Act 1972.
[4] Cmnd. 2471.

of costs. He also remarked that awards of costs on grounds of unreasonable behaviour would arise "only in very exceptional circumstances". In the same circular he indicated that where a postponement or adjournment of an inquiry was made necessary through the fault of any party, including a third party who had been allowed to appear, he would be prepared to consider applications by the other parties appearing for their extra costs, so far as occasioned by the postponement or adjournment, to be paid by the party at fault.

In *Regina v. Secretary of State for the Environment ex parte Reinisch*[1] the Divisional Court decided that the Secretary of State was entitled to have a policy that costs of planning inquiries should be awarded only against a party behaving unreasonably, provided that he did not apply such a policy blindly. R. had successfully appealed to the Secretary of State against an enforcement notice but although the notice was quashed the normal policy had been applied and costs had not been awarded against the authority. The circumstances in this case were a little unusual.

The enforcement notice required the demolition of a first-floor extension over part of the ground-floor of a house. Planning permission had in fact been given for such an extension but the plan with the application had contained an error in that it showed the existing ground floor as being twelve feet from the boundary, whereas it was in fact six. The planning authority had indicated that if the window in the extension were modified they would allow the extension to stay (and they had also attempted by what was clearly an unlawful condition to deal with the problem of the window in that way). The enforcement notice which the Secretary of State quashed rested on the basis that the extension was not authorised by the original permission because of the error in the plan.

Where there is an award the parties are given an opportunity to agree between themselves the amount to be awarded.

---

[1] (1971) 22 P. & C.R. 1022, D.C.

Under the original arrangements of Circular 73/65 the procedure followed was that where the party receiving costs was legally represented the responsible Minister would, without himself determining an amount, award payment of his costs of the inquiry to be taxed (in the High Court) in default of agreement. Where the party was not legally represented the Minister was prepared to make an order in such amount as the parties agreed and requested him to do. Failing agreement in such a case, the disputed claim for costs would be referred to the Department for settlement, upon consideration of the arguments of the parties, and an order made accordingly.

Thus there were two separate methods of determining costs where they had been awarded but the parties could not agree on the amount, the method depending on whether the party awarded costs was legally represented at the hearing. The Secretary of State, in Circular 69 of 1971, indicated that he considered this an unsatisfactory state of affairs and altered the procedure. In future (the Circular was dated 16th September 1971) the same procedure is to be adopted for parties who were not legally represented as has applied to parties who were, *i.e.* in default of agreement costs will be taxed in the High Court.

A delay of some months can be expected between the date of a hearing and the date of receipt of the Secretary of State's decision on an appeal, which is notified by letter to the appellant and the authority. It is the practice to send to both parties a copy of the Inspector's report.

Case for the High Court

At any stage of the proceedings on an appeal the Secretary of State may state any question of law arising in the course of the proceedings in the form of a special case for the decision of the High Court.[1]

---

[1] Section 246 (2).

DETERMINATION OF APPEALS BY MINISTERIAL INSPECTOR

Part III of the 1968 Act provided for the first time that certain prescribed classes of appeals from the local planning authority should, except as otherwise prescribed, or as might be specified in directions[1] given by the Minister be **determined by a person appointed by the Minister** instead of the Minister himself, *i.e.* the **person appointed** (referred to hereafter as "the Inspector") was to have power not only to consider the case and come to conclusions about it, but to **decide** the issue. Part III was in force from 1st January 1969.[2] It has now been repealed with effect from the 1st April 1972 by the Town and Country Planning Act 1971, but the provisions are re-enacted therein.

The Secretary of State may prescribe (*inter alia*) that appeals under section 88 of the 1971 Act against enforcement notices shall be dealt with in this way, and he exercised this power by the Town and Country Planning (Determination of Appeals by Appointed Persons) (Prescribed Classes) Regulations 1981[3] (replacing earlier Regulations).

The position now is that from 1st July 1981 when these regulations came into force all enforcement appeals (except listed building enforcement appeals, as to which see *post*, p. 265) are prescribed for decision by an inspector except that appeals by statutory undertakers are reserved for the Secretary of State.

In cases which are determined by an Inspector pursuant to the above provisions the procedure is as set out in Schedule 9 of the 1971 Act and described in the following paragraphs.

Notice of appeal must still be served on the Secretary of State who must ask the appellant and the local planning authority whether they wish to appear before and be heard by the Inspector. If **both** answer in the negative the appeal

---

[1] *See post* as to Minister's power to issue directions.
[2] S.I. 1968, No. 1909.
[3] S.I. 1981, No. 804.

may be determined without a hearing, but if either expresses a wish to be heard, an opportunity must be given to both parties to appear and be heard. The Inspector has power to hold a **local inquiry**, whether or not the parties have requested a hearing, and he **must** do so if so directed by the Secretary of State.

All the powers and duties of the Secretary of State described under the heading "Powers of the Secretary of State" in pages 169 to 187 (*ante*) become powers and duties of the Inspector and the Inspector's decision is to be treated as that of the Secretary of State.

An inspector determining a planning appeal must give adequate reasons for his decision so that an appellant can understand the grounds on which the decision has been made, but the Inspector is not bound to follow the practice of the Secretary of State as to amount of detail and the Court will interfere only if on their face the reasons given are unintelligible or bad.[1]

The Inspector also has the same powers as the Secretary of State (described previously) to disregard non-service of an enforcement notice in certain cases.

Paragraph 2 (3) (*b*) of Schedule 9 of the 1971 Act provides that it shall not be a ground of application to the High Court under section 245[2] of the Act or of appeal to that Court under section 246[2] of that Act, that the appeal ought to have been determined by the Secretary of State and not by the Inspector, unless the challenge to the Inspector's powers to determine the appeal was made (either by the appellant or the local planning authority) **before his decision on the appeal was given**.

Direction by the Secretary of State

The Secretary of State has power under Schedule 9 to direct that an appeal which would otherwise be determined

---

[1] *Ellis v. Secretary of State for the Environment* (1974) 31 P. & C.R. 130, D.C. *See also Hope v. Secretary of State for the Environment* (1975) 31 P. & C.R. 120.

[2] *See post*, p. 195, as to the detailed provision of s. 245 and *post*, p. 193, as to s. 246.

by an Inspector shall not be so determined but shall be determined by himself. His direction must state the reasons for which it is given and must be served[1] on the Inspector (if any) appointed, the appellant and the Local Planning Authority.

It seems clear that the Secretary of State may make his direction at any stage before the actual determination by an Inspector. If, however, he does exercise his power he must give to the appellant and the Local Planning Authority an opportunity of appearing before and being heard by an Inspector, if (*a*) his reasons for the direction raise any matters in respect of which they have not made representations, or, (*b*) if they had not yet been asked whether they wished to be heard or had been so asked but had expressed no wish or had expressed a wish to be heard, but had not yet been given an opportunity of doing so.

The Act expressly provides[2] that, where the Secretary of State issues a direction and himself determines an appeal as a result of it, he is not, except as described in the preceding paragraph, obliged to give any person an opportunity of a hearing, or of making fresh representations, or of making or withdrawing any representations already made, and that he may take into account any report made to him by the Inspector previously appointed to determine the appeal.

Substitution of Inspector

The Secretary of State is permitted to substitute one Inspector for another at any time before the determination of an appeal. If, before the new Inspector has been appointed, the Secretary of State has asked the parties whether they wish to be heard, he need not ask the question again, with reference to the new Inspector, and any answers previously given will stand in relation to the new Inspector; but if consideration of the appeal, or any inquiry or other hearing in connection with it has already begun, it must be recommenced. It is not, however, necessary to give any person an

---

[1] As to service, *see ante*, p. 121.
[2] Schedule 9, para. 3 (5).

opportunity of making fresh representations or modifying or withdrawing representations already made.

EFFECT OF APPEAL ON NOTICE

The effect of an appeal is to suspend the operation of the notice pending the final determination or withdrawal of the appeal.[1] The notice will come into effect when either of these events happens and if the notice is upheld the appellant will then have the period specified in the notice within which to comply with its terms (provided it is not open to challenge by other means dealt with below).

APPEAL FROM SECRETARY OF STATE TO[2] HIGH COURT

Section 246 (1) of the 1971 Act as amended by the 1981 Act provides that where the Secretary of State gives a decision in proceedings on an appeal against an enforcement notice the appellant or the local planning authority, or any person having an interest in the land to which the notice relates, may, according as Rules of Court may provide, either appeal to the High Court[3] against the decision on a point of law[4] or require the Secretary of State to state and sign a case for the opinion of the High Court.

The amendment by the 1981 Act regarding appeals to the Secretary of State confines the right of challenge to the local planning authority or a person having an interest in the land concerned, whereas formerly any person served with the notice had that right.

It was held in *Horsham District Council v. Fisher*[5] that a

---

[1] Section 88 (10).

[2] The same provisions apply to a determination of an appeal by an Inspector appointed under the provisions described, *ante*, p. 152, *See* Sched. 9, para. 2 (3).

[3] *See* R.S.C. (Revision) 1965, Orders 55 and 94. Notice of Motion, specifying the grounds of appeal must be served on the Minister and all parties within 28 days of the decision being communicated to the appellant.

[4] The exercise of a discretion of the Minister does not raise a point of law. *See Nelsovil v. Minister of Housing and Local Government* [1962] 1 W.L.R. 404.

[5] [1977] J.P.L. 178, Slynn, J.

decision of the Secretary of State to refuse to accept a notice of appeal was "proceedings on an appeal" so that an appeal to the High Court lay under section 246, and an appellant who had failed to exercise that right of appeal to the High Court could not thereafter raise the relevant point in other proceedings. In that case the Secretary of State had (wrongly) decided that a notice of appeal against an enforcement notice was defective. The defendant did not appeal under section 246, was convicted by magistrates for non-compliance with the enforcement notice and appealed to the Crown Court. It was held on the above basis that the validity of the enforcement notice could not be challenged in the Crown Court and that the conviction must stand.

The cases of *Button v. Jenkins* and *Wain v. Secretary of State for the Environment* noted *ante* at page 164 should also be referred to.

The Rules of the Supreme Court[1] provide that Notice of Motion specifying the grounds of appeal must be served on the Minister and all parties within 28 days of the decision being communicated to the appellant. It was held in *Ringroad Investments v. Secretary of State for the Environment*[2] that time runs from the date of **sending** of the letter of decision. In that case the decision of the Secretary of State dismissing an appeal against an enforcement notice had been conveyed in a letter dated March 6th 1979 and received by the appellant on March 7th 1979. He purported to appeal by Notice of Motion on April 4th 1979. The Secretary of State moved to strike out the appeal as being out of time and was successful on the basis set out above.

This provision was earlier contained in section 34 of the Caravan Sites and Control of Development Act 1960 and in *Hoser v. Minister of Housing and Local Government*,[3] a case under that section, the Court decided that since Rules of Court provided for an appeal by motion it was not open to an appellant to require the Minister to state a case. The

---

[1] R.S.C. (Revision) 1965, Orders 55 and 94.
[2] (1979) 40 P. & C.R. 99 D.C.
[3] [1962] 3 W.L.R. 1337.

selection of one of the alternatives referred to was for the Rules Committee and not an appellant.

On appeal to the High Court from the Minister an appellant is confined to the grounds of appeal actually taken before the Minister.[1]

In *Green v. Minister of Housing and Local Government*[2] the Divisional Court in an appeal under section 180 decided that the extended power of the Court to receive further evidence under the new R.S.C. Order 55, Rule 7 (2) and (3), did not allow the Court to hold a re-hearing of the primary facts and refused to allow the appellant to adduce evidence which was not before the Minister's Inspector.

If the High Court considers that the Minister's decision was wrong in law it will remit the matter to him with the opinion or direction of the Court for re-hearing and determination. The Court will not set aside or vary his decision.[3]

The Divisional Court in *Bendles Motors Ltd. v. Bristol Corporation*,[4] another case under the earlier provisions of the 1960 Act, decided that the Court will only interfere with a decision of the Minister if it is satisfied that, the Minister having properly directed himself as to the law, the decision was perverse in the sense that the evidence could not support it.

Further appeal from the High Court to the Court of Appeal and to the House of Lords will lie with leave of the Court.

When, on any appeal against a notice the Secretary of State decides, under the provisions noted, *ante*, page 169, to **grant planning permission** for the development to which an enforcement notice relates his action may be challenged under section 245 of the 1971 Act, re-enacting section 179 of the 1962 Act.

This section provides that if any person is aggrieved by

[1] *Miller-Mead v. Minister of Housing and Local Government* [1963] 2 Q.B. 196.
[2] [1967] 2 Q.B. 606.
[3] *See* R.S.C. (Revision) 1965, Orders 55 and 94.
[4] [1963] 1 W.L.R. 247.

any of certain defined[1] actions of the Secretary of State and desires to question the validity of the action on the grounds that it is not within the powers of the Act, or that any of "the relevant requirements" have not been complied with in relation to it, he may, within six weeks from the date on which the action is taken make application to the High Court. The Local Planning Authority has the same right.[2] Application to the High Court is by originating notice of motion.[3]

Persons appearing at a local inquiry by discretion of the Inspector, *e.g.* a local preservation society, may be aggrieved persons under section 245.[4]

The "relevant requirements" means[5] any requirements of the 1971 Act or of the Tribunals and Inquiries Act 1971 (consolidating earlier statutes), or any enactments replaced thereby, or of any order, regulations or rules made under these Acts which are applicable to the action in question.

On an application under this section the High Court:—

(*a*) may by interim order suspend the operation of the action in question until the final determination of the proceedings;

(*b*) if satisfied that the action in question is not within the powers of the Act **or** that **the interests of the applicant have been substantially prejudiced** by a failure to comply with any of the relevant requirements in relation to it, may quash that action.

Where an order is so quashed it is not open to the Court to substitute any other order. The appeal to the Secretary of State revives and is pending.[6]

---

[1] *See* s. 245 (3) and s. 242 (2) and (3).

[2] *See* s. 245 (2) and (7).

[3] *See* R.S.C. (Revision) 1965 (S.I. No. 1776), Orders 55 and 94. As to time see *Griffiths v. Secretary of State for the Environment, The Times*, January 28, 1982, C.A.

[4] *See Turner v. Secretary of State for the Environment* (1973) 72 L.G.R. 380, Ackner, J.

[5] Section 245 (7).

[6] *Hartnell v. Minister of Housing and Local Government* [1963] 1 W.L.R. 1141, affirmed [1965] 2 W.L.R. 474, H.L.

On a rehearing the Secretary of State should take full account of all matters relevant **as at the date of rehearing.**[1]

It is not for the Court, but for the Inspector, to decide what are the **relevant facts** on which a finding is required.[2]

Apart from challenge under section 245 as described above, the validity of a decision of the Secretary of State on an Enforcement appeal, to **grant Planning Permission** for the development to which the Enforcement Notice relates **cannot be questioned in any legal proceedings whatsoever.**[3]

LIMITATION ON METHODS OF CHALLENGE

Section 177 of the 1962 Act severely limited the right to challenge an enforcement notice. This section, and the appeal provisions with which it was linked, were altered in important respects by the 1968 Act.

However, in relation to an enforcement notice served before the commencement of Part II of the 1968 Act, *i.e.* before the 1st April 1969,[4] the effect of section 107 and paragraph 10 of Schedule 10 of the 1968 Act was that the 1962 Act provisions **as originally enacted** continued to apply to such notices. Only notices served on or after the 1st April 1969[5] were subject to the amended provisions.

That remained the position, despite the repeal by the 1971 Act of Part II of the 1968 Act. Section 243 of the 1971 Act re-enacted the provisions applying to enforcement notices served on or after the 1st April 1969 and by section 292 and Schedule 24, paragraph 31 the 1971 Act provided that in relation to enforcement notices served before 1st April 1969, notwithstanding their repeal or amendment by

---

[1] *See Price Brothers (Rode Heath) Limited v. Secretary of State for the Environment* (1978) 38 P. & C.R. 579.

[2] *See Continental Sprays v. Minister of Housing and Local Government* 67 L.G.R. 147; *William Boyer & Sons v. Minister of Housing and Local Government* (1968) 20 P. & C.R. 176; and *Deasy v. Minister of Housing and Local Government* (1970) 214 E.G. 415.

[3] Section 242 (1) and (3).

[4] *See* S.I. 1969, No. 275.

[5] Date of commencement of Part II of the 1968 Act. S.I. 1969 No. 275.

the 1968 Act the earlier statutory provisions had effect as they would have had, had the 1968 and 1971 Acts not been passed.

As noted presently the Local Government and Planning (Amendment) Act 1981 has further altered these provisions in an important respect.

The detailed position is as follows:—

In respect of enforcement notices served before 1st April 1969.[1]

With one exception to be noted presently the validity of an enforcement notice **which has been served on the owner and occupier of the land** "shall not, except by way of an appeal under Part IV of this Act (*i.e.* an appeal to the Secretary of State), be questioned in any proceedings whatsoever" on any grounds equivalent to those lettered (*b*), (*d*) and (*e*) on pages 153 to 154, *ante*.

The provision does not, however, apply to proceedings[2] brought in respect of failure to discontinue a use or comply with conditions or limitations as required by an enforcement notice against a person who—

(*a*) has held an interest in the land since before the enforcement notice was served, **and**

(*b*) did not have the notice served on him, **and**

(*c*) did not appeal against the notice.

It should be particularly noted that if the notice has not been served on the owner and occupier the limitation does not in any case apply.

In respect of enforcement notices served on or after the 1st April 1969.[2]

The 1971 Act provided that, with an exception noted hereunder the validity of an enforcement notice "shall not except by way of an appeal under Part V" of the Act of

[1] Date of commencement of Part II of the 1968 Act. S.I. 1969, No. 275.
[2] *See* Chapter 5, *post*.

1971 (*i.e.* an appeal to the Secretary of State), "be questioned in any proceedings whatsoever" on any of the grounds equivalent to those lettered (*b*) (*d*) (*e*) and (*f*) on pages 153 to 155, *ante*.

The provision does not apply to proceedings[1] brought in respect of failure to discontinue a use or comply with conditions or limitations as required by an enforcement notice against a person who:—

(*a*) has held an interest in the land since before the enforcement notice was served, **and**

(*b*) did not have the notice served on him, **and**

(*c*) satisfies the Court that—

(i) he did not know and could not reasonably have been expected to know that the enforcement notice had been served, and

(ii) his interests have been substantially prejudiced by the failure to serve him.

The most important difference between the 1962 Act and the 1971 provisions is that under the latter, failure to serve an enforcement notice as required by the Act is a matter for appeal to the Secretary of State[1] and cannot be the ground of appeal to the Courts.

The other difference is in the provisions relating to the exception to the general rule of section 243. Under the 1962 Act provisions, it is enough to secure exemption from the limitations of section 177 that the person in question held an interest in the land since before the notice was served, did not have it served on him and did not appeal against it.

Under the present Act, he must, in order not to be subject to section 243, satisfy the Court that he did not know and could not reasonably have been expected to know that the enforcement notice had been served and, further, that his interests have been substantially prejudiced by the failure to serve him.

---

[1] *See* Chapter 5, *post*.

As noted *post* (p. 206) the effect of the decision of the Divisional Court in *Smith v. King*[1] was that the validity of an enforcement notice **could** be challenged on what were grounds (f) and (g) (equivalent to the present grounds (g) and (h). The Local Government and Planning (Amendment) Act 1981[2] has removed this possibility by changing the provisions so that they now[3] say that validity is not to be challenged except by appeal under Part V of the 1971 Act (*i.e.* an appeal to the Secretary of State) "**on any of the grounds on which such an appeal may be brought**".

Consequential amendments provide that as from the same date[5] the words "issue" replaces the word "serve" in (a) and (c) (i) on p. 199 ante in relation to certain cases and the reference in (c) (ii) to "failure to serve" now refers to a copy of the notice instead of to the notice itself. Oddly Sub-Section 2A (inserted by the 1981 Act) provides that the earlier wording applies in respect of an enforcement notice served "before the passing of" the 1981 Act. It would appear that the intention was to refer to the **coming into operation** of the Act. The Act was passed on 27th July 1981 but the relevant provisions did not become effective until 27th August.[4]

An enforcement notice which has become effective is registrable as a local land charge. Section 198 of the Law of Property Act 1925 (as amended by the Local Land Charges Act 1975) provides that the registration of any instrument or matter in, (*inter alia*), any Local Land Charges Register is deemed to constitute **actual notice** thereof to all persons for all purposes connected with the land. However, it is submitted that, despite the unequivocal nature of this provision, mere registration would not be sufficient to impute knowledge to a person so as to prevent him from taking advantage of the above provision in defending himself from a criminal charge.

---

[1] (1970) 21 P. & C.R. 560.
[2] Section 1 and Schedule para. 18.
[3] On and after 27 August 1981. See section 2 (2).
[4] Section 2.

In *Jeary v. Chailey Rural District Council*[1] J had been served with an enforcement notice in respect of development consisting of a change of use of land from a caravan site to a breaker's yard. His contention was that the land had been used as a breaker's yard since before 1948[2] and that the enforcement notice was *ultra vires* and a nullity. The council contended that section 177 (1) (of the 1962 Act) (now replaced by section 243 of the 1971 Act) precluded her from questioning the validity of the notice, even though that might operate to deprive her of a vested right. On the assumption that there had been no development, it was held that in the absence of bad faith the Council had been entitled to serve the notice, which was not *ultra vires*, and that the fact that J had a vested right did **not** affect the prohibition in section 177 (1).

No person who has appealed to the Secretary of State against an enforcement notice can afterwards be heard in any other proceedings to allege that he was not duly served with such a notice, nor can any such allegation be made by any other person.[3]

A person who has applied for planning permission after service of an enforcement notice in respect of that development, or who has appealed to the Secretary of State on the footing of the validity of the enforcement notice is not by reason of that fact estopped from afterwards denying its validity.[4]

Despite the limitations mentioned there are still circumstances in which a person served with an enforcement notice may be able to pursue other courses of action instead of, or as well as, an appeal to the Secretary of State. These will now be discussed.

---

[1] (1973) 26 P. & C.R. 280, C.A.

[2] The 1st July 1948 was the appointed day for the coming into force of the 1947 Planning Act.

[3] Section 110 (2).

[4] *See Swallow and Pearson v. Middlesex County Council* [1953] 1 W.L.R. 422, and *Mounsdown v. Weymouth and Melcombe Regis Corporation* [1960] 1 Q.B. 645.

APPLICATION DIRECT TO THE HIGH COURT

There have been a number of cases in the past where an enforcement notice has been successfully challenged by means of an action in the High Court for a declaration that the notice is a nullity.[1] It would seem that proceedings can be begun either by writ or by originating summons.[2] In the case of *Rigden v. Whitstable U.D.C.*[3] it was decided that an originating summons could **not** be used, but this decision was on the terms of Order 54A of the Rules of the Supreme Court (now replaced[4]). The earlier Order referred to a person "interested under a deed will or other written instrument" and Danckwerts, J., held that the Plaintiff (who was asking under the Rule for a declaration that an enforcement notice was null and void), was not within this description, since he could not be interested under an enforcement notice. The new Order[5] is in wider terms, referring to "the construction of any . . . contract or other document", where this is the sole or principal question in issue.

The present provisions for appeal to the Secretary of State and the above restriction on questioning the validity of an enforcement notice except by way of such an appeal first appeared in the Caravan Sites and Control of Development Act 1960.[5]

It is clear that the provisions in question do not prohibit such recourse to the High Court on any ground with which the Secretary of State has no power to deal.[6]

The distinction of between nullity and invalidity and the powers of the Secretary of State and the Court having regard to the limitations on appeal to the latter were discussed at some length in the *Miller-Mead Case*. It would appear from

---

[1] *See e.g., Swallow and Pearson v. Middlesex County Council, supra; Burgess v. Jarvis* [1952] 2 Q.B. 41; *Francis v. Yiewsley and West Drayton U.D.C.* [1958] 1 Q.B. 478.

[2] R.S.C. 0.5 and 0.15 and 16.

[3] [1959] Ch. 422.

[4] *See* R.S.C. 0.5, r. 4 (2) (*a*).

[5] *See* s. 33 of that Act.

[6] *Per* Upjohn, L.J., in *Miller-Mead v. Minister of Housing and Local Government* [1963] 2 Q.B. 196.

this case that a notice will be a **nullity**, and liable to be declared such on application to the High Court, if **on its face** it appears not to comply with the requirements of the Act previously mentioned in Chapter 3. This will be so if it:—

(*a*) fails to specify a date when it is to take effect;
(*b*) fails to specify the matters alleged to constitute a breach of planning control[1];

(*c*) fails to specify clearly the steps to be taken;

(*d*) fails to specify the time within which those steps are to be taken.

In respect of a notice served under the original 1971 Act provisions (*i.e.* before 27th August 1981 on which date the amended provisions substituted by the 1981 Act came into effect) an additional ground would be that the notice failed to specify separately and distinctly the date when the notice was to take effect or that the date of taking effect specified was less than 28 days from service.

In *R. v. Hillingdon London Borough Council ex parte Royco Homes Ltd.*[2] one of the issues was whether it was open to an applicant for planning permission to apply to the High Court for *certiorari* to quash a planning permission which showed on its face that it was based on an error of law, or made without jurisdiction or was otherwise invalid. The question clearly is applicable to other exercises of powers under planning legislation *e.g.* the service of an enforcement notice. The Court indicated that *certiorari* **might** be granted **in a proper case** and Lord Widgery, C.J., said [3] that "a proper case" was one where "the decision in question is liable to upset as a matter of law because on its face it is clearly made without jurisdiction or made in consequence of an error of law".

---

[1] But mistaken allegations of fact do not make a notice which on its face complies with the section a *nullity*. *Per* Diplock, L.J., in *Miller-Mead v. Minister of Housing and Local Government (supra). See also Findlow v. Lewis* [1963] 1 Q.B. 151.
[2] [1974] 2 W.L.R. 805.
[3] At p. 649 B.

Where a notice is not a **nullity**, but is merely **invalid**, the normal remedy is appeal to the Secretary of State, but the Court may have jurisdiction when the notice, although not a nullity is invalid in that it offends against the requirements of the statute but not in respect of a matter which can be taken by way of appeal to the Secretary of State.[1]

Metallic Protectives v. Secretary of State for the Environment[2] concerned an Enforcement Notice which alleged a breach of a planning condition that no nuisance should be caused to residential properties by reason of noise etc. and required M.P. Company to install satisfactory soundproofing for a compressor and take "all possible action to minimise the effects of use of acrylic paint". On Appeal the Secretary of State modified the wording but on further Appeal to the Divisional Court it was held that the Notice was so defective that it was a nullity from the beginning and Lord Widgery C.J. said "there is no place for it but the waste paper basket". As the Notice was a nullity it was not open to the Secretary of State to amend it or take any other action.

(For another case where an enforcement notice was held to be a nullity and incapable of correction by the Secretary of State see *Hounslow London Borough Council v. Secretary of State for the Environment and the Indian Gymkhana Club.*[3])

It is suggested that either of the following grounds might be sufficient to found an action for a declaration:—

(1) That the notice is served by a body which is neither the planning authority nor a body possessing planning powers properly delegated to it by a planning authority.[4] (It will be rarely that this ground can be used.)

---

[1] *See* judgment of Upjohn, L.J., in *Miller-Mead v. Minister of Housing and Local Government* [1963] 2 Q.B. 196.

[2] [1976] J.P.L. 166, D.C.

[3] [1981] J.P.L. 510, D.C.

[4] *See ante*, page 47 as to delegation. A body exercising delegated powers cannot, in the absence of specific authority to do so, sub-delegate the functions entrusted to it. *See e.g., Allingham v. Minister of Agriculture and Fisheries*, 64 T.L.R. 290.

(2) That the authority serving the notice has improperly exercised its discretion.[1]

(3) That, where a notice served before the 27 August 1981[2] has been served on more than one person, its terms or the dates of service are such as to result in the notice purporting to come into effect on more than one date in relation to different persons. (*See Bambury v. London Borough of Hounslow*,[3] discussed at page 122, *ante*.)

(4) That a condition attached to a planning permission and in respect of an alleged breach of which the notice is served is not in fact a valid condition.

A further ground of challenge now[4] appears to be failure to comply with regulations of the Secretary of State under section 87 (12) (a) or (b) as to additional matters to be specified in an enforcement notice or as to the attachment to an enforcement notice of an explanatory note or as to the information to be included in such a note.

In respect of an enforcement notice served before the 1st April 1969[5] another ground available is that the notice has not been served on the owner and occupier. In such a case other grounds (*see* page 198, *ante*), will also be available since section 177 of the 1962 Act as originally enacted applied only to cases where the notice had been served on owners and occupiers.[6]

The availability of declaratory relief after previous criminal proceedings was the subject of a decision of the Court of Appeal in *Munnich v. Godstone R.D.C.*[7] The Court was

---

[1] *See ante*, page 91, as to matters to be properly taken into account. If the authority has acted *bona fide* the Court will not substitute its own view for that of the local planning authority as to whether a notice should have been served in a particular case. *See Goddard v. Minister of Housing and Local Government* [1958] 1 W.L.R. 1151.

[2] Date of coming into force of the substituted provisions of the 1981 Act.

[3] [1966] 2 All E.R. 532.

[4] *I.e.* after the coming into force of the 1981 Act.

[5] Commencement of Part II of 1968 Act.

[6] *See* discussion of the effects of section 177, *ante*, p. 197.

[7] [1966] 1 W.L.R. 427.

considering an appeal by the local planning authority against the decision of Mocatta, J.,[1] to grant a declaration of invalidity of an enforcement notice, in a case where the plaintiff had on three previous occasions been convicted of offences in proceedings based on the enforcement notice in question, on the basis that such notice was valid. He had not appealed against those convictions. The Court of Appeal held that although the Court would not grant declaratory relief to a litigant seeking to reverse a decision on **fact** in criminal proceedings such relief **could** be granted where the issue was one of **law** (i.e. the validity of the enforcement notice). In that case the Court, reversing the decision of Mocatta, J., decided that the enforcement notice **was** valid and a declaration was refused.

DEFENCE TO PROSECUTION OR OTHER PROCEEDINGS BY THE LOCAL PLANNING AUTHORITY

Subject to the limitations set out in section 243[2] the invalidity of the enforcement notice may be set up as a defence by a person (1) prosecuted[3] for failing to comply with an enforcement notice or (2) being sued by the local planning authority who have carried out the requirements of the notice themselves[3] and are seeking to recover their expenses.

The grounds of challenge suggested above in relation to an application for a declaration will apply.

It was held in *Smith v. King*[4] that the validity of an enforcement notice was open to challenge before justices (for penalties for non-compliance) on grounds (*f*) and (*g*) of section 46 (1) of the Act of 1962 (later grounds (*f*) and (*g*) of section 88 (1) of the 1971 Act)—these grounds related to an allegation of excessive steps required to be taken, or of too short a period for compliance—but that the reasonable-

---

[1] (1966) 110 S.J. 131 (1965) 63 L.G.R. 506.
[2] *See ante*, page 197.
[3] *See post*, Chapter 5.
[4] (1970) 21 P. & C.R. 560, D.C.

ness of time stated for compliance must be tested as at the **date of the notice** and not as at the date of trial.

As earlier noted (p. 200, *ante*) these grounds are not open after 27 August 1981.[1]

The principles of *res judicata* as developed in civil proceedings, do not apply with the same strictness to criminal proceedings, and on a second or subsequent prosecution a defence can possibly be taken although it had been available to prevent a previous conviction.[2]

ACTION AGAINST THE LOCAL PLANNING AUTHORITY

Subject again to the limitation of section 243,[3] where a local planning authority have exercised the power themselves to carry out the requirements of the notice[4] an occupier whose land has been entered upon may bring an action for damages for trespass and/or an injunction on the ground that the notice under which action was taken is invalid.

The grounds of challenge suggested above in relation to an application for a declaration will apply.

LIFE OF AN ENFORCEMENT NOTICE

Assuming that an enforcement notice has not been successfully challenged, it is necessary to consider the effect upon the notice of

(*a*) compliance with the notice;

and (*b*) a subsequent grant of permission for the development to which it relates.

---

[1] Date of coming into force of the 1981 Act provisions.

[2] *See* the Judgment of Lord Parker, C.J. in *Hailsham R.D.C. v. Moran* (1966) 64 L.G.R. 367, D.C.

[3] *See ante*, page 197.

[4] *See post*, Chapter 5.

COMPLIANCE WITH ENFORCEMENT NOTICE

Compliance with any requirement of an enforcement notice whether in respect of completion of demolition or alteration of buildings or works or the discontinuance of any use of land, or in respect of any other requirement, does not mean that it can in future be ignored. The position is as follows:—

Unauthorised uses

A requirement in an enforcement notice that a use shall be discontinued operates as a requirement that it shall be **permanently** discontinued in so far as it is a contravention of the Act.[1]

The resumption of an unauthorised use at any time after discontinuance in compliance with the notice is a contravention of the notice, and any person who himself uses or who causes or permits the land to be used for the offending purpose is liable to prosecution.[2]

Buildings or works

If any development is carried out on land by reinstating or restoring buildings or works which have been demolished or altered in compliance with an enforcement notice, the notice is to be deemed to apply to the buildings or works as reinstated or restored, as it applied to the buildings or works before they were demolished or altered, notwithstanding that the terms of the notice may not be apt for the purpose.[3]

The terms of section 93 (3) were considered by Judge Goldstone in the County Court case of *Broxbourne Borough Council v. Small*[4] when it was held that where a Dutch barn was the subject of an enforcement notice, a subsequently erected Nissen hut of smaller area and height but on substantially the same site and put to the same use was in fact

[1] Section 93 (2).
[2] Section 89 (5). *See post*, Chapter 5.
[3] Section 93 (3).
[4] Edmonton County Court. April 21st 1980, [1980] C.L. 2638.

a "reinstatement or restoration" of the Dutch barn as defined by section 93 (3).

In such a case two results may follow:—

(1) The local planning authority may themselves enter on the land and take steps to demolish or alter the buildings or works in accordance with the requirements of the notice[1] in the same way as they could have done originally, with the difference that, in this case, they must not less than 28 days before doing so, serve on the owner and occupier of the land a notice of their intention.[2] The provisions stated *post* as to recovery of expenses from the **owner**[3] and as to his right to recover from the person actually responsible apply.

(2) The local planning authority may prosecute any person[4] who, without a grant of planning permission has carried out the reinstatement or restoration and such a person is liable on summary conviction to a fine of up to £1000.[5]

The penalty is less heavy if the enforcement notice was served before 1st April 1969 (the date on which provisions of the 1968 Act increasing penalties came into effect). The maximum penalty in such a case is £100.

The owner as such is not liable to prosecution. The position is thus different from that on an initial failure to demolish or alter, when an owner served with an enforcement notice is liable to be prosecuted.[6]

---

[1] Section 93 (3) and s. 91 (1).
[2] Section 93 (4).
[3] *See ante*, page 119 as to meaning of "owner".
[4] As to offences by corporations, *see* p. 218, *post*.
[5] Section 93 (5). As amended by the 1981 Act with effect from 27th August 1981. The earlier maximum was £400.
[6] *See post*, Chapter 5.

Breach of condition or limitation

The two previous cases are dealt with specifically in section 93, but there is reference in subsection (1) to "any other requirements" contained in an enforcement notice and this appears to cover a requirement to comply with a condition or limitation subject to which planning permission was granted and which may not fall under either of the above heads. Again, compliance does not discharge the[1] notice and subsequent breaches will therefore result in liability to prosecution of any person[2] who either himself contravenes or who causes or permits the contravention by failure to comply with the condition or limitation in question.

Recovery by owner or occupier of expenses of compliance

Any expense incurred by an owner or occupier in complying with the requirements of an enforcement notice are recoverable[3] by him from the person who in fact committed the breach of planning control.[4]

RESUMPTION OF PREVIOUS USE

Section 23 (9) of the 1971 Act provides that where an enforcement notice has been served planning permission is not required for the resumption of any **lawful use** to which the land was put before the unauthorised development was carried out. (But for this provision, the "change back", if material, would need planning permission.) It is however important to note that **lawful use** here does **not** include a use which had continued long enough to acquire immunity from enforcement proceedings,[5] so that such a use **would** require a planning permission.[6]

It is not necessary for the lawful use to immediately pre-

---

[1] Section 93 (1).
[2] As to offences by corporations, *see* p. 218, *post*.
[3] By action in the County Court or the High Court.
[4] Section 91 (2).
[5] As to such immunity, *see* pp. 130 to 134, *ante*.
[6] *See L.T.S.S. Print and Supply Services v. Hackney London Borough Council*, *ante*, p. 43.

cede the unlawful use (in respect of which an enforcement notice has been served). Subject to any question of possible abandonment (as to which see *ante*, p. 31) a user can go back as far as he likes to find the lawful use which he may resume.[1]

EFFECT OF SUBSEQUENT GRANTS OF PLANNING PERMISSION

Enforcement proceedings are not affected by the mere **submission** of a planning application or even by the lodging of an **appeal against refusal**[2] of planning permission.

It may be, however, that a planning permission is **granted** after the service of an enforcement notice, either for the retention of the offending buildings or works, or for the continuance of the hitherto unauthorised use of land to which the enforcement notice relates. In that event the enforcement notice **ceases to have effect**, in so far as it requires steps to be taken for the demolition or alteration of the buildings or works, or for the discontinuance of the use in question.[3]

If the subsequent grant of planning permission permits retention of buildings or works or continuance of a use without complying with some condition subject to which a previous planning permission was granted (as it may do under section 32 of the Act) the enforcement notice **ceases to have effect** in so far as it requires steps to be taken to comply with the condition.[4]

The Act specifically provides[5] that liability remains in respect of any offence of failing to comply with the enforcement notice before the relevant provisions in the notice ceased to have effect.

---

[1] *Balco Transport Services v. Secretary of State for the Environment*, *The Times* June 24th 1981, D.C.
[2] *Davis v. Miller* [1956] 1 W.L.R. 1013.
[3] Section 92 (1).
[4] Section 92 (2).
[5] Section 92 (3).

CHAPTER 5

NON-COMPLIANCE WITH AN ENFORCEMENT NOTICE

OWNER PREVENTED FROM COMPLIANCE BY ANOTHER PERSON

If an owner of premises to which an enforcement notice relates, wishes to comply with its terms but is prevented by some other person, *e.g.* a tenant, having an interest in the land, he may on complaint to a court of summary jurisdiction obtain an Order of that court requiring any other person interested in the land to permit the execution of the work.[1]

COURSES OF ACTION OPEN TO LOCAL PLANNING AUTHORITY ON NON-COMPLIANCE

According to the circumstances of the particular case the authority may have one or more of the following courses open to them in the event of non-compliance with an enforcement notice which has either not been appealed against or which has been upheld on appeal.

1. They may enter on the land and do what the notice requires.[2]
2. They may institute a prosecution for penalties.[3]
3. They may seek an injunction restraining contravention of the notice.

These remedies will now be examined more fully.

---

[1] Section 289 of the Public Health Act 1936, as applied by s. 91 (3). *See also* the Town and Country Planning General Regulations 1976 (S.I. 1976, No. 1419), replacing earlier Regulations, as amended by S.I. 1981, No. 558.
[2] Section 91.
[3] Section 89.

Entry by local planning authority to carry out requirements of notice

Extent of this remedy

This remedy may be exercised only when the notice requires steps to be taken **other than discontinuance of a use**. It will be available, *e.g.* where demolition or alteration of buildings or works is required.

No doubt this is a remedy which will be used sparingly and its exercise calls for care on the part of the authority that the work done is strictly in accordance with what the notice requires.

It is clear from the case of *Arcam Demolition and Construction Co. v. Worcestershire County Council*[1] that when an enforcement notice requires a number of steps to be taken and the local planning authority are exercising the power themselves to carry out the requirements of the notice they are not bound to take **all** the steps specified in the notice, but may take any one or more of them. In that case a landowner moved for an injunction to restrain a local planning authority which intended to enter his land in order to do part of the works required by an enforcement notice. An injunction was refused and it was held that the authority were acting *intra vires*.

Recovery of expenses by authority

Having exercised the remedy described above the local planning authority may recover[2] from the person **who is then the owner**[3] of the land any expenses reasonably incurred by them in so doing.

The local planning authority may also:—

(i) sell any materials removed in carrying out the requirements of the notice and which are not within 3 days of removal claimed and taken away by the

[1] [1964] 1 W.L.R. 661; [1964] 2 All E.R. 286.

[2] As a simple contract debt in any court of competent jurisdiction, *i.e.*, in the County Court or the High Court. Section 91 (1).

[3] For definition, *see* p. 119, *ante*.

owner, recouping their recoverable expenses and accounting to the owner for the balance of the proceeds of sale[1];

(ii) include in their expenses of carrying out the requirements of the notice such sum in respect of establishment charges as appears to them to be reasonable.[2]

Position of owner from whom expenses recoverable

Agents or Trustees:

> The liability of a person receiving rent of premises merely as agent or trustee, in respect of recoverable expenses is limited to the amount of money which he has, or has had in his hands since receipt of the demand for payment. The principal or beneficiary is liable for the balance and the authority may recover that balance from the principal or beneficiary or alternatively may recover the whole from him in the first instance.[3]

As previously noted (page 119) the definition of "owner" in the 1971 Act **excludes** an agent, but the provision above is relevant to a notice served before the 1st April 1969, (the operative date of the relevant part of the 1968 Act), since the 1968 Act amended the definition in the 1962 Act to bring about the exclusion referred to. That position is preserved by section 292 and Schedule 24, paragraph 31, of the 1971 Act.

Development not in fact carried out by owner:

> If the breach of planning control was in fact committed by some person other than the owner, the owner

[1] Section 276 of the Public Health Act 1936 as applied by s. 91 (3) and S.I. 1976, No. 1419, *supra*.

[2] Local Government Act 1974, s. 36, replacing similar provisions in s. 292 of the Public Health Act 1936, applied by s. 91 (3) of the 1971 Act and Regulations thereunder, where however the sum for establishment charges was not to exceed 5% of the cost.

[3] Section 294 of the Public Health Act 1936 as applied by s. 91 (3) of the 1962 Act and S.I. 1976, No. 1419, *supra*.

may himself recover[1] from that person any sums he has had to pay to the authority.[2]

Prosecution for contravention

The local planning authority may prosecute[3] for contravention of an enforcement notice. The contravention may consist of:—

(*a*) failure to discontinue a use;

(*b*) failure to comply with a condition or limitation in respect of a use of land or the carrying out of operations thereon;

(*c*) failure to take steps required by the notice other than discontinuance of a use, *e.g.*, to demolish buildings or alter buildings or works.

In cases (*a*) and (*b*) proceedings may be brought against—

(i) Any person who himself **uses** the land or **carries out** the operations in question.

and (ii) Any person who **causes or permits** the use of the land or the carrying out of the operations.

To cause a use involves some express or positive mandate from the person causing to another person, or some authority from the former to the latter arising in the circumstances of the case (*per* Lord Wright in *McLeod* (*or Houston*) *v. Buchanan*[4]).

To "permit" means to allow someone else to do something,[5] but it may mean no more than a failure to take steps to prevent.[6] For a person to "permit" he must have knowledge of the offence and in this connection knowledge "includes the state of mind of a man who shuts his eyes to

---

[1] In the County Court or the High Court.
[2] Section 91 (2).
[3] Section 89.
[4] [1940] 2 All E.R. 179.
[5] *See Waddell v. Winter* (1967) 65 L.G.R. 370, D.C.
[6] *See James and Son Ltd. v. Smee* [1955] 1 Q.B. 78.

the obvious or allows his servant to do something in the circumstances where a contravention is likely not caring whether a contravention takes place or not".[1] The fact that the defendant is a limited company does not involve any different consideration regarding the inferring of knowledge.[2] A person does not "permit" unless it is in his power to forbid the act in question.[3]

When land is occupied by a tenant the owner is not liable to prosecution for non-compliance unless he himself uses the land for the purpose complained of, or causes or permits that use.[4]

In *Bromsgrove District Council v. Carthy*[5] an owner of land on which gypsies had parked their caravans had attempted to persuade them to move peacefully, but they had remained. He had not tried to use force, nor had he taken legal proceedings against them. The justices had acquitted him on a charge or permitting them to remain contrary to an enforcement notice. The prosecutor appealed. The Divisional Court dismissed the appeal, holding that the owner had not "permitted" the caravans to remain and that the justices had been entitled to find, as they had done, that the steps taken to try to remove the gypsies were reasonable.

Knowledge that an enforcement notice has taken effect[6] is an essential ingredient of an offence, but a person must take all appropriate care to inform himself of facts relevant to the lawfulness of his conduct. In *South Cambridgeshire District Council v. Stokes*[7] an appeal against acquittal of S. for non-compliance with an enforcement notice was allowed by the Divisional Court on this basis. S. (having been served

---

[1] *Per* Parker, J. (as he then was), in *James and Son Ltd. v. Smee*, [1955] 1 Q.B. 78 at p. 278.

[2] *See James and Son Ltd. v. Smee, supra.*

[3] *See Goodbarne v. Buck* [1940] 1 K.B. 771.

[4] *Johnston v. Secretary of State for the Environment* (1974) 28 P. & C.R. 424, D.C.

[5] (1975) 30 P. & C.R. 34, D.C.

[6] As to when an enforcement notice takes effect and the consequences of an appeal see *ante*, p. 116.

[7] [1981] Crim. L.R. 261, D.C.

with a notice) had not appealed against it but his tenant had done. However the tenant withdrew his appeal (thus ending suspension of the notice and bringing it into effect) but S. had been unaware of this withdrawal.

Care should be taken to state the offence correctly, *i.e.* to say whether "using" (or carrying out of an operation) or "causing" or "permitting" is charged. A wrong allegation will result in the proceedings failing, *e.g.* a person who himself uses cannot be charged with permitting a use.[1]

In case (*c*) proceedings may be brought against the person who was the **owner**[2] **of the land when the notice was served on him**.

If such a person can show that he had ceased to be the owner of the land before the end of the period specified in the notice for compliance he is entitled by section 89 (2) of the 1971 Act to have the new owner brought before the court in the proceedings. In order to do this he must lay an information and give the prosecution not less than three clear days' notice of his intention.[3]

If, after the prosecution have proved that the steps required by the enforcement notice have not been taken within the required period, the original owner proves that the failure to take those steps was wholly or in part attributable to the default of the new owner, the new owner may be convicted. If the original owner is able also to prove that he himself took all reasonable steps to secure compliance with the notice he is entitled to be acquitted. He is not deprived of this defence because the new owner is not in fact brought before the court, *e.g.* by failure of the police to serve the summons.[4]

---

[1] *See Waddell v. Winter* (1967) 65 L.G.R. 370, D.C. For a case in which a defective information resulted in convictions being quashed see *Drakes v. Coley* [1978] Crim. L.R. 493, D.C.

[2] For definition, *see* p. 119, *ante*.

[3] It is probable that the information must also be laid 3 clear days before the proceedings are heard. *Per* Goddard, L.C.J., in *Malcolm v. Cheek* [1948] 1 K.B. 400.

[4] *Malcolm and Cheek (supra)*.

In a case under the Food and Drugs Act 1955[1] which contains similar provisions for "third party procedure" it was held that although the third party information was laid after the expiry of the six month time limit under section 104 of the Magistrates' Courts Act 1952, (now section 127 of the Magistrates Courts Act, 1980), this did not deprive the original defendant of his defence although the third party could not be convicted, the magistrates having no jurisdiction to hear the information against him. See *post*, p. 219 as to the present position about time limits in a planning case.

These provisions were originally contained in the 1962 Act, section 47 (2).

In *Whitfield v. Gowling*[2] proceedings were taken against D for failing to comply with an enforcement notice served on him in December 1971. The prosecution could show that he was the owner in June 1970 and the owner and occupier in June 1971. The Divisional Court held, remitting the case to the justices to continue the hearing, that the evidence of ownership raised a presumption that D was the owner on the relevant date and it was for him to displace that presumption.

If, in the case of a contravention of an enforcement notice **by a corporate body** it is proved that the offence has been committed with the consent or connivance of, or to be attributable to any neglect on the part of, a director, manager, secretary or other similar officer of the corporate body, **or any person who was purporting to act in such a capacity** that person, as well as the corporate body itself, is guilty of an offence and may be proceeded against accordingly.[3] In the case of a corporate body established by or under statutory authority for the purpose of carrying on a nationalised industry or part of an industry or undertaking, and whose affairs are managed by the members of the body the term "director" means a member of the body in question.[4]

---

[1] *R. v. Bicester JJ., ex parte Unigate Ltd.* [1975] 1 All E.R. 449.
[2] (1974) 28 P. & C.R. 386, D.C.
[3] Section 285 (1).
[4] Section 285 (2).

The general principle which prevents disclosure of previous convictions before committal applies to corporations as to individuals. In *R. v. Colchester Justices ex parte North Essex Building Company*[1] evidence of a previous conviction of a company was tended to Justices after which they committed him to trial (for unlawful demolition of a listed building). They heard this evidence because section 29 of the Magistrates Courts Act 1952 (now section 38 of the Magistrates Courts Act 1980) which permits Justices to commit for sentence to the Crown Court if they consider their own powers inadequate in the particular case, does not apply to corporations. The committal was quashed by the Divisional Court and an order of *mandamus* granted requiring the Justices to hear and determine the case.[2]

The penalties prescribed[3] have been substantially increased[4] and are now heavy. The maximum penalty on summary conviction, previously £400, is now £1000 and there may be proceedings on indictment, in which case there is no statutory limit on the amount of the fine. The provisions as to penalties are now contained in section 89 of the 1971 Act. (See also the Criminal Law Act, 1977 Section 28 (2).)

In respect of any enforcement notice served under earlier statutes the penalties originally prescribed by the 1962 Act[5] will continue to apply.[6]

Section 127 of the Magistrates Courts Act, 1980 (formerly Section 104 of the Magistrates Courts Act, 1952) requires a prosecution for a summary offence to be brought within six months from the date of the alleged offence, but this does not apply to **continuing** offences. There can be argument as to when an offence is a continuing one. The Divisional Court considered such a question in *St Albans District*

---

1 (1977) 242 E.G. 696, D.C.
2 As to such an offence see *post*, p. ••.
3 Section 89 (1).
4 Criminal Law Act, 1977 Section 28 (2).
5 Section 47.
6 *See* s. 292 and Schedule 24, para. 31, 1971 Act.

Council v. Norman Harper Autosales Ltd.[1] The Council prosecuted a Company for failing to comply with an enforcement notice. Magistrates dismissed the information as proceedings were not begun within the six months period. The Council then, without any application by the company, purported to extend the period of compliance with the enforcement (under Section 89 (6) of the 1971 Act) and, when the company still did not comply with the notice even within the extended period, brought further proceedings. The case was dismissed and on the authority's appeal the Divisional Court held that the offence alleged was not a continuing one, time for complying with the enforcement notice could not be unilaterally extended to the detriment of the developer, and the authority's summons was out of time. The offence in question was one falling within section 89 (1) of the Act which relates to an enforcement notice requiring steps to be taken **other than the discontinuance of a use**. The Court expressly left open the question of whether offences against sub-section (5) were continuing offences. Subsection (5) relates to an offence by failure to comply with an enforcement notice which requires discontinuance of a use of land, or compliance with conditions or limitations (whether in respect of a use or the carrying out of operations). However the question is now an academic one, because the limitation of six months does not apply to an indictable offence and "indictable offence" includes an offence **triable either way**. (*i.e.* either summarily or on indictment). Offences consisting of breach of enforcement notices are triable either way. (See the Criminal Law Act, 1977.)

The procedure for dealing with an offence **triable either way** is now laid down in Sections 18 to 23 of the Magistrates Courts 1980. In broad terms, such a case starts in the magistrates court, and the court will decide (after hearing representations on the point from the prosecution and the defence) whether they consider the case more suitable for summary trial or for trial by the Crown Court. If the former is decided upon the defendant still has the right to elect for trial by the Crown Court (on indictment).

---

[1] (1977) 35 P. & C.R. 70.

"Further offences" were always continuing offences, although it was held in *R. v. Chertsey JJ., ex parte Franks*[1] that a fine in respect of such an offence must not be related to a period more than six months before the laying of the information. This case was before the coming into force of the Criminal Law Act, 1977.[2]

A person convicted by a Magistrates' Court has the right of appeal to the Crown Court and, on the ground that the decision is wrong in law or in excess of jurisdiction of appeal by way of case stated to a Divisional Court of the Queen's Bench Division direct from the magistrates' court[3] or from the Crown Court.[4]

A person convicted on indictment has a right of appeal to the Court of Appeal (Criminal Division) and thence to the House of Lords.

In cases (*a*) or (*b*) if the use is continued after conviction a further offence is committed. On summary conviction there may be a fine of up to £100 for every day on which the contravening use continues.[5] There may also be proceedings on indictment carrying a penalty of a fine of unlimited amount.

In rural areas in particular vehicle storage and breaking is a use which can cause considerable difficulties for planning authorities. The case of *Backer v. Uckfield R.D.C.*[6] is of interest in this connection. The defendant, having been served with an enforcement notice requiring discontinuance of a use of land for stationing vehicles (pantechnicons), had been convicted of contravening the notice. After that conviction the remains of two of the vehicles were still on the land, although the chassis of one was gone and neither had any wheels. He was further convicted of continuing the

[1] See *post*, s. 222.

[2] June 17 1978 by S.I. 1978, No. 712.

[3] *See* Magistrates' Courts Acts 1980, and Magistrates' Courts Rules 1968, rr. 65 to 68.

[4] Section 10, Courts Act 1971.

[5] Section 89 (5), as amended by Local Government and Planning (Amendment) Act, 1981 Section 1 and Schedule para. 2 (2).

[6] (1970) 114 S.J. 666, D.C.

unauthorised use after conviction and appealed to the Divisional Court. The Court dismissed his appeal, holding that the question was not whether the remains of the pantechnicons were "vehicles" for the purpose of the Road Traffic Acts but whether they were the offending objects referred to in the enforcement notice, and that the justices had been sensible in deciding that the vehicle without a chassis had ceased to be one of the "vehicles" referred to but that the other one still bore that character.

In case (*c*) if a person who has been convicted of an offence does not as soon as practicable do everything in his power to secure compliance with the enforcement notice he is guilty of a further offence carrying a penalty on summary conviction of up to £100 for each day following his first conviction on which any of the requirements of the enforcement notice (other than discontinuance of a use) remain unfulfilled. There may also be proceedings on indictment carrying a penalty of a fine of unlimited amount.[1]

Here again, in respect of the offences described in the preceding two paragraphs, the original 1962 Act penalties[2] will apply in respect of notices served before 1st April 1969.[3]

In *R. v. Chertsey Justices ex parte Franks*,[4] the Divisional Court considered the effect of what are now the provisions of the 1971 Act described in the preceding paragraphs. It was held that the (further) offence was a continuing one which occurred from day to day and that section 104 of the Magistrates' Courts Act 1952 precluded the hearing of an information in so far as it alleged an offence occurring more than six months before its date. No penalty could be imposed in respect of any day falling more than six months prior to the date of an information. The Criminal Law Act 1977 has, however, affected the position (see *ante*, p. 220).

---

[1] Section 89 (4), as amended by Local Government and Planning (Amendment) Act, 1981 Section 1 and Schedule para. 2 (2).

[2] £20 a day on summary conviction.

[3] *See* S.I. 1969, No. 275, bringing the 1968 Act provisions regarding enforcement notices into force.

[4] [1961] 2 Q.B. 152.

Injunction

Those acquainted with enforcement procedure will be well aware of the opportunity for delaying tactics which is open to any person determined not to comply with planning requirements. It may also be that convictions, fines and even imprisonment for non-payment of fines, do not deter in certain cases, so that the statutory procedure is ineffective. A possible remedy for a local authority faced with this kind of situation is to seek to prevent further infringement of the public right by means of an injunction from the High Court, to restrain further contravention of the enforcement notice.

Although the development of land without planning permission, being contrary to the Planning Act infringes a public right[1] it must be remembered that as an injunction is an equitable remedy it is discretionary. The Court will consider whether other available remedies have been exhausted. However, in *A.G. v. Bastow*,[2] Devlin, J. said "If he (the Attorney General) having surveyed the different ways that are open to him for seeing that the law is enforced and that it is not defied, has come to the conclusion that the most effective way is to ask this Court for a mandatory injunction—and I am satisfied that the very nature of a relator action means that he has surveyed those ways and has come to that conclusion—then I think that this court, once a clear breach of the right has been shown, should only refuse the application in exceptional circumstances. I am dealing, of course, purely with that type of case in which the only substantial ground for not giving an injunction is that there are other remedies available. In cases where other circumstances arise which are not primarily a matter for administrative discretion, then different considerations might apply and a different view be taken." In that case an injunction was granted perpetually restraining use of land as a caravan site.

In a later case[3] an injunction was granted restraining the defendant from using as a caravan site any land in a par-

---

[1] *A.G. v. Bastow, infra.*
[2] [1975] 1 Q.B. 514.
[3] *A.G. v. Smith* [1958] 2 Q.B. 173.

ticular Urban District. This defendant had endeavoured to flout the law by moving his caravans from one place to another ineffectually pursued by normal enforcement proceedings of the local planning authority.

In *Att.-Gen (ex rel East Sussex County Council) v. Morris*[1] the scope of the remedy of an injunction was further extended. M had failed to comply with an enforcement notice requiring cessation of use of land as a caravan site. He had been prosecuted and fined several times. He then moved the caravans to an adjacent part of the same plot of land. Another enforcement notice followed, and he was again prosecuted and fined. All this spread over some five years. An injunction was sought on the motion of the Attorney General at the relation of the planning authority perpetually restraining M from using as a caravan site that land or any other land not an authorised caravan site. The action was undefended. O'Connor, J., granted a perpetual injunction restraining the use of the land in question and any other land which was not an authorised caravan site **within the county of East Sussex**. He had indicated that he was not prepared to grant a perpetual injunction nationwide and there would have to be some restriction on the area.

It is to be noted that in all three cases mentioned where injunctions have been granted as a means of planning control the actions have been relator actions, involving the Attorney-General.

Under the Local Government Act 1933 a local authority was bound to sue on the relation of the Attorney-General and not in its own name.[2] That Act has however, been repealed by the Local Government Act 1972 and the provisions of the latter Act are different from those in the former Act. The 1972 Act, by section 222 provides[3] expressly that where a local authority consider it expedient for the promotion or protection of the interests of the inhabitants of their area they may prosecute or defend or appear in any

---

[1] (1973) 227 E.G. 991.

[2] *See Prestatyn Urban District Council v. Prestatyn Raceway Ltd. and Another* [1969] 3 All E.R. 1573, a case concerning a public nuisance.

[3] Subsection (1).

legal proceedings and in the case of civil proceedings **may institute them in their own name**. Now, therefore, a local authority had no need to seek the approval of the Attorney-General.

In *Solihull Metropolitan Borough Council v. Maxfern Ltd. and Another*[1] the council brought an action to restrain the holding of Sunday markets contrary to secition 47 of the Shops Act 1950. The defendants moved to strike out the writ as disclosing no reasonable cause of action and/or as being frivolous, vexatious and an abuse of the process of the Court. The motion was on the basis that being an action for enforcement of public rights it had to be constituted in the name of the Attorney-General. The Council relied on section 222 of the Local Government Act 1972. Oliver, J., held that the new enactment enabled the local authority to sue in its own name where previously it could not have sued without the assistance of the Attorney-General. It was the intention of Parliament to vest in the local authority the discretion formerly exercised by the Attorney-General, where they (the local authority) thought it necessary to protect public rights in their area.

It might reasonably be asked whether the courts might not adopt an attitude of less readiness to grant an injunction at the suit of a local authority acting by themselves than when (as formerly) the Attorney General was involved, especially as Parliament has provided specific remedies (and not insubstantial ones). Problems attend the use of civil injunctions to enforce the criminal law, as both Lord Wilberforce and Viscount Dilhorne pointed out in *Gouriet v. Union of Post Office Workers*.[2] However, Lord Denning, M.R. in *Stafford B.C. v. Elkenford Ltd.*[3] expressed the view that where there was a clear breach of a statute, a local authority could apply straight to the High Court for an injunction without bringing any other proceedings (this was a case under the Shops Act 1950).

---

[1] [1977] 1 W.L.R. 127.
[2] [1978] A.C. 435.
[3] [1977] 1 W.L.R. 324.

A later case appears to follow the same line. In *Kent County Council v. Batchelor (No. 2)*[1] no enforcement proceedings had been commenced for breach of a tree preservation order[2] but the authority obtained an injunction.

Subsequent committal proceedings for alleged breach of the injunction were dismissed by the Court of Appeal because of lack of evidence of breach. Later, the authority began further commital proceedings for further alleged breaches. The defendant applied to discharge the injunction and adjournment of the committal proceedings on the grounds (inter alia) that the authority could not sue in its own name. The application was refused, Talbot J. Lolding that as the Court of Appeal had previously accepted jurisdiction the court was bound to do so, and that under Section 222 the local authority could bring the proceedings in its own name as the purpose was to protect the interests of the inhabitants.

In another case in 1981[3] where the right of the local authority to sue in its own name was again challenged the decision was the same; that it was entitled to do so.

---

1 [1979] 1 W.L.R. 213.

2 See post as to breaches of Tree Preservation Orders.

3 *Westminster City Council v. Jones*, *The Times*, June 2 1981, Whitford J.

CHAPTER 6

TERMINATION OF AUTHORISED DEVELOPMENT

USES AND WORKS

A local planning authority[1] have power under section 51 of the Act, subject to confirmation by the Secretary of State, to make Orders requiring steps to be taken within a specified period for the discontinuance of authorised uses, or their continuance subject to conditions, or the alteration or removal of authorised buildings or works.

The Court of Appeal held in *Parkes v. Secretary of State for the Environment*[2] that the term "use of land" in section 51 was such that the planning authority could make an order under this section applying to the storing, sorting and processing of scrap metal in the Peak National Park notwithstanding the definition of "use" in section 290 as not including "the use of land for the carrying out of any building or other operations thereon".

The use, building or works may exist or have been carried out by virtue of a planning permission or in circumstances where such permission was not required, or in circumstances where permission was required but not obtained and enforcement action is impossible, *e.g.* because the development occurred before the end of 1963.

An order under this section may grant planning consent for any development to which the order relates, which may

---

[1] Normally the district planning authority, except for "county matters' as to which *see* p. 90, *ante*. The county planning authority may also act where county matters are concerned. Local Government Act 1972, Schedule 16, para. 24. *See also ibid.*, para. 51 (2).

[2] *The Times*, May 11 1978, C.A.

be conditional, and it may grant such consent (which again may be conditional) for the retention of buildings or works constructed or carried out before the date of submission of the order to the Secretary of State or for continuance of use begun before that date.

The power is exercisable if it appears to the local planning authority **expedient in the interests of the proper planning of their area (including the interests of amenity)**[1] regard being had to the development plan and to any other material considerations.[2]

Notice has to be given to owners and occupiers and any other persons thought by the authority to be affected by the order and such persons may within a time (not less than 28 days from service) specified in the order require a hearing by a person appointed by the Secretary of State.

The Secretary of State has power[3] to confirm an order subject to modifications, and is expressly[4] authorised to modify any provision of the order granting planning permission, or to include any grant of planning permission which might have been included in the order as submitted.

On confirmation of an order a copy must be served[5] on the owners and occupiers.

If an order involves displacement of residents in premises and there is no other residential accommodation available on reasonable terms it is the duty of the authority to secure the provision of such accommodation in advance of the displacement.

For default powers of the Secretary of State, *see* page 149, *ante*.

As to whether there is other residential accommodation

---

[1] "Amenity" appears to mean pleasant circumstances, features, advantages, *per* Scrutton, L.J., in *Re Ellis and Ruislip Northwood U.D.C.* [1920] 1 K.B. 343.

[2] As to **material considerations** see *ante*, p. 171.

[3] Section 51 (4).

[4] Section 51 (5).

[5] The method of service is the same as for an enforcement notice, *see* p. 121, *ante*.

suitable to the reasonable requirements of people to be displaced it would seem that the numerous cases under the Rent Acts will provide guidance.

ORDERS PROHIBITING RESUMPTION OF MINERAL WORKING

Under section 51A of the 1971 Act[1] (inserted by section 10 of the Town and Country Planning (Minerals) Act 1981) where it appears to the mineral planning authority (the county council) that development consisting of the winning and working of minerals has been carried out in on or under land but that it has permanently ceased they may by order (which requires confirmation by the Secretary of State):—

(1) prohibit the resumption of such development and

(2) impose, in relation to the site, requirements specified (as to which see below).

They may assume that the mineral development has permanently ceased **only** when either no such development has been carried out to any substantial extent anywhere in on or under the site of which the land forms part for a period of at least two years and it appears to them on the evidence available at the time when they make the order that resumption of such development in on or under the land is unlikely.[2]

The requirements they may impose are as follows:—

(a) To alter or remove plant or machinery which was used for the purpose of the mineral working or for any ancillary purpose.

(b) To take steps (as specified in the order) within a period to be specified for the purpose of removing or alleviating injury to amenity caused by the mineral workings (other than injury due to subsidence caused by underground mining operations).

---

[1] Coming into force on a date to be appointed. No date has yet been appointed

[2] Section 51A (2).

(c) That any condition subject to which the planning condition had been granted or which had been imposed under any provision of the Act shall be complied with and

(d) A restoration condition.

The order may also impose aftercare conditions as the mineral planning authority think fit if the order includes a restoration condition or a restoration condition has previously been imposed in relation to the site by virtue of any provision of the 1981 Act.[1]

In a case where the use specified is use for agriculture **and** the land was used for agriculture immediately before the mineral development began, or it had previously been used for agriculture and not used for any authorised purpose since the use for agriculture ceased **and** if the Minister of Agriculture Fisheries and Food (or in Wales the Secretary of State) has notified the mineral planning authority of the physical characteristics of the land when it was last used for agriculture, the land is brought to the required standard when its physical characteristics are restored, so far as is practicable to do so, to what they were when it was last used for agriculture. In any other case, where the use specified is use for agriculture, the land is brought to the required standard when it is reasonably fit for that use.

SUSPENSION ORDERS—MINERAL WORKINGS

Where it appears to the mineral planning authority—

(a) that development consisting of the winning and working of minerals has been carried out in, on or under any land; **but**

(b) that it has been **temporarily suspended**,

the mineral planning authority may under section 51B by order referred to in the Act as a "**suspension order**" require that steps shall be taken for the protection of the environ-

[1] Section 51A (4).

ment. An order requires confirmation by the Secretary of State.

The mineral planning authority may assume that development consisting of the winning and working of minerals has been temporarily suspended only when—

(a) no such development has been carried out to any substantial extent anywhere in, on or under the site of which the land forms part for a period of at least twelve months; but

(b) it appears to the mineral planning authority, on the evidence available to them at the time when they make the order, that a resumption of such development in, on or under the land is likely.

"Steps for the protection of the environment" means steps for the purpose—

(a) of preserving the amenities of the area in which the land in, or under which the development was carried out is situated during the period while operations for the winning and working of minerals in, on or under it are suspended;

(b) of protecting that area from damage during that period; or

(c) of preventing any deterioration in the condition of the land during that period.

A suspension order must specify a period, commencing with the date on which it is to take effect, within which any required step for the protection of the environment is to be taken and may specify different periods for the taking of different steps.

At any time when a suspension order is in operation the mineral planning authority may by order (Act referred to as a "**supplementary suspension order**") direct—

(a) that steps for the protection of the environment shall be taken in addition to or in substitution for any of the steps which the suspension order or a previous supplementary suspension order specified as required to be taken; or

(b) that the suspension order or any supplementary suspension order shall cease to have effect.

Where a suspension order or supplementary suspension order has been confirmed by the Secretary of State, the mineral planning authority must serve a copy of the order on every person who was entitled to be served with notice by virtue of subsection (3) of this section.

A supplementary suspension order revoking a suspension order or a previous supplementary suspension order and not requiring that any fresh step shall be taken for the protection of the environment takes effect without confirmation.

A suspension order or a supplementary suspension order is registrable as a local land charge.

Neither a suspension order nor a supplementary suspension order prevents recommencement of development consisting of winning or working of minerals in, on, or under the land in question[1] but a person intending to recommence must give notice to the mineral planning authority specifying the date on which he intends to recommence.

The mineral planning authority must revoke the order if development consisting of the winning and working of minerals has recommenced to a substantial extent in, on or under the land in relation to which the order is in effect.

If the authority do not revoke the order before the end of the period of two months from the date specified in the notice, the person who gave that notice may apply to the Secretary of State for the revocation of the order.

Notice of such an application shall be given by the applicant to the mineral planning authority.

If he is required to do so by the person who gave the notice or by the mineral planning authority, the Secretary of State, before deciding whether to revoke the order, must

[1] Section 51F.

afford to that person and to the mineral planning authority an opportunity of appearing before, and being heard by, a person appointed by the Secretary of State for the purpose.

If the Secretary of State is satisfied that development consisting of the winning and working of minerals in, on or under the land has recommenced to a substantial extent, he must revoke the order.

If the Secretary of State revokes an order, he must give notice of its revocation to the person who applied to him for the revocation and to the mineral planning authority.

CHALLENGE OF ORDERS

If any person aggrieved by an order made under section 51 51A or 51B (or the authority concerned) wishes to question the validity of the order on the grounds that it is not within the powers of the Act or that any of the relevant requirements have not been complied with in relation to it, he may within six weeks from the date of its confirmation apply to the High Court under section 245[1] of the Act. Apart from this the validity of an order cannot be questioned in any legal proceedings whatsoever.

ENFORCEMENT OF ORDERS UNDER SECTIONS 51, 51A AND 51B

Any person who without the grant of a planning permission uses land, or causes or permits it to be used for any purpose for which an order under section 51 has required that use to be discontinued, or in contravention of a condition imposed by an order or resumes, or causes or permits resumption of development consisting of winning and working of minerals where resumption is prohibited by an order under section 51A or contravenes or causes or permits to be contravened requirements specified in sections 51A (3) or (4) of the Act is guilty of an offence. Similarly any person who contravenes the requirement of the suspension order

---

[1] See *ante*, p. 197.

or a supplementary suspension order, or who causes or permits any such requirement to be contravened is guilty of an offence.[2]

In either of the above cases the offender is liable on summary conviction to a fine not exceeding the statutory maximum[1] or on conviction on indictment to a fine of unlimited amount.[2]

If any step required by an order under section 51 to be taken to alter or remove buildings or works or plant or machinery, or any step required to be taken under an order under section 51A for alterations or removal of plant or removal or alleviation of any injury to amenity, or any step for the protection of the environment required to be taken by a suspension order or a supplementary suspension order has not been taken within the period specified by the order (or within such extended period as the authority may allow) the local planning authority may enter the land and take the required steps and recover their expenses from the owner. Section 276 of the Public Health Act 1936 will apply to the works they executed as it applies in relation to works executed by the authority under the Act. The local planning authority for these purposes is the mineral planning authority.[2]

It is a defence for a person charged with an offence under the provisions to prove that he took all reasonable measures and exercised all due diligence to avoid commission of the offence by himself or by any person under his control. If in any case his defence involves an allegation that the commission of the offence was due to the act or default of another person, or due to reliance on information supplied by another person, the person charged is not, without the leave of the Court, entitled to rely on that defence, unless, within seven clear days before the hearing he has served on the prosecutor a notice in writing giving such information

---

[1] As to the meaning of this see *post*, p. 235.

[2] Section 108 substituted by the Town and County Planning Minerals Act, 1981, Section 11.

identifying or assisting in the identification of the other person, as was then in his possession.

Whether or not the accused has exercised all due diligence will be a question of fact. The failure of directors of a limited company to exercise due diligence is the failure of the company. See *Pearce v. Cullen.*[1] In the case of large scale business the failure of subordinate managers or similar employees to exercise due diligence will not necessarily amount to a failure by the company. See *Tesco Supermarkets Limited v. Nattrass.*[2]

For the statutory maximum see section 290 (1) of the 1971 Act as amended by the Town and Country Planning (Minerals) Act 1981 section 34 and schedule 1, paragraph 11.

COMPENSATION

Under section 170 of the Act, as amended by the Town and Country Planning (Minerals) Act 1981, any person who has suffered damage in consequence of an Order by—

> depreciation[3] of the value of an interest to which he is entitled in the land or in minerals in, on, or under it

or by

> being disturbed in his enjoyment of the land, or in minerals in, on, or under it

may claim compensation from the local planning authority who made the order.[4]

In addition any person who carries out works in compliance with the Order is entitled to recover from the local planning authority compensation in respect of expenses reasonably incurred by him in so doing.

---

[1] (1952) 96 Sol. J. 132.

[2] [1972] A.C. 153, H.L.

[3] Compensation for depreciation is assessed in accordance with the provisions of the rules in s. 5 of the Land Compensation Act 1961. (See Section 178 of the 1971 Act.) *i.e.* The prescribed sum under Section 32 of the Magistrates Courts Act 1980 (£1000 at present).

[4] See Section 290 (1) of the 1971 Act as amended by the Town and County Planning (Minerals) Act 1981 Section 34 and Schedule 1, para. 11.

Any compensation is to be reduced by the value to the claimant of any timber, apparatus or other materials removed for the purpose of complying with the order.[1]

If an interest in land is **subject to a mortgage** (which includes any charge or lien on property for securing money or money's worth)[2] compensation for depreciation of the value of the interest is assessed as if the interest were not subject to the mortgage. A mortgagee may make a claim in respect of the whole interest in the land and not merely his mortgage interest. No compensation is payable in respect of the mortgagee's interest as such. Any compensation in respect of the interest subject to the mortgage must be paid **to the mortgagee**, or if there is more than one mortgagee, to the first mortgagee, and the mortgagee must apply such compensation as if it were proceeds of sale.[3]

The right to compensation under section 170 may be lost by a person who takes advantage of the Purchase Notice provisions described below.[4]

Section 170A and 170B[5] 178A, 178B and 178C provide specially for compensation in regard to mineral workings.

Time for submission of claim and method of claiming

The claim must be in writing and must be made within six (calendar) months from the date of the order, but the Minister has power to extend the period.[6] It must be served on the authority by delivering it at their offices or by sending it by pre-paid post.[5]

Disputes

Questions of disputed compensation are to be referred to and determined by the Lands Tribunal[7] and the provisions

---

[1] Section 170 (4).
[2] Section 290.
[3] Section 178 (3). A mortgagee is trustee of the proceeds of sale. *See* s. 105 of the Law of Property Act 1925, as to application of the proceeds of sale.
[4] *See* s. 189 (4).
[5] Added by the Town and Country Planning (Minerals) Act, 1981.
[6] Town and Country Planning General Regulations 1976 (S.I. 1976, No. 1419), replacing earlier Regulations amended by S.I. 1981, No. 558.
[7] *See* note,[3] p. 101, *ante*.

of sections 2[1] and 4 of the Land Compensation Act 1961 (as amended)[2] (as to certain aspects of procedure and as to costs) will apply.[3]

PURCHASE NOTICE

If any person entitled to an interest in land in respect of which an order is made under the provisions now under discussion is able to show that, after the requirements of theorder have been complied with, the land will be incapable of reasonably beneficial use in its then existing state and cannot be rendered capable of such use by the carrying out of any development for which planning permission has been granted, he may require the council of the London Borough or county district[4] in which the land is situate to purchase his interest in the land.[5]

He must do this by means of a **purchase notice** served within twelve months, in the same manner as in the case of a compensation claim.[6]

The subsequent procedure is as follows[7]:—

The authority has three months from the service of the purchase notice within which to serve on the person who served the purchase notice, a notice stating either—

(*a*) that they, or some other authority, or some statutory undertakers, are willing to comply with the notice (in which case at that date the authority or undertakers are deemed to be authorised to acquire the owner's interest compulsorily, and to have served a notice to treat);

or (*b*) that for the reasons specified in their notice they are unwilling to comply with the purchase notice

[1] As amended by Local Government, Planning and Land Act, 1980, Section 193 and Schedule 33, paras. 5 (1) and (2).

[2] See footnote 5, p. 101, *ante*.

[3] Section 179.

[4] Note that this may not be the authority which made the order.

[5] Section 189.

[6] *See* p. 236, *ante*.

[7] *See* s. 189 (2) applying ss. 181 to 184 and ss. 186 and 187.

and have not found any other authority or statutory undertakers willing to comply with it.

In case (*b*) they must send a copy of the purchase notice to the Secretary of State with a statement of their reasons.

If the Secretary of State is satisfied that the statutory conditions for service of the purchase notice are fulfilled, he must confirm the notice (in which case a notice to treat is deemed to have been served on such date as he may specify), but if it appears to him expedient to do so, he may, in lieu of confirming the purchase notice, revoke or amend the order which gave rise to it, so far as appears to him to be required to ensure that the land is not rendered incapable of reasonably beneficial use. He also has power to direct that permission is to be granted for other development by which the land could be rendered capable of reasonably beneficial use.

If it appears to him that, having regard to the probable ultimate use of the land, it is expedient to do so, he may, if he confirms the notice, modify it, either in relation to the whole or to part of the land to which it relates, by substituting another local authority or statutory undertakers for the Council on whom the notice was served (and a notice to treat is deemed to have been served on such date as he specified).

Before doing either of these things he must give notice of his proposed course of action to the person who served the purchase notice, to the council on which it was served, to the local planning authority, and, if he proposes to substitute any other local authority or statutory undertakers as mentioned above, to that local authority or the statutory undertakers concerned. He must give them a period of not less than 28 days within which either of them may require a hearing before a person appointed by the Secretary of State.

If before the expiration of a period of nine months beginning with the date of service of the purchase notice, or within a period of six months beginning with the date on which a copy of that notice was sent to him by the local authority (whichever period first expires), the Secretary of State has neither confirmed the notice nor taken any other action open to him, and has not notified the owner that he does not intend to confirm the purchase notice, the notice is deemed to be confirmed at the end of the period in question. In such an event a notice to treat is deemed to have been served at the end of the period.

Although under section 31 of the Land Compensation Act 1961 a notice to treat may, subject to certain conditions, be withdrawn, the constructive notices to treat referred to above can **not** be withdrawn. Section 208 of the 1971 Act, re-enacting earlier provisions, expressly provides that the power of withdrawal is not to be exercisable in the case of a notice to treat deemed to have been served by virtue of the purchase notice provisions. (If it were otherwise, the object of the purchase notice procedure would, of course, be defeated.)

CHAPTER 7

PLANNING AGREEMENTS

A local planning authority, as a corporate body, has the right to enter into agreements with another person, but in the planning field it has some specific statutory rights to do so which have assumed a substantial importance in the application of the concept of "positive planning". The subject is not free of controversy,[1] but an examination of the merits and demerits of achieving planning objectives by agreement is outside the scope of this book. Powers exist and have been widely used.

The relevant statutory provisions are contained now in Section 52 of the Town and Country Planning Act 1971 and Section 126 of the Housing Act 1974, but these enactments are merely the successors of similar provisions in planning legislation going back as far as 1932.[2]

When in 1st July 1948 the Town and Country Planning Act 1947 came into force a provision about planning agreements was to be found in Section 25.

The two sets of statutory powers which now exist are complementary and are as follows.

SECTION 52 AGREEMENTS

Section 52 of the 1971 Act enables a local planning authority[3] to enter into an agreement with any person[4] inter-

---

[1] See for example discussions in Articles in the Journal of Planning and Environment Law [1977] J.P.L. 414 [1978] J.P.L.8, 290 and 806 and [1979] J.P.L. 661.

[2] Town and Country Planning Act 1932.

[3] By sub-section (4) this includes in relation to land in a county district the council of that district and, in relation to land in the area of a joint planning board, the county or district council.

[4] This includes any body of persons corporate or unincorporate. Interpretation Act, 1978, Section 5, and Schedule 1.

ested in land in their area for the purpose of **restricting or regulating the development or use of the land**, either permanently or for a limited period (specified in the agreement) and the section specifically[1] authorises "such incidental and consequential provisions (including provisions of a financial character) as appear to the local planning authority to be necessary or expedient for the purposes of the agreement".

Sub-section (2) provides that any such agreement is enforceable by the local planning authority against persons deriving title under the other party, as if the authority possessed adjacent land and as if the agreement had been expressed to be made for the benefit of such land. Restrictions included in a Section 52 agreement therefore run with the land in respect of which they are imposed in the same way as a restrictive covenant and will be enforceable against successive owners. The **burden** of a restrictive covenant runs with land in equity under the Rule in *Tulk v. Moxhay*,[2] but this principle has never been extended to positive covenants *i.e.* covenants actually to **do** something in respect of the land[3]. Although there are views to the contrary,[4] it is generally accepted that Section 52 is effective against successive owners only so far as concerns **negative** covenants and that the section can not be used to impose obligations to do **positive** acts so as to bind successors in title. (See however the provisions of Section 126 of the Housing Act, 1974 discussed *post*).

A Section 52 Agreement is registrable as a local land charge[5] and registration under the Land Charges Act 1925 constitutes notice to all the world[6] but as against a purchaser for money or money's worth of the legal estate failure to register will make the agreement unenforceable against him even if he has actual knowledge.[7] The registration must be before completion of the purchase.[8]

---

[1] Section 52 (1).
[2] (1848) 2 Ph. 774.
[3] See *Re Nisbett and Potts' Contract* [1905] 1 Ch. 391.
[4] See the Article by M. Aves at [1976] J.P.L. 216.
[5] See Land Charges Act, 1925 Section 15 (7).
[6] *Ibid.*, Section 198.
[7] *Ibid.*, Section 199.
[8] *Ibid.*, Section 15 (2).

AGREEMENTS UNDER SECTION 126 OF THE HOUSING ACT 1974

Section 126 of the Housing Act 1974, effective from 2nd December, 1974[1] empowers county and district councils to enter into agreements with a person[2] having an interest in land in their area[3] which, in certain circumstances, are enforceable[4] against successors in title of the original owner, even in respect of **positive** covenants.

The circumstances which must exist for an agreement to be so enforceable are that:—

(1) The agreement must be by deed.[5]

(2) It must[6] be entered into for the purpose of securing the carrying out of works on the land specified or of facilitating the development of that land or of other land in which the "other party" has an interest.

(3) The agreement must be registered in the local land charges register of the area in which the land is situate.

(4) The agreement must contain a covenant by a person having an interest in the land[7] to carry out works or to "do any other thing on or in relation to the land".

(5) The covenant must be expressed (in the agreement) to be one to which Section 126 applies.

(6) The agreement must define the land to which the covenant relates[8] (preferably, it is suggested, by means of an accurate plan).

---

[1] Housing Act, 1974 (Commencement No. 3) Order, 1974, S.I. 1974 No. 1791.

[2] This includes a body or persons corporate or unincorporate. Interpretation Act, 1978 Section 5 and Schedule 1.

[3] The interest must exist at the time the agreement is executed. See Section 126 (2) (b).

[4] Section 126 (2).

[5] Section 126 (1).

[6] *Ibid.*

[7] At the time of execution of the agreement. See Section 126 (2) (b).

[8] Section 126 (2) (b).

Subject to these conditions covenants are enforceable without any limit of time against any person deriving title from the original covenantor in respect of his interest in any of the defined land and against any person deriving title under him in respect of any lesser interest in the land, as if that person had himself been the original covenanting party.[1]

In addition to the normal remedy of action in the courts to enforce a covenant the act, in Section 126 (3), gives to a council a further remedy for breach. If there is breach of a positive covenant then they may enter on the land and carry out the requirements of the covenant and recover any expenses incurred from the person against whom the covenant is enforceable. However, before exercising this remedy the council must under sub-section (4) give not less than 21 days[2] notice notice of their intention to any person having at that time an interest in the land on or in relation to which they intend to carry out the act in question, and similar notice to any person against whom the covenant is enforceable. Certain provisions of the Public Health Act, 1936 are applied by sub-section (5).[3]

There is of course nothing to prevent one agreement dealing with matters under both the Section 52 provisions and the Section 126 provisions, provided that the requirements for a valid agreement under both statutory provisions are observed.

RESTRICTION OF POWERS OF COUNCIL

It is well established that a local authority cannot so bind itself by contract as to fetter the future exercise of its statutory powers[4] and this principle has to be borne carefully in

---

[1] See Section 126 (2).

[2] This means clear days *i.e.* exclusive of the date of service and the date of exercise of the power *R. v. Turner* [1904] 1 K.B. 1 and *Re Hector Whaling Ltd.* [1936] Ch. 208.

[3] These relate to power to require information about ownership, notices, penalties for obstruction, charging expenses on premises and power to order payment by instalments.

[4] See *ante*, p. 50.

mind when considering the preparation or the enforcement of agreements under the statutory powers described above.

For example in the case of *Ransom and Luck Ltd. v. Surbiton Borough Council*[1] the Court of Appeal had to consider an agreement under an earlier planning statute, Section 34 (1) of the Town and Country Planning Act, 1932 (which gave power to a local authority to enter into agreements restricting the use of land) under which agreement, as the plaintiffs contended, the council had assumed a contractual obligation that they would not exercise existing or future statutory powers so as to restrict development of the plantiffs land to a greater extent than that provided for in the agreement. The plantiffs failed, the Court holding that Section 34 was or very limited application and did not empower the council to undertake not to use its planning powers or to fetter its discretion under the Planning Acts.

However, a recent case on the subject illustrates that the authority's power may be **limited** by an agreement into which they have entered. *Windsor and Maidenhead Royal Borough v. Brandrose Investments*[2] concerned a Section 52 agreement the terms of which were such that it was clear that P agreed to the demolition by D of certain buildings. (The agreement did not in fact expressly so provide but in the course of his judgment the Learned Judge said that he treated the agreement as if it provided in terms for the demolition.) However, subsequent to the agreement the site became designated as a conservation area under the Town and Country Planning Act 1971 with the result that the consent of the Council was necessary for the demolition of any buildings (see post page 280). In proceedings by P a declaration was claimed that D was not and had at no time since the land was included in a conservation area, been entitled to demolish the buildings without obtaining P's consent as the Local Planning Authority (under Section 277 (a) of the Town and Country Planning Act 1971). In determining the question of whether P could lawfully enter into an agreement which had the effect of disentitling them to re-

---

[1] [1949] 1 All E.R. 185, C.A.
[2] *The Times*, February 13, 1981, Fox, J.

quire consent under Section 277 (a) to the demolition of the buildings, the Court (Fox J.) considered the *Ransom and Luck* case and distinguished it and followed the case of *Dowty Boulton Paul v. Wolverhampton Corporation*. (*See post*.) In considering the *Ransom and Luck* case the Learned Judge said that he bore in mind observations of Lord Greene as to the improbability that Parliament would authorise a Local Authority to tie its hands with regard to its statutory duties and to contract itself out of them but (said the Learned Judge) plainly Parliament could in appropriate language authorise a planning authority to enter into agreements which limited the subsequent exercise of the planning authorities powers and the real question was whether Section 52 had done so. His lordship found there to be a fundamental difference between Section 34 and Section 52 in that the latter section (in sub-Section 3 (a)) provided that nothing in Section 52 or in any agreement entered into under it should be construed "as restricting the exercise in relation to land which is the subject of any such agreement, of any powers exercisable by any Minister or Authority under this Act so long as those powers are exercised in accordance with the provisions of the Development Plan or in accordance with any directions which may have been given by the Secretary of State as to the provisions to be included in any such plan". Having considered the detailed provisions of the Section his Lordship decided that Parliament had contemplated the existence, in consequence of a Section 52 Agreement of fetters upon the powers of the local planning authority. It was common ground in the case under consideration that there was no development plan or direction by the Secretary of State and it followed that if upon its true construction the agreement in question limited the exercise of P's powers to take steps to prevent the demolition of the properties there was nothing in law to prevent the agreement having that effect. Although P could not simply fetter their own discretion they could limit it by the exercise of another statutory power (Section 52) and (as the Judge found) they had done so in the particular Section 52 Agreement under consideration. The result was that P could not enforce their powers under Section 277 (a) in relation to extension of the conservation area so as to prevent the demolition of the building in question.

As was pointed out in that case there is nothing in Section 52 to prevent an authority inserting a provision in the agreement itself preserving all or any of its powers in full but where an authority is attempting to reach agreement with a developer an agreement containing such a clause is likely to be of little attraction to the developer. It has to be borne in mind that in the particular case in question there was no relevant Development Plan or Ministerial direction. In a case where there is a Development Plan and /or a Ministerial direction it appears clear that it is still open to a planning authority to use their powers in accordance therewith contrary though such exercise may be to the provisions of a Section 52 Agreement into which they have entered. Indeed it appears from the judgment in this case that local planning authorities can **not** bind themselves not to use their powers in accordance with the Development Plan or any directions of the Secretary of State.

Dowty Boulton Paul v. Wolverhampton Corporation[1] was a case concerning a local authority which had in 1936 conveyed land to an aircraft company and had granted the company the right to use the authority's adjoining airfield for certain purposes for a term of 99 years, there being covenants by both parties expressed to be binding for the same period, these covenants including one by the local authority which effectively provided that they should not unreasonably affect the company's rights to use the airfield in accordance with the agreement.

The company issued proceedings and sought an interlocutory Injunction seeking to restrain the Council from doing anything which would cause the Board of Trade to determine the Licence enabling the airfield to be used as such and from doing anything to prevent the company from using the airfield. The Council relied (*inter alia*) upon Section 163 (1) of the Local Government Act 1933 (now repealed by the Local Government Act 1972 but replaced by other sim-

[1] [1971] 1 W.L.R. 204, Pennycuick, V-C.

ilar provisions), which Section gave them power, in respect of land belonging to them and not required for the purposes for which it was acquired or had since been appropriated, to appropriate that land for any other purpose approved by the Minister for which the Council were authorised to acquire land. The authority had maintained the airport for over 30 years when it decided that it would not renew the Board of Trade Licence which would expire on the 24th June 1971 nor would it renew a management agreement with a management company for the running of the airfield which would expire on the 31st December 1970. The Corporation intended to close the airfield and develop it as a housing estate.

The Court (Pennycuick V-C), having referred to the contention of Counsel for the authority that the principle was that a body entrusted with statutory powers could not by contract fetter the exercise of those powers and having referred to the case "which established beyond all doubt that principle", decided that this was a principle "wholy inapplicable to the present case". The principle did not apply where, as in that case, a statutory powers was validly exercised in such a way as to create a right extending over a term of years, even though the existence of the right pro tanto excluded the exercise of other statutory powers in respect of the same subject matter. The principle previously referred to was confined to attempts to fetter in advance, otherwise than by the exercise of a statutory power, a future exercise of a power.

A Section 52 Agreement is often used where the carrying out of development is to be delayed pending the construction of public works, *e.g.* sewage works. That an agreement may have a limited efficacy in this situation, so far as a developer is concerned, is illustrated by the case of *L. A. H. Ames Limited v. North Bedfordshire Borough Council* the facts of which are set out *ante* at page 59.

DISCHARGE OR MODIFICATION OF RESTRICTION

A restriction imposed by a Section 52 Agreement may be discharged or modified by the Lands Tribunal[1] if it is such as to fall under Section 84 (1) of the Law of Property Act 1925 (which, subject to detailed provisions to which reference should be made, gives the Tribunal the power to discharge or modify restrictive covenants affecting land).[2]

[1] (1979) 253 E.G. 55, C.A.
[2] See *Beecham Group's application* (1980) 256 E.G. 829.

Part II
Additional Controls

CHAPTER 8

BUILDINGS OF SPECIAL ARCHITECTURAL OR HISTORIC INTEREST

The statutory provisions for the preservation of buildings of special architectural or historic interest now contained in the Town and Country Planning Act 1971, a consolidating measure, had earlier been completely re-cast and greatly strengthened by Part V of the Town and Country Planning Act 1968 which, with other related provisions, came into force in the whole of England and Wales on 1st January 1969.[1]

Prior to this Act the basic provision, contained in the 1962 Act, was that such buildings should be listed and notice of this fact given to their owners and occupiers, whose duty it was to give a specified period of notice[2] to the local planning authority of any works for demolition of a listed building or its alteration or extension in such a manner that its character would be seriously affected. Listing imposed no other obligations on owners or occupiers and the only penalty to which such a person might be subject as a result of the Planning Acts was for failing to give the required notice. (If he had contravened this provision he could also be required to restore the building to its former state.)

If the local planning authority wished to restrict the demolition, alteration or extension of a building of special architectural or historic interest **whether listed or not** they had to make a **Building Preservation Order** which required confirmation by the Minister of Housing and Local Govern-

---

[1] *See* the Town and Country Planning Act 1968 (Commencement No. 2) Order 1968 (S.I. 1968, No. 1909).

[2] Two months, later changed to six months by the Civic Amenities Act 1967, s. 2. In the case of certain urgent works notice could be given after work had started.

ment. This they could do on their own initiative without there being any immediate intention of the owner to do works, or after receiving notice under the provisions outlined above. There were penalties for contravening a Building Preservation Order, but any requirements as to consents being obtained for works, or as to the restoration of a building to its former state after contravening works, depended on the terms of the Order itself. If no order had been made, and provided notice of intention had been given as described above, a listed building could be demolished or substantially altered without any penalty or other repercussion, so far as the Planning Acts were concerned, unless, of course, planning permission was necessary and had not been obtained.

The Civic Amenities Act of 1967 substantially increased the penalties for failing to give notice of works or for contravening a Building Preservation Order and contained certain other provisions designed to strengthen control.

Part V of the 1968 Act, which came into force on the first of January 1969[1] made a fundamental change in the machinery by repealing the provisions relating to the making of Building Preservation Orders[2] so that in general[3] control rested on listing alone. The present position regarding preservation of buildings of special architectural or historic interest is now as described below:—

LISTING OF BUILDINGS

The Secretary of State is charged by section 54 of the 1971 Act (re-enacting section 32 of the 1962 Act) with the duty of compiling lists of buildings of special architectural or historic interest, or approving with or without modifications, lists compiled by others.

---

[1] *See* the Town and Country Planning Act 1968 (Commencement No. 2) Order 1968 (S.I. 1968, No. 1909).

[2] As to the position regarding Building Preservation Orders made earlier, *see post*, p. 284.

[3] Certain steps are open to a local planning authority, even if a building is not listed. *See post*, p. 276.

In the case of *Iveagh (Earl) v. Minister of Housing and Local Government*[1] it was decided that in considering whether a particular building is in this category the building need not be viewed in isolation, but the architectural or historic interest of related buildings, *e.g.* of a square, might be taken into account. The 1968 Act by section 54 provided, and section 54 (2) of the 1971 Act now provides, that in considering whether to include a building in a list there may be taken into account not only the building itself but also—

(*a*) any respect in which its exterior contributes to the architectural or historic interest of any group of buildings, of which it forms part and

(*b*) the desirability of preserving, on the grounds of its architectural or historic interest, any feature of the building consisting of a manmade object or structure fixed to the building or forming part of the land and comprised within the curtilage of the building.

In *Corthorn Land and Timber Co. v. Minister of Housing and Local Government*[2] a Building Preservation Order had been made under section 30 of the 1962 Act prohibiting removal of carvings and panels bearing murals which were affixed to a building of outstanding architectural interest. This order was held to be *intra vires*, the issue being confined to whether the carvings and panels had become part of the building.

The 1968 Act, by section 40 (3), specifically provided, and section 54 (9) of the 1971 Act now provides, that for the purposes of the statutory provisions relating to listed buildings and preservation notices[3] any object or structure fixed to a building or forming part of the land and comprised within the curtilage of a building is to be treated as part of the building.

---

[1] [1963] 3 W.L.R. 974.
[2] (1965) 63 L.G.R. 490.
[3] As to which, *see post*, p. 276.

A building may be included in a list compiled or approved by the Secretary of State under section 54, notwithstanding that it is Crown land.[1] This provision was first contained in section 60 of the 1968 Act, a provision to the contrary in section 199 (2) (*b*) of the 1962 Act being repealed by the 1968 Act.

Certified copies of parts of any such list relating to any London Borough or county district have to be deposited with the proper officer[2] of the borough or district council and, outside Greater London, with the proper officer of the county planning authority whose area or any part of whose area includes the district or any part of it and where the district council are not the district planning authority, the proper officer of that authority.[3] A copy of anything so deposited with the proper officer[3] of a London Borough has also to be deposited with the proper officer[3] of the Greater London Council.

The Secretary of State must also keep available for public inspection free of charge at reasonable hours and at a convenient place copies of all lists and amendments of lists compiled, approved or made by him, and every local authority with whose proper officer[3] lists are deposited must similarly keep available copies of so much of any such list or amendment as relate to buildings in their area.[4]

An entry has to be made in the Register of Local Land Charges.[5]

As soon as may be after any building is included in or excluded from a list, the council of the London borough or county district in whose area the building is situated, on being informed of the fact by the Secretary of State must

---

[1] Section 266 (1) (*c*), 1971 Act.

[2] *i.e.* an officer of the council appointed for that purpose. Local Government Act 1972, s. 270 (3). The term "proper officer" is to be read for the former word "clerk". *ibid.*, s. 251 and Schedule 29.

[3] Section 54 (4) as amended by the Local Government Act 1972 from 1st April 1974, *ibid.*, Sched. 30 and Sched. 16, para. 28.

[4] Section 54 (8).

[5] *See* s. 54 (6) and Local Land Charges Rules 1977 (S.I. 1977, No. 985).

serve a notice intimating that fact on every owner and occupier of the building.[1]

Section 54A of the 1971[2] Act inserted by the Local Government Planning and Land Act, 1980, now enables anyone who wishes, in certain circumstances, to obtain a certificate of the Secretary of State that he does not intend to list a building. This may be done[3] where either "application has been made for planning permission[4] **for any development involving the alteration, extension or demolition of a building or any such planning permission has been granted**."[5] It seems that the applicant for the certificate need not be the person who applied for or was granted the planning permission. The effect[6] of the Secretary of State's certificate, where one is granted, is that for a period of five years thereafter the building cannot be listed and the local planning authority are for a like period precluded from serving a Building Preservation Notice.[7]

Effect of Listing

With certain exceptions noted later, once a building is listed no works of demolition or alteration or extension in any manner which would affect its character as a building of special architectural or historic interest can lawfully be carried out after 1st January 1969[8] unless that work has been **authorised** under the relevant statutory provisions.

Circumstances in which works are authorised

Works of the kind described in the proceding paragraph are **authorised** if, the Local Planning Authority[9] or the Sec-

[1] Section 54 (7), as amended by the Local Government Act 1972, *ibid.*, Schedule 30 and Schedule 16, para. 28, w.e.f. 1st April 1974.

[2] Inserted by the Local Government, Planning and Land Act, 1980 Schedule 15, para. 5.

[3] A person applying for a certificate must at the same time give notice to the local planning authority Section 54A (3).

[4] Section 54A (a).

[5] Section 54A (b).

[6] Section 54A (2).

[7] As to Building Preservation Notice see *post*, p. 276.

[8] The date of coming into operation of Part V of the 1968 Act.

[9] By the Local Government Act 1972, Schedule 16, para. 25 (1), this is the district planning authority, except in Greater London *ibid* para 52.

retary of State has granted written consent (referred to in the Act and hereafter as "listed building consent") for the execution of the works **and the works are executed in accordance with the terms of that consent and of any conditions attached to that consent** under section 56 of the Act[1] (as to which, *see* below).

In considering whether to grant planning permission for development which affects a listed building **or its setting** or whether to grant listed building consent for any works the local planning authority or the Secretary of State must[2] have special regard to the desirability of preserving the building or its setting or any features of special architectural or historic interest which it possesses.

In the case of demolition there is a further requirement. Notice of the proposal must be given to the Royal Commission on Historical Monuments (England) or the Royal Commission on Ancient and Historical Monuments (Wales and Monmouthshire) as appropriate,[3] and the works will not be **authorised** for the purpose of the section unless **either** for a period of at least a month following the grant of listed building consent and before the commencement of works, reasonable access to the building has been made available to Members or Officers of the Commission for the purpose of recording it **or** the Commission have by their Secretary or other authorised officer stated in writing that they have completed their recording of the building or that they do not wish to record it.

By an amendment made by the Local Government Planning and Land Act 1980,[4] section 55 (2A) now provides that the local planning authority or the Secretary of State may give a written consent ("listed building consent") for the retention of works for the demolition of a listed building or

---

[1] Section 55 (2).

[2] Section 56 (3) as amended by the Local Government Planning and Land Act 1980, Schedule 15, para. 7.

[3] The Secretary of State has power by s. 55 (3) by order made by statutory instrument to provide that from a date he specifies another body shall be substituted for either Royal Commission.

[4] Schedule 15, para. 6.

its alteration or extension which has been executed unlawfully, *i.e.* without prior listed building consent. The authorisation dates from the grant of consent[1] and not retrospectively so that the offence of having done the work without authority remains.

Prior to 13th November 1980[2] a planning permission in certain circumstances could operate as a listed building consent and no separate consent was required. From that date however the relevant provision of the 1971 Act[3] was repealed and now in every case a planning permission **and** a listed building consent will be necessary. Listed building consent may[4] be granted subject to conditions which may include conditions as to:—

(*a*) the preservation of particular features of the building either as part of it or after severance therefrom;

(*b*) the making good, after the works are completed of any damage caused to the building by the works;

(*c*) the reconstruction of the building or any part of it following the execution of any works, with the use of original materials so far as practicable and with such alterations of the interior of the building as may be specified in the conditions.

Where listed building consent is given for the demolition of a building it may be granted subject to a condition that demolition shall not take place before a contract for the work of redevelopment of the site has been made and a planning permission has been granted for that redevelopment.[5]

Applications for listed building consent have to be made to the Local Planning Authority in accordance with

---

[1] Section 54 (2A).
[2] Coming into force of the Local Government Planning and Land Act 1980, Schedule 15.
[3] Section 56 (2).
[4] Section 56 (4) substituted by *ibid.*, para. 9.
[5] Section 56 (5).

regulations[1] made by the Secretary of State under section 56 (6) and Schedule 11 of the 1971 Act. The Secretary of State may give directions to Local Planning Authorities to refer applications to him for decision[2] and so that he may have an opportunity of exercising this power there is provision[3] for him to be notified of applications. A London Borough Council is subject to the authority or direction of the Greater London Council, to whom they must give notice of any application.[4] The Greater London Council must in turn notify the Secretary of State so that he can consider exercising his power of "calling in" the application.[4]

A listed building consent, **unless the consent itself otherwise provides**, enures for the benefit of the building in question and of all persons for the time being having an interest in it.[5]

It has a life of five years or such other period (longer or shorter) as the consent specifies[6] and lapses if the work is not begun within that period. Any consent granted before 1st January 1978 without a time limit is deemed subject to a limit of three years beginning with 13th November 1980.[7] A consent granted without a time limit on or after 1st January 1978 and before 13th November 1980 is subject to a deemed condition requiring the beginning of works not later than 12th November 1985.

Revocation or modification of Listed Building Consent

A local planning authority may[8] subject to certain conditions, and subject to confirmation by the Secretary of State[9]

---

1 *See* the Town and Country Planning (Listed Buildings and Buildings in Conservation Areas) Regulations 1977 (S.I. 1977, No. 228).

2 Schedule 11, para. 4.

3 *See* Schedule 11, paras. 5, 6 and 7.

4 Unless they decide to refuse it.

5 See Schedule 11, para. 1 (2).

6 See Section 56A inserted by the Local Government Planning and Land Act 1980, Schedule 15, para. 11.

7 Date of coming into force of Schedule 15 of Local Government Planning and Land Act, 1980.

8 Section 56 and Part II of Schedule 11, 1971 Act, as amended by Local Government Planning and Land Act 1980, Schedule 34, Part X.

9 There are some exceptions to this. *See post.*

by order revoke or modify a listed building consent. Where such an order is submitted to the Secretary of State for confirmation notice has to be served[1] on the owner and occupier of the building and on any other person who, in the opinion of the authority will be affected by the order, and such persons have a right to be heard by a person appointed by the Secretary of State.[1]

The power of revocation or modification may be exercised at any time before the works in question have been **completed**, but revocation or modification does not affect so much of the works as has previously been carried out.

The Secretary of State may himself make such an order.[1]

There is a right to compensation for expenditure in carrying out works which are rendered abortive by the revocation or modification and for other loss or damage directly attributable to such revocation or modification[2] and in certain cases an owner may require the London borough or district council to purchase his property.[3]

Subject to certain safeguards, revocation and modification orders of local planning authorities which are unopposed do **not** require confirmation by the Secretary of State.[4]

Where an application for listed building consent is refused or no decision upon the application is made within the specified time[5] or there is a conditional consent, the applicant may appeal to the Secretary of State.[6] In certain cases an owner may also require the London borough or district council (who may not be the planning authority) to purchase his land, or persons having an interest in the land may be

---

[1] As to service, *see ante*, p. 121.
[2] *See* s. 172. *See also* the Local Government Act 1972, Schedule 16, para. 34.
[3] *See* s. 190. The provisions are similar to those concerning termination of authorised development, as to which *see post*, pp. 237 to 239.
[4] *See* para. 12 of Schedule 11, 1971 Act as amended by the Local Government Planning and Land Act, 1980.
[5] *See* the Town and Country Planning (Listed Buildings and Buildings in Conservation Areas) Regulations 1977 (S.I. No. 228).
[6] *See* Schedule 11, paras. 8 and 9.

able to claim compensation from the Local Planning Authority.[1]

Exceptions

As previously stated, there are certain exceptions to the provisions set out above. Section 56 (1) of the Act provides that the requirement that works shall be authorised in the manner described above does not apply to certain kinds of building, namely—

(*a*) *an ecclesiastical building which is for the time being used for ecclesiastical purposes or would be so used but for the works in question.*

The section specifically provides that for this purpose, a building used or available for use, by a minister of religion wholly or mainly as a residence from which to perform the duties of his office, is to be treated as **not** being an ecclesiastical building.

In *Phillips v. Minister of Housing and Local Government*,[2] a case turning on a similar exemption clause of the 1962 Act for the purposes of Building Preservation Orders, the Court of Appeal, reversing a decision of the Divisional Court, had held that the term, "ecclesiastical building" could, and did in that case, include a rectory, but the effect of this decision had, in fact been nullified even before the 1968 Act by section 9 of the Civic Amenities Act 1967, which amended the section of the 1962 Act in question.

The meaning of "ecclesiastical building" and the effect of this exemption was considered by the House of Lords in *A.-G. ex rel Bedfordshire County Council v. Howard United Reformed Church Trustees, Bedford.*[3] A Congregational Church which had ceased to be used for regular services was proposed to be demolished. It became listed and therefore consent for its demolition was required unless it was

---

[1] *See* ss. 190 and 171. *See also* the Town and Country Planning (Listed Buildings and Buildings in Conservation Areas) Regulations 1977. *See also* the Local Government Act 1972, Schedule 16, para. 34.

[2] [1964] 3 W.L.R. 378.

[3] [1975] 2 All E.R. 337 H.L.

within the meaning of section 56 (1) (*a*). It was still used for certain purposes—monthly church meetings, elders' meetings, an annual carol service and church social meetings, some of which concluded with prayers. At first instance Willis, J., had granted a declaration that it was not exempted, and an injunction restraining demolition. On the trustees' appeal this decision was reversed, the Court of Appeal holding that the church was an "ecclesiastical building" and was being used for "ecclesiastical purposes" (although social gatherings ending in prayer were not such purposes) and that but for the intended demolition the church "would be so used but for the works" and the exemption would apply on this ground also.

The decision of the Court of Appeal was reversed by the House of Lords, on an appeal by the planning authority. It was held that the church would not be used for ecclesiastical purposes when it was being demolished. The expression "or would be so used but for the works" in section 56 (1) (*a*) was limited to works of partial demolition necessitating temporary closure and did not extend to total demolition.

Under section 2 of the Redundant Churches and Other Religious Buildings Act 1969 (as amended), the provisions of section 55 of the 1971 Act, described above, do not apply to the execution of works for the demolition of the whole or part of a redundant church, pursuant to a pastoral scheme or a redundancy scheme under the Pastoral Measure 1968.

(*b*) *a building for the time being included in the Schedule of monuments compiled and maintained under section 1 of the Ancient Monuments and Archaeological Areas Act 1979.*[1]

The Act also provides in subsection (6) of section 55 that in any proceedings for an offence under that section (as to which *see post*) it is a defence to prove[2] that the works in question were urgently necessary in the interests of safety

[1] Amendment made by the 1979 Act.

[2] This will be on a preponderance of probability, which is not as onerous a burden as in the case of proof "beyond reasonable doubt". *See R. v. Carr-Briant* [1943] K.B. 607. *R. v. Dunbar* [1958] 1 Q.B. 1.

or health or for the preservation of the building **and** that notice in writing of the need for the works was given to the Local Planning Authority as soon as reasonably practicable.

ENFORCEMENT

The remedies of the Local Planning Authority against a person offending against the provisions described above are of two kinds—

(1) a prosecution for penalties;

(2) a requirement to carry out works of restoration or otherwise to the building.

Prosecution

(1) Section 55 (1) of the 1971 Act provides that any person[1] who executes or causes to be executed any works for the demolition of a listed building, or for its alteration or extension in any manner which would affect its character as a building of special architectural or historical interest, and the works are not authorised under Section 55 (2) of the Act, is guilty of an offence. The circumstances in which work is "authorised" are set out on page 255, *ante*.

(2) Section 55 (4) also provides that without prejudice to the above provision, any person[1] who is executing or causing to be executed works in relation to a listed building under a listed building consent and who fails to comply with any condition attached to the consent for those works under section 56 of the Act (as to which, *see* page 258, *ante*) is guilty of an offence.

Either offence is punishable summarily[2] or on indictment. In the former case the penalty is imprisonment for not more than 3 months or a fine of up to £1000[3] or both imprisonment and fine. In the latter, a term of up to twelve months' imprisonment or a fine of unlimited amount, or both, may

---

[1] As to offences by corporation, *see* p. 218, *ante*.
[2] *See ante* as to summary proceedings.
[3] Criminal Law Act, Section 28 (2).

be imposed.[1] In determining the amount of fine to be imposed on a person convicted on indictment, the court is directed by the Act,[1] in particular to have regard to any financial benefit which has accrued or appears likely to accrue to the offender in consequence of the offence.

Listed Building Enforcement Notice

Where it appears to the Local Planning Authority[2] that any works have been, or are being, executed to a listed building in their area and are such as to involve either of the offences described under (1) or (2) above, they may, if they consider it expedient to do so, having regard to the effect of the works on the character of the building as one of special architectural or historic interest, issue[3] a "listed building enforcement notice".[4]

If the Secretary of State, after consulting the Local Planning Authority, and also, in Greater London, the Greater London Council, considers that such a notice should be served, he may himself issue such a notice. His notice has the same effect as if it had been served by the Local Planning Authority,[5] and in the event of non-compliance with the notice, he has the same powers to take proceedings against the offender and to execute works and recover the cost as the Local Planning Authority would have.[5]

A listed building enforcement notice must[6] specify four things as follows:—

(1) the alleged contravention. Particulars of the contravention must be given and, where appropriate, the relevant consent and conditions should be recited;

---

[1] Section 55 (5).
[2] *See* footnote 9, p. 255, *ante*. The Greater London Council have, in respect of any London Borough, the same powers in this matter as the local planning authority. *See* 1971 Act, Schedule 3, para. 4.
[3] As to service, *see ante*, p. 118.
[4] Section 96 (1), as amended by the Local Government and Planning (Amendment) Act, 1981, Section 1 and Schedule para. 9.
[5] Section 100 as amended. *ibid*., para. 11.
[6] Section 96 (1) as amended by the Local Government and Planning (Amendment) Act 1981 and Schedule para. 9.

(2) (a) the steps the Local Planning Authority requires to be taken (a) for restoring the building to its former state or, (b) where the authority considers such restoration would be undesirable or not reasonably practicable, steps for executing such further (specified) works as they consider necessary to alleviate the effect of the works carried out without listed building consent or (c) for bringing the building to the state in which it would have been if the terms and conditions of any listed building consent granted for the works had been complied with. Except where the requirement is merely to require the building to be restored to its proper state listed building consent is by virtue of section 96 (7) deemed to be granted for any works of demolition, alteration or extension of the building executed as a result of compliance with the notice.

(3) the period within which the required steps are to be taken. The time allowed must be reasonable and the period will not begin to run until the notice takes effect (*see* next paragraph). As the date the notice is, in fact, to take effect, will depend on whether or not there is an appeal, the only effective way of specifying a period for compliance is to state a period, *e.g.* one month "from the date when this notice takes effect". As in the case of an ordinary Enforcement Notice, the period for compliance may be extended as the direction of the Local Planning Authority[1] but see *ante*, p. 116 as to the effect of this provision.

(4) a date on which it will take effect.

Although there is no statutory requirement, the notice should draw the attention of the recipient to his right of appeal (as to which *see post*).

The provisions relating to service of the notice, as to the persons to be served with a listed building enforcement

---

[1] *See* s. 98 (5).

notice and as to Crown land and as to the withdrawal of such a notice are the same as in the case of ordinary Enforcement Notices.[1]

By section 99A of the 1971 Act (inserted by the Local Government Planning and Land Act 1980 section 90 and schedule 15 para. 17) a listed building consent under section 55 (2A) for retention of work to which the enforcement notice relates or consent granted to permit retention without complying with a condition, the enforcement notice ceases to have effect to the extent covered by such permission but without prejudice to liability of any person for an offence of failure to comply with the listed building consent before the relevant provisions of the notice ceased to have effect.

APPEAL

Grounds

Any person who has an interest in the building to which such a notice relates may, at any time before the notice takes effect,[2] appeal to the Secretary of State against the notice on any of the grounds listed below.[3]

It should be noted that such a person need not have been served with the notice in order for him to have the right of appeal, and conversely a person who has been served but has no interest in the land can not appeal.

If an appeal is lodged, it suspends the operation of the notice pending the final determination or withdrawal of the appeal.[4] The manner of lodging and hearing of an appeal is the same as in the case of Enforcement Notices.[5] The possible grounds are as follows:—

(*a*) that the building is not of special architectural or historic interest;

---

[1] See Section 96 (3), Section 266 and Section 96 (5) as amended.

[2] As to which *see ante*, p. 116.

[3] Section 97 (1) as amended by the Local Government and Planning (Amendment) Act, 1981 Section 1 and Schedule para. 9.

[4] Section 97 (a).

[5] Section 97.

(*b*) that the matters alleged to constitute a contravention of section 55 do not involve such a contravention;

(*c*) that the contravention of that section alleged in the notice has not taken place.

(*d*) that the works were urgently necessary in the interests of safety or health or for the preservation of the building;

(*e*) that listed building consent ought to be granted for the works or that any relevant condition of such consent which has been granted ought to be discharged or different conditions substituted;

(*f*) that copies of the notice was not served as required by the Act (*i.e.* was not served on the owner and occupier of the building, and on any other person having an interest in the building, which in the authority's opinion is materially affected by the notice);

(*g*) that, except in relation to requirements listed under 2 (b) or (c) *ante*, the requirements of the notice exceed what is necessary for restoring the building to its condition before the works were carried out;

(*h*) that the period specified in the notice as the period within which any steps required by it are to be taken, falls short of what should reasonably be allowed;

(*i*) that the steps required by the notice to be taken to restore the character of the building to its former state would not serve that purpose.

(*j*) that the steps required to be taken under 2 (b) *ante* exceed what is necessary to alleviate the effect of the works executed to the building;

(*k*) that the steps required to be taken under 2 (c) *ante* exceed what is necessary to bring the building to the state in which it would have been if the terms and conditions of the listed building consent had been complied with.

Powers of the Secretary of State

The Secretary of State has under section 97[1] the same powers in relation to a listed building enforcement notice as he has in relation to an ordinary enforcement notice.[2] He may:—

(1) make regulations prescribing appeal procedures;

(2) dismiss or as the case may be allow an appeal on failure of an appellant or the authority to comply with certain statutory requirements or requirements of regulations.

See *ante*, p. 162 as to regulations made under these provisions and see also in the same place Rules governing the procedure where a local Inquiry is held.

On determining an appeal, the Secretary of State must[3] give directions for giving effect to his determination including, where appropriate, directions for quashing the notice or for varying the terms of it.

He has the same powers to correct errors and in certain cases to disregard failure to serve a copy of a listed building enforcement notice on a particular person as he has in relation to an ordinary enforcement notice.

He may:—

(*a*) grant listed building consent for the works to which the notice relates or for part only of those works or, as the case may be, discharge any condition subject to which the consent was granted and substitue any other condition **whether more or less onerous**;

---

[1] As substituted by Section 1 and the Schedule to the Local Government and Planning (Amendment) Act, 1981.

[2] See pp. 169 to 187, *ante*.

[3] Section 97A.

Any planning consent or listed building consent which he grants on appeal has effect as if granted on an ordinary application and his decision is final.

If any person aggrieved by the Secretary of State's decision to grant listed building consent or to grant planning consent pursuant to these provisions, wishes to question the validity of his decision on the grounds that it is not within the powers of the Act or that any of the relevant requirements have not been complied with in relation to it, he may within six weeks from the date of the decision apply to the High Court under section 245 of the 1971 Act. Apart from this the validity of his decision cannot be questioned in any legal proceedings whatsoever. The Local Planning Authority has a similar right.

(*b*) Remove the building in question from the relevant list.

(*c*) In the case of a building which was subject to a preservation order under section 54 (10) of the Act,[1] direct that that subsection shall cease to apply to it.

The case of *Shop Properties v. Minister of Housing and Local Government*[2] is relevant in regard to the powers of the Secretary of State in this connection. This was a case concerning a Building Preservation Order (as to which *see ante*, page 251) and the powers of the appropriate Minister on an appeal. A local planning authority, on the basis that certain buildings helped to maintain the quality of an old market town, although in themselves having no great architectural merit, had made a preservation order in respect of them and had refused planning permission to re-develop. Following an inquiry the inspector had recommended that the order should not be confirmed, but his recommendation was rejected by the Minister. An appeal to the High Court failed, Willis, J., holding that the Minister was entitled to

[1] *See post*, p. 284, as to the application of this subsection.
[2] (1969) 211 E.G. 161.

place a different emphasis on the opinions of the Inspector and to arrive at a conclusion different from his.

In prescribed cases,[1] a Ministerial Inspector may determine the appeal. The provisions relevant in such a case are the same as for Enforcement Notices which are set out on pages 190 to 193, *ante*.

Limitations on challenge

As in the case of other Enforcement Notices, there are limitations on the right to challenge a listed building enforcement notice.[2]

No person who has appealed to the Secretary of State against the notice can afterwards be heard in any other proceedings to allege that he was not duly served with such a notice. Nor can any such allegation be made by any other person.[3]

Appeal from Secretary of State to High Court

As in the case of other Enforcement Notices, section 246 of the 1971 Act provides for an appeal from the Secretary of State to the High Court on a point of law.[4]

Other means of challenge

A person affected by a notice may also be able to challenge its validity by applying direct to the High Court, or by setting up its invalidity as a defence to proceedings, or may use it as a basis for action against a Local Planning Authority seeking to enforce it directly.[5]

NON-COMPLIANCE WITH A NOTICE

In the event of non-compliance with a listed building enforcement notice which has either not been appealed

---

[1] *See* s. 97 and Schedule 9. At the time of publication no Regulations have been made to prescribe any classes of appeal under these provisions.

[2] See *ante*, pp. 197 to 201.

[3] Section 110 (2).

[4] *See* p. 193, *ante*.

[5] *See ante*, pp. 202 to 207, as to relevant points and other matters in relation to enforcement notices.

against or which has been upheld on appeal, the Local Planning Authority[1] may—

1. Prosecute for penalties.
2. Enter on the land and do the necessary work themselves.

Prosecution

Where a notice has been served on the person **who, at the time when the notice was served on him, was the owner of the building** to which it relates and any steps required by the notice to be taken have not been taken within the period allowed for compliance,[2] that person[3] is liable on summary conviction to a fine of up to £1000[4] or on conviction on indictment to a fine of unlimited amount.[5]

If a person against whom proceedings are brought under the above provisions can show that he had **ceased** to be the owner of the land before the end of the period specified in the notice for compliance he is entitled to have the new owner brought before the court in the proceedings.[6] In order to do this he must lay an information and give the prosecution not less than three clear days notice of his intention.[7]

If, after the prosecution have proved that the steps required by the enforcement notice have not been taken within the required period, the original owner proves that the failure to take those steps was wholly or in part attributable to the default of the new owner, the new owner may be convicted. If the original owner is able also to prove that

---

[1] The Greater London Council have, in respect of any London Borough, the same powers in this matter as the local planning authority. *See* 1971 Act, Schedule 3, para. 4.

[2] *See ante*, p. 264.

[3] As to offences by corporations, *see* p. 218, *ante*.

[4] Criminal Law Act 1977, Section 28 (2).

[5] Section 98 (1).

[6] Section 98 (2).

[7] It is probable that the information must also be laid 3 clear days before the proceedings are heard. *Per* Lord Goddard, L.C.J., in *Malcolm v. Cheek* [1948] 1 K.B. 400.

he himself took all reasonable steps to secure compliance with the notice he is entitled to be acquitted.[1]

If a person[2] who has been convicted of an offence does not as soon as practicable do everything in his power to secure compliance with the notice, he is guilty of a further offence and liable to be proceeded against either summarily or on indictment. On summary conviction he is liable to a fine of up to £100 for each day following his first conviction on which any of the requirements of the notice remain unfulfilled. On conviction on indictment he is liable to a fine of unlimited amount.[3]

Carrying out of works by Local Planning Authority

If, within the period allowed for compliance[4] with a listed building enforcement notice any steps required by the notice to be taken have not been taken, the Local Planning Authority may enter on the land and take those steps and may recover[5] from the person **who is then the owner**[6] of the land any expenses reasonably incurred by them in so doing.

The consequential powers of the local planning authority, as to sale of materials and other matters are the same as in respect of an ordinary enforcement notice and are as set out on pp. 213 to 215 *ante*.

Position of person from whom expenses are recoverable

Provisions under this head are the same as those relating to an ordinary enforcement notice and are as set out on pp. 214 to 215 *ante*.

---

[1] Section 98 (3). See the discussion at p. 217, *ante* regarding similar provisions concerning ordinary enforcement notices.

[2] As to offences by corporations, *see* p. 218, *ante*.

[3] Section 98 (4) as amended by Section 1 and the Schedule to the Local Government and Planning (Amendment) Act, 1981.

[4] *See ante*, p. 264.

[5] As a simple contract debt in any court of competent jurisdiction, *i.e.* in the County Court or the High Court. Section 99 and s. 111.

[6] For definition, *see* p. 119, *ante*.

WILFUL DAMAGE TO A LISTED BUILDING

The Civic Amenities Act of 1967 (amended by the 1968 Act) contained new provisions designed to prevent wilful damage to listed buildings. These provisions have been repealed and re-enacted in the 1971 Act, section 57.

If a building is included in a list compiled or approved as previously mentioned **and is not a building of a description specified in section 56 (1) of the 1971 Act** (as to which *see ante*, pages 260 to 262, then any person who, but for these statutory provisions would be entitled to do so, does or permits[1] the doing of any act which causes or is likely to result in damage to the building other than an act for the execution of "excepted works", and he does or permits[1] it with the intention of causing such damage, is liable to prosecution and on summary conviction to a fine of up to £100. Proceedings will be in the Magistrates' Court and must be brought within six months of the commencement of the offence.[2]

If, after conviction of such an offence, he fails to take such reasonable steps as may be necessary to prevent any damage or further damage resulting from his offence, he is guilty of a further offence and liable on summary conviction to a fine of up to £20 for every day on which the failure continues. Here again, proceedings will be in the Magistrates' Court, but the offence will be a continuing one, occurring from day to day, and the six month limit will not apply. The effect of the decision in *R. v. Chertsey Justices ex parte Franks*[3] should however be noted. In that case, having considered the effect of similar provisions relating to Enforcement Notices, the High Court decided that section 104 of the Magistrates' Court Act 1952 precluded the hearing of an information in so far as it alleged an offence occurring more than 6 months before its date and that no penalty could be imposed in respect of any day falling more than six months prior to the date of the information. A person

---

[1] *See ante*, p. 215.
[2] Section 127, Magistrates' Courts Act 1980.
[3] [1961] 2 Q.B. 152.

convicted of either of the offences mentioned has a right of appeal to the Crown Court and, on the ground that the decision is wrong in law or in excess of jurisdiction of appeal by way of case stated to a Divisional Court of the Queen's Bench Division direct from the Magistrates[1] or from the Crown Court.[2]

"Excepted works" means[3]:—

(*a*) works authorised by planning permission granted or deemed to be granted in pursuance of an application under the Planning Acts,

(*b*) works for which listed building consent has been given under the 1971 Act or the Town and Country Planning Act 1968.

COMPULSORY ACQUISITION OF LISTED BUILDINGS

The powers set out in the preceding pages are extensive but there remains one further power, namely, for the local authority (the county or district council or, in the case of a building situated in Greater London, the Greater London Council or the London Borough Council) to acquire compulsorily any listed building (subject to the exceptions in section 58 (2) of the 1971 Act (the same as those listed on pages 260 to 262, *ante*) in respect of which reasonable steps are not being taken for its proper preservation. If the Secretary of State is satisfied that such is the case he may authorise the compulsory acquisition of the building and any land comprising or contiguous or adjacent to it which appears to him to be required for preserving the building or its amenities, or for affording access to it, or for its proper control or management.[4] The Secretary of State may himself purchase compulsorily under similar conditions. These steps are now authorised by section 114 of the 1971 Act.

[1] *See* Magistrates' Courts Act 1952, 1980, and Magistrates' Courts Rules 1968, rr. 65–68.

[2] Section 10, Courts Act 1971.

[3] Section 57 (2) and *see* s. 292 and Schedule 24, para. 1 of the 1971 Act.

[4] Section 114 (1).

The Acquisition of Land Act 1981 will apply to any such compulsory purchase.

Before either a local authority or the Secretary of State start any compulsory purchase proceedings they must, at least two months previously, have served[1] on the owner of the building, and not withdrawn, a **repairs notice**—specifying the works which they consider reasonably necessary for the proper preservation of the building and explaining the effects of sections 114 to 117 of the 1971 Act.[2]

Once a repairs notice has been served the demolition of the building does not prevent further action. Section 115 (2) provides that in such a case the **site** of the building may be acquired compulsorily if the Secretary of State is satisfied that he would have confirmed, or as the case may be would have made, a Compulsory Purchase Order in respect of the building itself had it not been demolished.

The Council or the Secretary of State may at any time withdraw a repairs notice and if they do so, must forthwith give notice of the withdrawal to the person served with it.[3]

Where a person is served with a repairs notice he is precluded by section 180 (5) of the 1971 Act as applied by section 190 (4) of the 1971 Act from serving a purchase notice[4] until the expiration of three months beginning with the date of service of that notice. If during that three months the Council or the Secretary of State start the compulsory acquisition of the building he continues to be so precluded unless and until the compulsory acquisition is discontinued.

For the above purposes the "start" of compulsory purchase proceedings is **not** the date of making the order, but the date when the Council or the Secretary of State, as the case may be, serve notice as required by paragraph 3 (1) of Schedule 1 to the Acquisition of Land Act 1981.[5] Discontinuance occurs in the case of acquisition by a Council

---

[1] As to service, *see ante*, p. 121.
[2] Section 115.
[3] Section 115 (3).
[4] As to purchase notices, *see ante* p. 237.
[5] Section 12 (1).

when they withdraw the order or the Secretary of State decides not to confirm it, and in the case of acquisition by the Secretary of State, when he decides not to make the order.[1]

Where a Compulsory Purchase Order is made, a person having an interest in the building proposed to be acquired may within 28 days after service of notice under paragraph 3 of Schedule 1 to the Acquisition of Land Act 1981, apply to a Magistrates' Court for the Petty Sessions area in which the building is situated, for an order staying further proceedings on the Compulsory Purchase Order.[2] If the court is satisfied that reasonable steps have been taken for properly preserving the building, the court **must** make such an order.[1] Any person aggrieved by the decision of the Magistrates may appeal to the Crown Court.[3]

Having regard to the decisions in *Ealing Corporation v. Jones*[4] and *R. v. Dorset Quarter Sessions Appeal Committee ex parte Weymouth Corporation*[5] it appears that this right of appeal to the Crown Court is **not** open to the Secretary of State or local authority whose Compulsory Purchase Order is in question. These cases concerned appeals against Enforcement Notices relating to unauthorised advertisements.[6] Such appeals were then to magistrates and there was, as in the circumstances now under consideration, a further appeal to Quarter Sessions by any "person who is aggrieved" by the decision of the magistrates. In the former case the Court decided that a local planning authority whose notice had been quashed by the Magistrates was **not** "a person aggrieved" and in the latter that this was so, even when an order for costs had been made against the authority.

Compensation on compulsory acquisition will be assessed in accordance with the provisions of the Land Compensation Act 1961, but section 116 of the 1971 Act as amended by

---

1 Section 180 (6) (*b*), as applied by s. 190 (4).
2 Section 114 (6).
3 Section 114 (7).
4 [1959] 1 Q.B. 384.
5 [1960] 2 Q.B. 230.
6 *See post*, p. 318.

the Town and Country Amenities Act 1974, section 6, contains special provisions regarding assumptions to be made in calculating such compensation and section 117 provides that subject to certain conditions, and to a right of appeal to Magistrates, when a building has been deliberately allowed to fall into disrepair for the purposes of justifying its demolition and the development or re-development of the site or an adjoining site, the order for compulsory purchase may contain a direction for "minimum compensation", which will have the effect of excluding from the assessment of compensation any possible development or re-development value of the site.

GENERAL CONTROL OVER UNLISTED BUILDINGS [1]

Subject to certain exceptions,[2] where a building is **not** listed, but it appears to the District Planning Authority in whose area it is,[3] that it is of special architectural or historic interest **and is in danger of demolition or of alteration in such a way as to affect its character as such**, they may take steps under section 58 of the 1971 Act which have the interim effect of bringing it with the minimum of delay under the same control as if it were listed. Where under section 54A of the 1971 Act[4] (added by the Local Government Planning and Land Act 1980 schedule 15 para. 5) the Secretary of State has issued a certificate that he does not intend to list the building, no steps can be taken under section 58 for a period of five years thereafter. The procedure is as follows:—

The authority must request the Secretary of State to consider including the building in a list compiled or approved

[1] For control over demolition of unlisted buildings in conservation areas, *see post*, p. 280.

[2] The exceptions are the same as the exceptions from the requirement of authorisation for works to listed buildings, which are set out on pp. 260 to 262, *ante*.

[3] In London the Greater London Council or the London Borough Council (who have concurrent powers). The word "district" was substituted for the word "local" by the Local Government Planning and Land Act 1980 section 90 and schedule 15 para. 12 excluding the County planning authority.

[4] See *ante*, p. 255.

under section 54 of the Act. They must then serve[1] on the owner[2] and occupier of the building a **building preservation notice**. This notice must:—

1. State that the building appears to the authority to be of special architectural or historic interest and that they have requested the Secretary of State to consider including it in a list.

2. Explain the effect of subsection (3) and (4) of section 58 (which is as follows).

A building preservation notice comes into force as soon as it is served[3] on both the owner and occupier and remains in force until the happening of one of the following events, **whichever first occurs**:—

1. The expiry of a period of six months from the date when it was served or, as the case may be, last served.

2. The Secretary of State includes the building in a list.

3. The Secretary of State notifies the Planning Authority **in writing** that he does not intend to include the building in a list.

As to service, **time** is important and it is open to the intended recipient of a building preservation notice served by post to prove that he never received it, in which case it will be ineffective.[4] Personal service is desirable where possible (but see post for urgent cases).

While a building preservation notice is in force the provisions described in this chapter have effect in relation to the building as if it were a listed building, except that the provisions of section 57 of the Act (which relates to wilful damage to listed buildings) do not apply,[5] but if a listed building consent is refused or granted subject to conditions

[1] For methods of service, *see* p. 121, *ante*.
[2] For definition of "*owner*", see p. 119, *ante*.
[3] For methods of service, *see* p. 121, *ante*.
[4] *Maltglade Ltd. v. St. Albans R.D.C.* [1972] 3 All E.R. 129, for a full note of which case *see ante*, p. 127.
[5] Section 58 (4). For the provisions of s. 57, *see* p. 272, *ante*.

the compensation provisions[1] do not apply unless and until the building is included in a list, except that a claim for compensation may be lodged.[2]

If the notice ceases to be in force by reason of event (2) above, the control will, of course, continue by virtue of the listing.

If, following the service of a building preservation notice, the Secretary of State notifies the Planning Authority that he does not propose to list the building, the authority must forthwith give notice of his decision to the owner and occupier of the building and the authority are precluded from serving another building preservation notice in respect of the building in question for a period of twelve months beginning with the date of the Secretary of State's notification.[3]

If a building preservation notice ceases to be in force by reason of either of the events numbered (1) or (3) above, the following is the position[4]:—

(*a*) the fact that the notice has ceased to be in force does not affect the liability of any person to be prosecuted and punished for an offence under section 55 or 98,[5] committed by him while the notice was in force;

(*b*) any proceedings on or arising out of an application for listed building consent made while the notice was in force, lapse, as does any listed building consent granted with respect to the building while the notice was in force;

(*c*) any listed building enforcement notice[6] served by the Local Planning Authority while the Building Preservation Notice was in force ceases to have effect and any proceedings thereon lapse. If, however, matters have progressed so far that the au-

---

[1] *See* s. 171.
[2] Section 173 (2).
[3] Section 58 (5).
[4] Section 58 (4) and Schedule 11, Part III.
[5] As to such offences, *see* pp. 262 and 270, *ante*.
[6] As to such notices, *see* p. 263, *ante*.

thority have exercised their power under section 99 of the Act to execute works themselves[1] their power under that section to recover from the then owner the expenses incurred in so doing, remains. Similarly, any expenses incurred by an owner or occupier in complying with a listed building enforcement notice and sums paid by an owner to the authority may still be recovered from the person who, in fact, carried out the work to which the listed building enforcement notice relates[2];

(*d*) any person who at the time when the notice was served had an interest in the building is entitled to compensation by the authority in respect of any loss or damage directly attributable to the effect of the notice.[3] This may include any sum payable in respect of breach of contract caused by the necessity of discontinuing or countermanding any works to a building on account of the building preservation notice being in force in respect of it.[4]

Urgent Cases

Section 58 (6) (inserted by the Town and Country Planning (Amendment) Act 1972), provides that if it appears to the planning authority to be urgent that a building preservation notice should come into force they may, instead of serving the notice on the owner and occupier of the building, "affix the notice conspicuously to some object on the building" and this is to be treated for all relevant purposes as service of the notice.

---

[1] As to this *see* p. 271, *ante*.

[2] As to this *see* p. 271, *ante*.

[3] *See* s. 173 (3) and the Town and Country Planning (Listed Buildings and Buildings in Conservation Areas) Regulations 1977 (S.I. 1977, No. 228).

[4] Section 173 (4).

CONTROL OVER DEMOLITION OF UNLISTED BUILDINGS IN CONSERVATION AREAS

Under the Town and Country Planning (Amendment) Act 1972 it was possible for directions to be made by local planning authorities, with the consent of the Secretary of State, which had the effect of requiring listed building consent to be obtained for demolition of buildings in a conservation area.

Those provisions have been repealed and replaced by others[1] wider in scope, by the Town and Country Amenities Act 1974. The control is now applied to **all** demolitions of buildings in conservation areas, with some exceptions, by the provisions described below.

Under section 277 of the 1971 Act, as substituted by section 1 of the 1974 Act, every local planning authority[2] must from time to time determine which parts of their area are areas of **special architectural or historic interest**, the character of which it is desirable to preserve or enhance and must designate such areas **conservation areas**. The authority must review the situation again from time to time.[3] After consultation with a local planning authority the Secretary of State may himself designate a conservation area. There are provisions in subsection (5)[4] for consultations between authorities.

The designation of an area as a conservation area is to be registered as a Local Land Charge.[5]

Section 277A of the 1971 Act, inserted by section 1 of the 1974 Act, provides the control machinery.

It applies to all buildings in conservation areas other than:—

---

[1] Operative from 1st September 1974. *See* the 1974 Act, s. 13 (3).

[2] In Greater London the G.L.C. and in relation to a London Borough the London Borough Council, in a National Park the county planning authority, elsewhere the district planning authority or the county planning authority. Section 277 (11).

[3] Section 277 (2) as amended by the Local Government, Planning and Land Act, 1980. Section 90 and Schedule 15, para. 26.

[4] Section 277 (5) as amended *ibid.*

[5] Section 277 (9).

(*a*) Listed buildings (which are of course subject to the other controls earlier discussed)

(*b*) excepted buildings within the meaning of section 58 (2) (*see ante*, p. 276)

(*c*) buildings in relation to which a direction by the Secretary of State under subsection (4) is in force (*see* below).

A building to which the section applies must not be demolished without the consent of the "appropriate authority". This is the local planning authority or the Secretary of State, or, in the case of applications by local planning authorities themselves, the Secretary of State.

Where there are proposals for redevelopment the merit of proposed development is a relevant consideration in deciding whether consent to demolition should be given.[1]

The Secretary of State may direct that the section shall not apply to a description of buildings specified in his direction.

A direction as to a description of buildings may be given either to an individual local planning authority or to local planning authorities generally.[2] A direction may be varied or revoked by a further direction.[3]

Section 277A provides that various sections of the 1971 Act are to apply to buildings covered by the section, as if they were listed buildings, but that regulations may provide for them to have effect subject to such exceptions and modifications as may be prescribed.[4]

These sections, which are dealt with *ante*, are:—

Section 55 (listed building consents and offences).

Section 56 (3), (5) and (6) and Schedule 11, Parts I and

---

[1] *Richmond-upon-Thames London Borough Council v. Secretary of State for the Environment* (1979) 37 P. & C.R., 151, Sir Douglas Frank Q.C.

[2] Section 277A (5).

[3] Section 277A (6).

[4] Subsection (8).

II (procedure on application, appeals and revocation of consent).

Sections 96 to 99 (listed building enforcement notices and consequential matters).

Sections 172 and 190 and Schedule 19 (compensation, purchase notices, and related matters).

Section 266 (1) (*b*) (Crown land).

By subsection (10) of section 277A any proceedings on or arising out of an application for listed building consent made while section 277A applies to a building lapse when the section ceases to apply to it and any listed building consent granted also lapses, but the fact that the section has ceased to apply to a building does not affect the liability of any person to be prosecuted and punished for an offence under section 55 or 98 of the Act committed by him with respect to the building while the section did apply to it. (Section 55 and section 98 are described *ante* at pages 262 and 270 respectively.)

Under subsection (4) the Secretary of State has issued a direction (in Circular 23/77, paragraph 71) that section 277A shall not apply to the following descriptions of buildings:—

(i) buildings with a cubic content not exceeding 115 cubic metres, or any part of such a building;

(ii any building within the curtilage of a dwelling-house and erected in pursuance of the permission granted by article 3 of the Town and Country Planning General Development Order 1977 as coming within any of the descriptions in Class I of Schedule 1 to that order;

(iii) gates, fences, walls or other means of enclosure erected in pursuance of the permission granted by article 3 of the Town and Country Planning General Development Order 1977 as coming within the description given in Class II of Schedule 1 to that Order;

(iv) temporary buildings erected in pursuance of the permission granted by article 3 of the Town and Country Planning General Development Order 1977 as coming within the description given in Class IV.I of Schedule 1 to that Order;

(v) agricultural buildings erected in pursuance of the permission granted by article 3 of the Town and Country Planning General Development Order 1977 as coming within the description given in Class VI.I of Schedule 1 to that Order;

(vi) industrial buildings erected in pursuance of the permission granted by article 3 of the Town and Country Planning General Development Order 1977 as coming within the description given in Class VIII.I of Schedule 1 to that Order;

(vii) any building required to be demolished by virtue of a discontinuance order made under section 51 of the Town and Country Planning Act 1971;

(viii) any building required to be demolished by virtue of any provision of an agreement made under section 52 of the Town and Country Planning Act 1971;

(ix) any building in respect of which the requirements of an enforcement notice served under section 87 or section 96 of the Town and Country Planning Act 1971 require its demolition, in whole or in part, however expressed;

(x) any building required to be demolished by virtue of a condition of planning permission granted under section 29 of the Town and Country Planning Act 1971;

(xi) any building included in an operative clearance order or compulsory purchase order made under Part III of the Housing Act 1957, or to which a Demolition Order made under Part II of that Act applies; and one building purchased by a local authority by agreement where Part III applies to the building.

(xii) ecclesiastical buildings in respect of which a redundancy scheme has been drafted under the Pastoral Measure 1968.

EFFECT OF BUILDING PRESERVATION ORDERS MADE PRIOR TO 1968 ACT

As previously stated, control under the Planning Acts over buildings of architectural or historic interest prior to the coming into force on 1st January 1969 of the provisions in the 1968 Act, rested in the main on Building Preservation Orders. After 1st January 1969[1] such orders cannot be made, but orders made prior to that date under the 1962 Act and still subsisting immediately before the coming into force of the 1968 Act provisions, **did not**, and **still do not** lapse. They continue to have effect for a number of purposes. The position is as follows[2]:—

1. Every building which immediately before the 1st January 1969[1] was subject to a Building Preservation Order but was not then listed is **deemed to be a listed building** and therefore subject to all the controls mentioned in this chapter.

   The Secretary of State may, however, at any time direct in the case of any building that this provision is not to apply to it. If he does so the council of the London borough or county district in whose area it is, on being notified of the Secretary of State's direction, must give notice of it to the owner and occupier of the building.[3]

   Before giving any such direction the Secretary of State must consult with, in Greater London, the local planning authority, in a National Park the

---

[1] The date of commencement of Part V of the 1968 Act provisions.
[2] *See* s. 54 (10) and Schedule 24, 1971 Act.
[3] Section 54 (10), 1971 Act.

county planning authority, elsewhere the district planning authority, and in any case the owner and the occupier of the building.[1]

2. Any consent under a Building Preservation Order given before the 1st January 1969[2] (whether by the Local Planning Authority or by the Minister on appeal) for the execution of any works operates as a listed building consent.[3] If it is a conditional consent the conditions still apply.

3. If consent under a Building Preservation Order was given before the 1st January 1969[4] for **demolition** works it is **not** necessary to give notice to the Royal Commission on Historical Monuments (England) or the Royal Commission on Ancient and Historical Monuments (Wales and Monmouthshire).[5]

4. If before the 1st January 1969[2] application had been made for consent under a Building Preservation Order for any works and any proceedings on it were pending at that date, all necessary steps regarding the making of applications, the decision of the Local Planning Authority thereon and any appeals against a decision could be proceeded with under the corresponding provisions of Part V of the 1968 Act.

5. Section 62 (2) of the 1962 Act (now repealed) provided that a Building Preservation Order could (*inter alia*) contain powers enabling the authority concerned, where contravening works had been carried out, to require restoration of the building to its former state, and for this purpose the order could apply with necessary modifications and adaptations the provisions of the 1962 Act relating to Enforcement Notices. The 1968 Act[6] enabled any such provisions

---

[1] Section 54 (11), as amended by the Local Government Act 1972 w.e.f. 1st April 1974.

[2] Date of commencement of Part V of the 1968 Act.

[3] *See ante*, p. 255.

[4] Date of commencement of Part V of the 1968 Act.

[5] *See ante*, p. 256, as to the necessity for such notice in normal cases.

[6] Section 107 and Schedule 10, para. 20.

in a Building Preservation Order to be enforced despite the repeals effected by that Act, and the relevant provisions maintaining this enforcement power are now contained in paragraph 40 of Schedule 24 of the 1971 Act.

URGENT WORKS FOR PRESERVATION OF UNOCCUPIED BUILDINGS

Under section 101 of the 1971 Act as substituted by the Town and Country Amenities Act 1974 a local authority[1] may carry out any works urgently necessary for the preservation of a listed building which is **unoccupied**. They must previously have given to the owner[2] not less than 7 days' notice in writing of the proposed execution of the works. This action cannot be taken in respect of an excepted building as defined in section 58 (2) (as to which *see ante*).

A notice must specify in detail the works considered to be urgently necessary and the purpose of the 7 days notice is to enable the owner, if he wishes to make representations or possibly offer to do the works himself. It appears that the "works" which may properly form the subject of a notice cannot include works which could involve the owner in a continuing liability e.g. maintenance of scaffolding erected to give structural support to a building.[3]

If it appears to the Secretary of State that in the case of a building which is **not** a listed building, but is situated in a conservation area, it is important to preserve that building for the purpose of maintaining the character or appearance of the conservation area, he may direct that section 101 shall apply to the building. If he does so, the local authority have the same powers in relation to it as those described in the preceding paragraph.

---

[1] For definition, *see* s. 290 (1).

[2] If the building is ecclesiastical property a notice must also be served on the Church Commissioners. *See* p. 118, *ante*.

[3] *See R. v. Secretary of State for the Environment ex. P. Hampshire County Council.* (1981) J.P.L. 47.

The Secretary of State has the same powers as the local authority.

The local authority or, as the case may be, the Secretary of State may give notice to the owner of the building requiring him to pay the expenses of any work executed under these powers.[1]

In that event the amount specified in the notice is recoverable[2] from the owner subject to the following provisions of subsections (7) to (9) of section 101:—

(1) Within 28 days of the date of the notice (as to expenses) the owner may represent to the Secretary of State—

(*a*) that the amount specified is unreasonable; or

(*b*) that recovery of it would cause him hardship; or

(*c*) that some or all of the works were unnecessary for the building's preservation.

(2) The Secretary of State must then determine the extent, if any, to which these representations are justified.

(3) He must then give the owner and the local authority notice of any determination under (2) and of the reasons for it and of the amount (if any) which is to be recoverable from the owner, and no sum is recoverable from him unless it is so notified.[3]

LOCAL PLANNING AUTHORITY AND CROWN LAND

As to listed buildings owned by local planning authorities or by the Crown, the position is as follows:—

---

[1] Section 101 (6).

[2] As a simple contract debt in a court of competent jurisdiction. Section 111, *i.e.* in the county court or the High Court.

[3] Section 101 (9).

Local Planning Authorities

The Act's provisions apply by virtue of section 271 as substituted by section 7 of the Town and Country Amenities Act 1974 and Part VI of Schedule 21, subject to any exceptions and modifications prescribed by regulations made by the Secretary of State. The effect of the Town and Country Planning (Listed Buildings and Buildings in Conservation Areas) Regulations 1977[1] is that applications which would in the ordinary way go to the local planning authority go to the Secretary of State, for determination, and the Secretary of State may serve any notice which a local planning authority could serve if the building were not one which they owned.

Crown Land

The provisions apply to Crown land[2] to the extent of any interest therein for the time being held otherwise than by or on behalf of the Crown, but no listed building enforcement notice can be issued in respect of works executed by or on behalf of the Crown in respect of a building which was Crown land at the time when the works were executed.[3] No listed building enforcement notice can be issued except with the consent of the appropriate authority.[4]

It may be noted that prior to the 1971 Act, the provisions noted on page 286, *ante*, as to the powers of local authorities to carry out urgent works for the preservation of unoccupied listed buildings did not apply at all to Crown land. These provisions were originally contained in section 6 of the Civic Amenities Act 1967, which Act contained nothing applying the section to such land. The provisions of section 266 of the 1971 Act are now such that Crown land **is** covered (to the extent mentioned in the preceding paragraph). This small amendment to remove an anomaly was made on the

---

[1] S.I. 1977, No. 228.
[2] *See ante*, p. 138, as to definition of Crown land.
[3] Section 266.
[4] As to "appropriate authority", *see* p. 139, *ante*.

recommendation of the Law Commission in their Report to the Lord Chancellor on the consolidating measure.[1]

[1] Cmnd. 4684.

CHAPTER 9

TREE PRESERVATION

TREE PRESERVATION ORDERS

Making of order

A local planning authority[1] are empowered by section 60 of the Act, in the interests of amenity to preserve individual trees, groups of trees or woodlands, in their area, by means of a "tree preservation order". The functions may be delegated. *See* page 47, *ante*.

A county planning authority may, however from 13 July 1981 only make an order if they do so pursuant to Section 59 (b) of the Act. (As to the provisions of this section see *post*, p. 292),[1] or in respect of land which does not lie wholly within the area of a single district planning authority, or in respect of land in which the county planning authority hold an interest, or in respect of land in a National Park.

Such an order may prohibit, subject to any exemptions specified in the order, "the cutting down, topping, lopping, uprooting, wilful damage[2] or wilful destruction of trees" except with the authority's consent and for enabling them to give such consent subject to conditions. There is a right of appeal against a refusal or against conditions [3].

---

[1] Both county and district planning authorities. Section 1 (2A) of the Town and Country Planning Act 1971 (inserted by the Local Government Act 1972) and s. 182 (5) of the Local Government Act 1972. As to the position in Greater London see Schedule 3 of the 1971 as amended by the Local Government Planning and Land Act, 1980.

[2] The words "uprooting" and "wilful damage" were inserted by s. 10 of the Town and Country Amenities Act 1974, operative from 1st September 1974, *ibid.*, s. 13 (3).

[3] See the prescribed form of Order S.I. 1969, No. 17 as amended by S.I. 1975, No. 148 and S.I. 1981, No. 14.

In *Regina v. Bournemouth Justices ex parte Bournemouth Corporation*[1] the Divisional Court refused to uphold a contention that the order-making power was restricted to the precise words within quotation marks and decided that a tree preservation order may prohibit not only **cutting, etc.**, of trees but also **causing or permitting** such cutting and other activites.

The meaning of "wilful destruction" has been the subject of a case in the High Court in *Barnet London Borough Council v. Eastern Electricity Board.*[2] The Council had made a Tree Preservation Order. The Board, in digging a trench had damaged and severed the roots of several of the trees the subject of the order. There was no evidence that the trees would necessarily die within a given period. The Board were prosecuted, and the magistrates' court dismissed the charges on the ground that the alleged damage could not amount to wilful destruction. On appeal by the Council it was held that such damage **could** amount to wilful destruction and the case was remitted to the magistrates to continue the hearing. "Wilful destruction" of a tree is the inflicting on it of so radical an injury that a reasonably competent forester would in consequence decide that it ought to be felled.

It was decided in *Bullock v. Secretary of State for the Environment*[3] that a tree preservation order may validly be made in respect of a coppice and that it was not objectionable for the Secretary of State (whose confirmation of the order was at that time necessary) to defer the question of felling for future in the hope that a practical scheme of management might in due course be agreed.

An order may require and prescribe the manner of replanting of any part of a woodland area felled in the course of permitted forestry operations.

It may, by virtue of section 174 of the 1971 Act, provide for compensation to be paid by the local planning authority,

---

[1] (1970) 114 S.J. 150, D.C.
[2] [1973] 2 All E.R. 319, D.C.
[3] [1980] J.P.L. 461.

subject to specified exceptions and conditions, for loss or damage caused by refusal of any consent the order requires, or by conditions imposed on a grant. Under section 175, where a direction is given for re-planting of a woodland area felled in the course of forestry operations permitted by or under the order the local planning authority are also liable to pay compensation, in certain circumstances.

An order may also include the "purchase notice" provisions of the Act, under which an owner may in certain circumstances require his land to be bought by the district council.[1]

Section 59 (a) of the Act imposes on local planning authorities a duty to ensure, wherever it is appropriate, that in granting a planning permission adequate provision is made, by the imposition of conditions, for preservation or planting of trees and also (Section 59 (b)) to make such tree preservation orders as appear to the authority to be necessary in connection with the permission (whether for giving effect to conditions imposed or otherwise). The section operates only in relation to planning permissions granted on or after 28th August 1967.[2] In relation to trees planted pursuant to any conditions so imposed a tree preservation order may be made in advance so as to apply to those trees as from the time when they are planted.[3]

There are restrictions on the making and effect of a tree preservation order in respect of any land which is subject to a forestry dedication covenant or in respect of which the Forestry Commissioners have made advances.[4]

Tree Preservation Orders normally take effect only when confirmed[5] but if it appears to the authority making the order that the order should take effect immediately they may include in the order a **direction** that the provisions of section 61 of the Act shall apply to it. An order containing such a

---

[1] *See* s. 60 (1) and (2) and s. 191, 1971 Act. *See also* pp. 237 to 239, *ante*.
[2] *See* s. 292 and Schedule 24 para. 25, of 1971 Act.
[3] Section 60 (3).
[4] *See* s. 60 (7) and (8) of the 1971 Act, and the Forestry Act 1967.
[5] As to confirmation see *post*, p. 294.

direction comes into effect provisionally on such date as is specified in the order and continues in force by virtue of section 61 for a period of six months **beginning with the date on which the order is made**, or until the order is confirmed.[1]

If in such a case the six months' period elapses without the order being confirmed it appears that, although the order ceases to operate, it does **not** become a nullity, but remains a valid order which may be confirmed subsequently and which will, upon such confirmation, again become effective. The 1962 Act contained provisions relating to Building Preservation Orders[2] which, though different in terms from those now under discussion, were in substance the same in relation to an order having provisional effect. These provisions had to be construed by the Divisional Court in *Cass v. Platford*,[3] when the Court decided that confirmation of an order by the appropriate Minister after the expiry of the period of its provisional operation was effective to bring it into operation again.

The form of Order has been prescribed.[4]

Notice of the making of the Order must be served on the owners and occupiers of land affected by the Order and on any other person known to the authority making the Order to be entitled to work by surface working any minerals in that land or to fell any of the trees affected by the Order, and they must be sent a copy of the Order. They must be told (*inter alia*) the grounds for making the Order, the method of making objections to it[5] and that if no objections or representations are duly made or any so made are withdrawn then not less than 42 days from the date of the service

---

[1] Section 61 (2).

[2] As to such Orders, *see* Chapter 8, *ante*.[3] *Cass v. Platford, Cass v. Charles Griffiths Ltd.* (1968) 20 P. & C.R. 58.

[3] *Cass v. Platford, Cass v. Charles Griffiths Ltd.* (1968) 20 P. & C.R. 58.

[4] Town and Country Planning (Tree Preservation Order) Regulations 1969 (S.I. 1969, No. 17), Reg. 4. These Regulations are effective from 10th February 1969 and replace earlier and similar provisions. They continue to have effect under the 1971 Act under s. 292 and Schedule 24 of that Act. The prescribed form was amended by the S.I. 1975, No. 148, with effect from 12th March 1975. The Regulations are further amended by S.I. 1981, No. 14.

[5] *See ibid.*, Reg. 7.

of the Notice the Order may be confirmed (but without any modification) as an Unopposed Order by the authority who made it instead of being confirmed by the Secretary of State. The power for the authority themselves to confirm an Unopposed Order is conferred by section 60 of the 1971 Act (re-enacting section 81 of the 1968 Act which was effective from the 10th February 1969 by virtue of the Town and Country Planning Act 1968 (Commencement No. 3) Order 1969[1]), and Regulation 6 of the Town and Country Planning (Tree Preservation Order) Regulations 1969.[2] Notice of the confirmation of an Order has to be given to owners and occupiers of the land to which the Order relates and to any persons served with notice of the making of the Order.

Where the Order contains a Direction under section 61 (*see* above) the Notice of the making of the Order must contain a statement of the effect of the Direction.[3]

Opposed tree preservation orders formerly required the confirmation of the Secretary of State but by an amendment of section 60 (4) effected by the Local Government Planning and Land Act 1980[4] this requirement no longer applies as from 13th January 1981. The local planning authority themselves may confirm the order either without modification or subject to such modifications as they consider expedient.

Exceptions may be specified in an order, but without prejudice to any such exceptions, no Order applies[5]:—

(*a*) to the cutting down, uprooting,[6] topping or lopping of trees which are dying or dead, or have become dangerous;

or (*b*) the cutting down, uprooting,[2] topping or lopping of any trees in compliance with any statutory requirements, *e.g.* a requirement by the highway authority under the Highways Act 1980,

---

[1] S.I. 1969, No. 16.
[2] S.I. 1969, No. 17.
[3] *Ibid.*, Reg. 5.
[4] Section 90 and Schedule 15, para. 13.
[5] Section 60 (6).
[6] The word "uprooting" was inserted by s. 10 of the Town and Country Amenities Act 1974, operative from 1st September 1974, *ibid.*, s. 13 (3).

or (*c*) any cutting down, topping or lopping of trees which may be necessary for the prevention or abatement of a nuisance.

Subject to certain conditions a licence to fell trees granted by the Forestry Commissioners under section 15 of the Forestry Act 1967, overrides the provisions of any Tree Preservation Order. Similarly any Ministerial consent under the Opencast Coal Act 1958, for the opencast working of coal overrides (subject to certain conditions) any Tree Preservation Order.

For default powers of the Minister, see *ante*, page 140.

Crown Land

By virtue of section 266 of the Act a Tree Preservation Order can be made in respect of Crown land so as to apply to the extent of any interest in the land held otherwise than by or on behalf of the Crown, provided that the consent of the appropriate authority[1] is first obtained.

Registration as Land Charge

A Tree Preservation Order is registrable as a Local Land Charge.[2]

Challenge of Order

In respect of an order made on or after 16th August 1959, if any person aggrieved by an order (or the authority concerned) wishes to question the validity of the order on the grounds that it is not within the powers of the Act, or that any of the relevant requirements have not been complied with in relation to it, he may within six weeks from the date of its confirmation apply to the High Court under section 245 of the Act. Apart from this, the validity of an order cannot be questioned in any legal proceedings whatsoever.[3]

A full statement of the provisions of section 245 is set out

---

[1] *See* p. 139, *ante*.

[2] *See* Local Land Charges Act 1975 and Local Land Charges Rules 1977, (S.I. No. 985).

[3] Section 242.

on page 195, *ante*. In relation to Tree Preservation Orders, the Court has, however, no power to make an interim order, but in finally determining the matter may quash or, where applicable, suspend the operation of the order, either in whole or in part.[1]

Enforcement

Prosecution

The penalties for contravention of a Tree Preservation Order are substantial, and there may be proceedings on indictment.

If any person, in contravention of a Tree Preservation Order, cuts down, uproots or wilfully destroys[2] a tree, or wilfully damages, tops or lops a tree in such a manner as to be likely to destroy it, he is guilty of an offence and liable on summary conviction to a fine of up to £1000, or twice the sum which appears to the court to be the value of the tree, whichever is the greater.[3]

On conviction on indictment he is liable to a fine of unlimited amount[1] and in determining the fine in such proceedings the court is expressly directed in particular to have regard to any financial benefit which has accrued or appears likely to accrue to him in consequence of the offence.[4]

Any person[5] who contravenes the provisions of an Order otherwise than as mentioned above is guilty of an offence[6] and liable on summary conviction to a fine of up to £200. In the case of a continuing offence, contravention after conviction results in liability to a further fine of £5 per day.[7]

It is an offence to contravene a tree preservation order

[1] *See* proviso to s. 245 (4) and (5).
[2] As to the meaning of this term, *see ante*, p. 291.
[3] Section 102 (1), as amended by the Town and Country Amenities Act 1974 and the Criminal Law Act, 1977.
[4] Section 102 (1) (*b*).
[5] As to offences by corporations, *see* p. 218, *ante*.
[6] Section 102 (2).
[7] Section 102 (3).

with or without knowledge of the existence of the order. It is an absolute offence.[1]

Injunction

Where trees are protected by a Tree Preservation Order but cutting down is commenced, the authority, if they learn of the infringement and can act in time, may be able to prevent further destruction of, or damage to, the protected trees by applying for an injunction. This was the situation in *A.-G. v. Melville Construction Co.*[2] where it was held that notwithstanding that no prosecution had been brought an injunction would be granted, since the threatened damage would be irremediable. For further observations concerning injunctions see *ante*, p. 223.[3]

REPLACEMENT OF TREES

In addition to the above, an offender against a Tree Preservation Order may be subject to a requirement to **replace** trees. This requirement, contained in section 62 of the Town and Country Planning Act 1971, was first contained in the Civic Amenities Act 1967 (section 13). The section was amended by the Town and Country Amenities Act 1974.

Section 62 applies to any tree in respect of which a Tree Preservation Order is for the time being in force **other than a tree to which the Order applies as part of a woodland**. It provides that if any such tree is removed, uprooted or destroyed in contravention of the order or is removed, uprooted or destroyed or dies at a time when its cutting down or uprooting is authorised only by section 60 (6) of the Act relating to trees which are dying or dead or have become dangerous (as to which *see ante*, page 294), it is the duty of the owner of the land (unless he applies to the local planning authority for, and they grant, a dispensation from the requirement), to plant another tree of an appropriate size and

---

[1] *Maidstone Borough Council v. Mortimer* [1980] 3 All E.R. 552, D.C.
[2] (1968) 118 New L.J. 814.
[3] Section 60 (1) (A) inserted by Local Government Planning and Land Act, 1980, Section 90 and Schedule 15, para. 13.

species at the same place, as soon as he reasonably can. The relevant Tree Preservation Order will apply to any tree so planted as it applied to the original tree.[1]

The duty described above attaches to the person who is from time to time the owner of the land.[2]

Enforcement

The duty may be enforced as provided by section 103 of the 1971 Act, and described below, **and not otherwise.**[2]

If it appears to the local planning authority that the provisions of section 62 of the Act described above, or any conditions of a consent given under a Tree Preservation Order which require the replacement of trees, are not complied with in the case of any tree or trees, the authority may serve on the owner[3] of the land anotice requiring him to plant within a period to be specified in the notice a tree or trees of such size and species as may be specified in the notice.[4]

Before serving a notice it should be considered whether the trees required are required in the interests of amenity, whether the planting would accord with the practice of good forestry and whether the place on which the trees are required to be planted is suitable for the purpose. Unless each of these questions can be answered affirmatively the notice is liable to be quashed on appeal.[5]

Such a notice must be served **within four years** from the date of the alleged failure to comply with the provisions of the Act or the conditions, as the case may be.[4]

As in the case of an enforcement notice the notice must specify two periods (*a*) a period (not less than 28 days after service of the notice) at the expiration of which it is to take effect and (*b*) a period for compliance.

---

[1] Section 62 (2).
[2] Section 62 (3).
[3] If the land is ecclesiastical property a notice must also be served on the Church Commissioners. *See ante*, p. 118.
[4] Section 103 (1).
[5] *See post*, p. 299.

In relation to these two periods, the same important considerations as those for enforcement notices have to be borne in mind.[1]

Appeal

Under section 103(3) of the Act any person on whom the notice is served may, within the period specified in the notice as that as the end of which it is to take effect, appeal against it to the Secretary of State.

An appeal may be on any of the following grounds:—

(*a*) that the provisions of section 62, or the conditions as the case may be, are not applicable or have been complied with;

(*b*) that the requirements of the notice are unreasonable in respect of the period or the size or species of trees specified therein;

(*c*) that the planting of a tree or trees in accordance with the notice is not required in the interests of amenity or would be contrary to the practice of good forestry;

(*d*) that the place on which the tree or trees is or are required to be planted is unsuitable for that purpose.

Section 103 (3A) inserted by the Local Government and Planning (Amendment) Act, 1981, provides that an appeal shall be made by notice in writing to the Secretary of State and sub-section (3B) similarly inserted, that the notice "shall indicate the grounds of the appeal and state the facts on which it is based". A hearing may be required by the appellant or the local planning authority and sub-sections (3D), (3E) and (3F) as to the following matters, contains provisions which are the same as those relating to enforcement notices.

---

[1] *See* pp. 115 and 116, *ante*.

1. Suspension of notice pending determination or withdrawal of appeal.[1]
2. Secretary of State's powers to correct errors (but **not** the power to disregard non-service of the notice on a particular person).[2]
3. Secretary of State's duty to give directions for giving effect to his determination of the appeal.[3]

Under Section 246(1A), inserted by the 1981 Act, a decision of the Secretary of State on an appeal against a notice under Section 103 may be challenged in the High Court by the appellant on whom the notice was served. Such a person may appeal to the High Court on a point of law or require a case to be stated (See *ante* p. 193 as to the effect of a provision in these terms).

Challenging a Notice

There is no provision limiting the right to challenge a notice requiring the replacement of trees, as there is in the case of an enforcement notice.[4] It is therefore open to a person served with such a notice to challenge it by an action in the High Court for a declaration that the notice is a nullity or is invalid. The grounds which might found a successful action in the case of an enforcement notice are discussed on pages 202 to 206, *ante*, but to such of these grounds as are relevant, it would seem that the following may be added:—

(1) That the provisions of section 62 of the Act or the conditions as the case may be are not applicable or have been complied with.

(2) That the notice was not served on the owner, or within the four year period specified in section 103 (1) of the Act.

Where the local planning authority have exercised the

---

[1] *See* p. 117, *ante*.
[2] *See* pp. 179 and 155, *ante*.
[3] *See* p. 169, *ante*.
[4] *See* p. 197, *ante*.

power themselves to carry out the requirements of the notice and are seeking to recover their expenses[1] the invalidity of the notice may be set up as a defence by the person being sued and the grounds of challenge suggested above in relation to an action for a declaration will apply. It will also be open to an occupier whose land has been entered upon by the authority in these circumstances to bring an action for damages for trespass and/or an injunction on the ground that the notice under which action was taken was invalid or a nullity.

Powers of Local Planning Authority in default

If the requirements of a notice under section 103 are not complied with the authority may carry out the work themselves and recover from the then owner the expenses incurred in so doing. The supplementary powers of the authority described on pages 213 and 214, *ante*, are the same as is the case in respect of enforcement notices.[2]

Expenses of compliance with notice

If an owner incurs expenses in complying with the requirements of a notice under section 103 or the authority have recovered expenses from him under the above provisions he may recover[3] these expenses from the person who in fact was responsible for the cutting down, destruction or removal of the original tree or trees. The position of persons from whom expenses are recoverable and who are agents or trustees is the same as is the case in respect of enforcement notices.

Owner prevented from compliance by another person

If the owner of premises to which a notice under section 103 applies wishes to comply with it but is prevented by some other person, *e.g.* a tenant, interested in the land, he may on complaint to a court of summary jurisdiction obtain

[1] *See below.*
[2] Section 103 (5).
[3] In the County Court or the High Court.

an Order of that Court requiring any other person interested in the land to permit the execution of the work in question.

The provisions in the last three paragraphs are operative by virtue of section 91 of the 1971 Act and Regulations[1] under it, as applied to notices under section 103 by section 103 (5).

Crown Land

As earlier noted, the provisions about replacement of trees originated in the Civic Amenities Act 1967 and when contained in that Act they did not relate to Crown land.[2] This was an anomalous situation, and in their Report to the Lord Chancellor on the consolidating measure of 1971[3] the Law Commission recommended that it be rectified. This has been done and the effect of section 266 (1) (*b*) of the 1971 Act is such that the provisions about replacement of trees, in common with various other enforcement provisions, apply to Crown land to the extent of any intent therein for the time being held otherwise than by or on behalf of the Crown.

TREES IN CONSERVATION AREAS

The Town and Country Amenities Act 1974 increased controls over trees by adding a new section, section 61A, to the Town and Country Planning Act 1971, dealing with trees in conservation areas. (As to such areas, *see ante*, page 280.)

The section applies generally to any tree in a conservation area, but in respect of which no tree preservation order is for the time being in force.[4] The Secretary of State may be regulations direct that the section is not to apply to specified cases.[5] The effect of the current regulations so made is noted *post*.

Subject to the defences listed below, any person who, in

---

[1] S.I. 1976, No. 1419.
[2] *See ante*, p. 138, as to definition of Crown land.
[3] Cmnd. 4684.
[4] As to tree preservation orders, *see ante*, p. 290.
[5] *See* ss. (4), (5) and (6).

relation to a tree to which section 61A applies, does any act which, under section 60 (1) (*a*) might be prohibited by a tree preservation order[1] is guilty of an offence.[2] The penalties are the same as for contravention of a tree preservation order.[3]

The following defences are available by section 61A (3), the onus of proof being on the defendant[4]—

(1) That the defendant served notice of his intention to do the act in question, with sufficient particulars to identify the tree, on the council of the district or London Borough in whose areas the tree is or was situated **and**

(*a*) that he did the act in question with the **consent** of the local planning authority in whose area the tree is or was situated

or

(*b*) that he did the act in question **after the expiry of six weeks** from the date of his notice **and before the expiry of two years** from that date.

The council of a district or a London Borough has a duty to compile and keep available for public inspection free of charge at all reasonable hours, and at a convenient place, a register of notices affecting trees in their area.[5]

Section 61A (8) provides for **replacement** of trees to which the section applies. If such a tree is removed, uprooted or destroyed, or dies, at a time when its cutting down or uprooting is authorised only by virtue of the provisions of regulations made by the Secretary of State exempting cases to which Tree Preservation Orders do not apply by section 60 (6)[6] it is the duty of the owner of the land, unless he

---

[1] *See ante*, p. 290.
[2] Section 61A (1).
[3] Section 102 (4).
[4] This will be on a preponderance of probability which is not as onerous a burden as in the case of proof "beyond reasonable doubt". *See R.* v. *Carr-Briant* [1943] K.B. 607; *R.* v. *Dunbar* [1958] 1 Q.B. 1.
[5] *See* s. 61A (7).
[6] These are cases (*a*), (*b*) and (*c*) set out *ante*, p. 294.

applies to the local planning authority for, and they grant, a dispensation from this requirement, to plant another tree of appropriate size and species at the same place as soon as he reasonably can. This duty may be enforced only as provided by section 103 of the Act (as to which *see ante*, page 298).

The current regulations made by the Secretary of State[1] contain provisions exempting from section 61A all the cases covered by section 60 (6). These are cases (*a*), (*b*), (*c*) listed *ante*, page 294.

The effect of section 61A (8) and the Regulations is that the provisions about replacement of trees in conservation areas is substantially the same as those about replacement of trees (other than trees forming part of a woodland) which are the subject of Tree Preservation Orders.

In those cases listed (*a*), (*b*) and (*c*), *ante*, page 294, an owner may cut down or remove a tree, but he must replace it.

In the following cases an owner of land in a conservation area on which a tree is situate is under no restriction as to dealing with the tree and under no duty to replace[2]:—

(1) the cutting down of a tree in the circumstances mentioned in paragraph (1) or (2), or the cutting down, uprooting, topping or lopping of a tree in the circumstances mentioned in paragraph (3), of the Second Schedule to the Form of Tree Preservation Order contained in the Schedule to the Town and Country Planning (Tree Preservation Order) Regulations 1969 (as amended)[3];

(2) the cutting down of a tree in accordance with a felling licence granted by the Forestry Commissioners;

---

[1] Town and Country Planning (Tree Preservation Order) (Amendment) and Trees in Conservation Areas (Exempted Cases) Regulations 1975 (S.I. 1975, No. 148).

[2] Section 61A (4), (5) and (6), and S.I. 1975, No. 148, *supra*, Reg. 3 (ii), (iii), (iv) and (v).

[3] S.I. 1969, No. 17. S.I. 1975, No. 148. S.I. 1981, No. 14.

(3) the cutting down, uprooting, topping or lopping of a tree on land in the occupation of a local planning authority and the act is done by or with the consent of that authority;

(4) the cutting down, uprooting, topping or lopping of a tree having a diameter not exceeding 75 millimetres, or the cutting down or uprooting of a tree having a diameter not exceeding 100 millimetres where the act is carried out to improve the growth of other trees, the reference to "diameter" being construed as a reference to the diameter, measured over the bark, at a point 1.5 metres above the ground level.

Among those cases falling under (1) is a tree the cutting down of which is immediately required for the purpose of carrying out development authorised by a specific planning permission, or a planning permission deemed to be granted. As to deemed permissions, *see ante*, page 44.

For offences under section 61A the penalties are the same as for contravention of a tree preservation order (as to which *see ante*, page 296).

CHAPTER 10

ADVERTISEMENTS

CONTROL OF ADVERTISEMENTS

Section 63 of the 1971 Act, re-enacting earlier provisions, provides for the making by the Secretary of State of regulations for restricting or regulating the display of advertisements so far as appears to him to be expedient in the interests of **amenity** or **public safety**. Such regulations may make different provisions for different areas.

Where the display of advertisements is in accordance with the regulations and involves development[1] of land planning permission is deemed to be granted by section 64 of the Act and no planning application is necessary.

The Town and Country Planning (Control of Advertisements) Regulations 1969,[2] which came into force on 1st January 1970,[3] replaced earlier Regulations made in 1960 and 1965, and substantially altered the earlier provisions. These 1969 Regulations were made by the Minister of Housing and Local Government under relevant sections of the Town and Country Planning Act 1962, now repealed by the Town and Country Planning Act 1971, but are saved by section 292 and Schedule 24 of that Act, and continue to have effect as if made under the 1971 Act. They contain a comprehensive set of rules concerning display of advertisements, on any land in England and Wales.

"Advertisement" is very widely defined by Regulation 2 to mean "any word, letter, model, sign, placard, board,

---

[1] *See* page 44, *ante*.

[2] S.I. 1969, No. 1532, as amended by S.I. 1972, No. 489, by S.I. 1974, No. 185 and by S.I. 1975, No. 898.

[3] Regulation 1.

notice, device or representation, whether illuminated or not, in the nature of and employed wholly or partly for the purposes of advertisement, announcement or direction (excluding any such thing employed wholly as a memorial or as a railway signal)", and without prejudice to the foregoing "includes any hoarding or similar structure used or adapted for use for the display of advertisements".

For the purpose of the regulations and hereafter, reference to a person displaying an advertisement is to be construed[1] as reference to the person who himself, or by his servant or agent, undertakes or maintains the display of such advertisement and is deemed to include:—

(1) the owner[2] and occupier[3] of the land on which the advertisement is displayed and

(2) any person to whose goods, trade, business or other concerns publicity is given by the advertisement.

In *John v. Reveille Newspapers Ltd.*[4] the Divisional Court refused to disturb a finding of magistrates that a billposter employed by a newspaper company to distribute advertisements at so much a hundred was **not** a servant or agent but an independent contractor.

The Regulations contain a wealth of detail and need to be referred to carefully, but their general effect is as follows:—

Exceptions

Regulation 3 provides for a number of exceptions to the otherwise universal application of the Regulations to the display of advertisements. These excepted advertisements are:—

(*a*) advertisements displayed on "enclosed land" and not readily visible from land outside the enclosure,

---

[1] Regulation 2. *See also* s. 109 (3).

[2] This expression has the same meaning as for the purposes of enforcement of planning control generally. Regulation 2. *See ante*, p. 119.

[3] This expression is not defined. *See ante*, p. 119.

[4] (1955) 5 P. & C.R. 95.

or from any part of the enclosure over which there is a public right of way or to which the public has a right of access. "Enclosed land" means[1] land wholly or for the most part enclosed within a hedge, fence, wall, or similar screen or structure, and is deemed to **include** railway stations and their yards and bus stations and their forecourts (whether or not in fact enclosed) but **not** to include a public park, public garden, or other land held for the use or enjoyment of the public or, except as above mentioned, enclosed railway land normally used for the carriage of passengers or goods by rail.

(*b*) advertisements displayed within a building,[2] **unless**[3] the advertisement is illuminated; is displayed in a building used principally for the display of advertisements; or is an advertisement any part of which is within one metre of an external door, window or other opening through which it is visible from outside the building. (The last exclusion enables control to be exercised over such things as "window stickers".) No advertisement is to be deemed to be displayed within a building unless there is access to the advertisement from inside the building.

(*c*) advertisements displayed on or in a vehicle ("vehicle" means[4] a vehicle "normally employed as a moving vehicle on any highway or railway, or a vessel normally employed as a moving vessel on any inland waterway" but does not[5] include any such vehicle or vessel during any period when it is used primarily for advertisement display.

(*d*) advertisements incorporated in, and forming part

---

[1] Regulations 3 (2) (*b*).

[2] An advertisement on the forecourt of a building is not "displayed within a building" within the meaning of this regulation. *Dominant Sites Ltd. v. Berkshire County Council* (1956) 6 P. & C.R. 10.

[3] *See* reg. 12.

[4] *See* reg. 3 (2).

[5] *See* reg. 3 (2).

of, the fabric of a building, other than a building used principally for advertisement display or a hoarding or similar structure. An advertisement is not to be deemed to form part of the fabric by reason only of being fixed to, or painted on, a building.[2]

(*e*) small unilluminated advertisements (not exceeding 0.1 square metre in area) relating to articles for sale, displayed on the goods themselves or the containers or dispensers from which they are sold. "Articles" includes a gas or liquid, *e.g.* petrol.

Advertisements existing on 1st August 1948

Advertisements existing on 1st August 1948 and sites[1] so existing may under Regulation 11 continue to be displayed or used without consent, but they are subject to the "discontinuance" procedure described later. Standard conditions set out in the First Schedule to the Regulations and other conditions and limitations set out in the proviso to Regulation 11 (3) apply.

Permitted advertisements

Certain advertisements are permitted by the Regulations themselves[2] but these too are subject to the discontinuance procedure, to the standard conditions in the First Schedule and the other conditions set out in the Regulations. (*See* in particular, Regulations 14 (2) and (4) and the provisions of Regulation 14 (3) as to definitions of various expressions. The limitations on size and number should also be carefully noted.)

Regulation 14 (2) (*a*) imposes on the deemed consent for advertisements of the classes specified in that Regulation a condition that no such advertisements (other than those in Class I) shall "contain letters, figures, symbols, emblems, or devices" of a height exceeding that specified. In *McDon-*

---

[1] "Site" is defined in Reg. 2 to mean any land, or any building other than an advertisement as above defined, on which an advertisement is displayed.

[2] *See* regs. 12 (2) and 14.

ald v. Howard Cook Advertising Ltd.[1] the Divisional Court had to consider the meaning of the words quoted. The defendants had displayed on certain public house walls advertisements for cigarettes and beer, two containing a picture of an open packet of cigarettes, and one a picture of a man holding up a glass of beer and another picture of a glass of beer and the words "Thirst prize". The cigarette packets, the figure of the man and the beer glass all exceeded the stipulated height, but the respondents, having been charged with contravening the Regulations had argued before the justices that the depicted objects did not fall within any of the categories to which the height limitation applied. This argument had been upheld and the charges dismissed. The prosecutor appealed. The Divisional Court dismissed the appeal, having concluded that the objects in question, which were obviously not "letters", were not "figures", which in the context meant numerical figures, and were not "symbols, emblems, or devices". In adopting this narrow construction the Court decided that, as a penal enactment, the Regulations should be strictly construed.

Advertisements conditionally permitted by the Regulations are as follows:—

(*a*) Election notices, statutory advertisements and traffic signs (Regulation 9).

(*b*) Advertisements of local planning authorities (Regulation 10).

(*c*) Certain advertisements within buildings (Regulation 12).

(*d*) Functional advertisements of local authorities, statutory undertakers and public transport undertakers (Regulation 14, Class I).

(*e*) Miscellaneous advertisements relating to premises on which they are displayed, *e.g.* professional nameplates; direction or warning signs; church, school, hospital, village hall, etc., notice boards (Regulation 14, Class II).

---

[1] [1971] 3 All E.R. 1249.

(*f*) Temporary advertisements, *e.g.* "For Sale" or "To Let" Boards; advertisements of sales of goods or livestock; builders' boards on land on which they are working; advertisements of local events, *e.g.* fetes, meetings, football matches; notices about demonstrations of agricultural methods or processes (Regulation 14, Class III).

(*g*) Advertisements on business premises[1] relating to the business carried on, the goods sold or services provided (Regulation 14, Class IV).

(*h*) Advertisements on the forecourts[1] of business premises relating to the same matters as in (*e*) above (Regulation 14, Class V).[1]

(*i*) Flag advertisements fixed to a flagstaff on a roof and displaying merely the name or emblem of the building's occupiers (Regulation 14, Class VI).

There is provision in Regulation 15 for a direction by the Secretary of State, on representations to him by the local planning authority or otherwise, that the display of advertisements of any of the classes specified in Regulation 14 shall not be undertaken in any particular area or in any particular case without express consent. Where this power is exercised in respect of an area public notice has to be given. In respect of a particular case notice has to be served by the local planning authority on the owner and occupier of the land concerned and on any other person who, to the authority's knowledge, proposes to display on the land advertisements of the specified class in question. A direction in respect of an area must specify a date when it comes into force, which must not be less than 14 nor more than 28 days after the first publication of the notice. A direction in respect of a particular case comes into force on the date on which notice is served on the occupier, or, if none, on the owner.

---

[1] As to the forecourts of petrol filling stations, *see Heron Service Stations v. Coupe* [1973] 2 All E.R. 110, H.L.

Discontinuance Notice

Regulation 16 sets out the procedure under which, subject to its terms, a local planning authority[1] may, if they think it expedient in the interest of amenity or public safety, require the discontinuance of display of an advertisement in respect of which consent is deemed to be granted under the regulations (other than election notices, statutory advertisements and traffic signs). In relation to advertisements displayed pursuant to Regulation 14 (*see* page 309) they must not use this procedure unless satisfied that it is required to remedy a **substantial** injury to amenity or danger to the public.

A discontinuance notice must be served[2] on the advertiser,[3] and on the owner and occupier of the land on which the advertisement is displayed and *may*, if the authority think fit also be served on any other person displaying the advertisement.

It must specify the advertisement to which it relates, and contain a full statement of the **reasons why** the authority consider it expedient in the interests of amenity and public safety that the display should be discontinued.

It must specify two periods (*a*) a period at the end of which it is to take effect (this cannot be less than one month[4] after service) and (*b*) a period within which the display is to be discontinued.

If there is an appeal to the Secretary of State as there may be under Regulation 22, the notice has no effect pending final determination or withdrawal of the appeal (*see* below as to extension of the period for appeal).

---

[1] This term means in respect of each London Borough the London Borough Council, in the City of London the Common Council, in an area outside Greater London and not in a National Park the district planning authority and in an area in a National Park the county planning authority. *See* S.I. 1969. No. 1532, Reg. 2, as amended by S.I. 1974, No. 185. *See also* Local Government Act 1972, Schedule 16, para. 25 (1), the 1971 Act, Schedule 3, and the Local Government Act 1972, s. 182 (4), (5) and (6) and Schedule 17.

[2] *See* p. 121, *ante*.

[3] *See* p. 307, *ante*.

[4] This will be a calendar month. *See* the Interpretation Act 1978, and Reg. 2 (4).

A discontinuance notice may be withdrawn by notice served on the advertiser[1] at any time before it takes effect. A copy of any withdrawal notice must be sent to every person served with the discontinuance notice.

Provided no appeal to the Secretary of State has been lodged and is pending, the local planning authority may also from time to time **vary** a discontinuance notice by extending the period within which it is to take effect and this extends the period during which an appeal may be lodged by the number of days by which the first mentioned period is extended. There may be a second or further extension in the same circumstances.

It would seem, however, that once a notice has taken effect the power cannot then be exercised.[2]

A copy of any notice varying a discontinuance notice as described above must be served[2] on the advertiser[3] and a copy sent to every other person served with the discontinuance notice.

All the above provisions relating to a discontinuance notice in respect of the display of an advertisement apply also to use of land for such display.[4]

Under Regulation 22 a person served with a discontinuance notice may appeal to the Secretary of State as if he had applied for consent to display the advertisement (or use the site) and the local planning authority had refused to give it. In determining any such appeal the Secretary of State must give directions for giving effect to his determination including, where appropriate directions for quashing the discontinuance notice or varying it in favour of the appellant.

Other advertisements

In respect of the display of all advertisements not excepted by Regulation 3 or included in one of the categories

---

[1] See *ante*, p. 307.
[2] *See* p. 115, *ante*.
[3] *See* p. 121, *ante*.
[4] *See* reg. 16 (7).

above, the consent of the local planning authority (or the Secretary of State on appeal) must be obtained. The local planning authority may delegate this power. Application has to be made on a form obtainable from the authority and the authority has power to grant or refuse consent.[1] Their powers are exercisable only in the interests of amenity and public safety.[2] They are expressly directed by Regulation 5 to have regard to certain particular matters in this respect.

They must, in the interests of amenity, determine the suitability of a site in the light of the general characteristics of the locality, including the possible presence of features of historic, architectural, cultural or similar interest, and when assessing general characteristics of a locality may disregard any advertisements then being displayed. In the interests of public safety they must have regard to the safety of people who may use any road, railway, waterway (including coastal waters), dock, harbour, or airfield affected or likely to be affected by advertisement display and in particular must consider whether the display of advertisements is likely to obscure, or hinder the ready interpretation of, any road traffic sign, railway signal or aid to navigation by water or air.

Consent may be granted subject to Part I of the standard conditions before referred to (which in fact apply to all advertisements) and to such additional conditions (if any) as the local planning authority think fit. If an application relates to a display in accordance with any provisions of Regulation 14 (*ante*) they must not refuse consent or impose a condition more restrictive in effect than any provision of that Regulation in relation to advertisements of that class unless such refusal or condition is required to prevent or remedy a **substantial** injury to the amenity of the locality or a danger (not necessarily a substantial danger) to members of the public.[3] Consent must be for a fixed period, which

---

[1] A fee is payable. See the Town and Country Planning (Fees for Applications and term Applications) Regulations 1981, S.I. 1981, No. 369, effective 1st April 1981 as amended by s.1. 1982. No 716 effective 1 June 1982.

[2] Regulation 5.

[3] *See* proviso to Reg. 19.

cannot, without the consent of the Secretary of State, be longer than five years. It cannot be shorter than five years unless so required by the application or considered expedient by the authority in the light of the provisions of Regulation 5. In the latter circumstance the authority must give their reasons in writing and the time limitation is to be regarded as a condition[1] (and therefore can be appealed against). If no period is specified a consent has effect for 5 years. (Temporary consent may be given under Regulation 23 for display on unspecified sites in the area of a local planning authority of posters of travelling fairs, circuses and similar entertainments and in such cases the standard conditions in Parts I and II of the First Schedule and other conditions in the Regulation apply.)

Consents may be renewed on application within six months before the expiry date, but Regulation 13 provides that in the absence of anything to the contrary in the consent, or refusal of a renewal application, an advertisement may continue to be lawfully displayed after the expiry of the period of consent granted, subject to the conditions imposed on the consent. In this event it is, however, subject to the "discontinuance" procedure.

Except in the case of certain statutory advertisements it is a condition of every consent given by or under the Regulations (whether expressly imposed or not) that before any advertisement is displayed on land, the permission of the owner of the land, or other person entitled to grant such a consent (*e.g.* a lessee) must be obtained.[2]

There is provision for appeal to the Secretary of State against refusal of consent or against conditions attached to a consent. His decision is final.

---

[1] *See* reg. 20 (2).
[2] Regulation 6 (4).

Areas of special control

By Regulation 26 every local planning authority[1] must from time to time consider whether any part of their area, or any additional part, should be defined as an area of special control. There must be reviews every five years. Section 63 (3) of the 1971 Act as substituted by the Town and Country Amenities Act 1974, section 3, provides that Regulations may make special provisions with regard to conservation areas (as to conservation areas, *see ante*, page 280).

In areas of special control the further restrictions upon advertisement display detailed in Regulation 27 will apply.

Briefly, this does not affect the display of advertisements of the classes specified in Regulations 9, 12, 14 and 23 as described earlier, but it limits[2] the power of the local planning authority to permit advertisements, to those advertisements specified in Regulation 27 (2).

The effect of the coming into force of an order defining and area of special control over advertisements **then being displayed in accordance with the regulations** is as follows:—

(1) Advertisements specified in Regulations 9 (Election notices, statutory advertisements and traffic signs), 12 (certain advertisements within buildings) and 23 (advertisements relating to travelling circuses and fairs) may continue to be displayed in accordance with the provisions of those regulations respectively.

(2) Advertisements of the classes specified in Regulation 14 and advertisements which would fall into

---

[1] In this case the term "local planning authority" means the district planning authority only. See Local Government Planning and Land Act 1980 section 90 and schedule 15, para. 15 amending earlier provisions of the Local Government Act 1972 under which county planning authorities also had this power. The order making power of a county planning authority remains in respect of land in a national park. See section 182 (4) of the Local Government Act 1972. There is no change in the provisions for Greater London.

[2] *See* reg. 27 (3).

one of those classes but for non-compliance with a condition or limitation as respects size, height from the ground, number or illumination imposed by Regulation 14 and for which the local planning authority has granted express consent, may continue to be displayed **with or without express consent** subject, after the term of any express consent has expired, to the discontinuance procedure described earlier.

(3) Any other advertisement may continue to be displayed for six months from the date the special control order comes into force, or for the remainder of the term of any express consent, whichever is the longer, and then for a further two months within which it must (without further notice) be removed unless express consent is granted for its continued display in accordance with Regulation 27.

If, however, a discontinuance notice[1] has been served before the coming into force of the special control order, or a particular advertisement is the subject of an express consent which contains a condition requiring the advertisement to be removed, neither the notice nor the condition is affected by the above provisions, which are in either case overridden.[2]

Compensation

Where, for the purpose of complying with the Regulations, a person carries out works for removing an advertisement which was being displayed on 1st August 1948 or for discontinuing the use for advertisement display of a site used for that purpose on that date he is entitled to compensation for expenses reasonably so incurred.[3]

---

[1] As to such notices, *see* p. 312, *ante*.
[2] *See* reg. 27 (5) (*a*) and (*b*).
[3] *See* s. 176, 1971 Act (re-enacting s. 126 of the 1962 Act) and reg. 30.

ENFORCEMENT

Section 109 of the 1971 Act enables Regulations as to advertisement control to apply any of the provisions of the Act respecting enforcement notices, but the current Regulations of 1969 do not do so. There is, therefore, no power to serve an enforcement notice and the local planning authority's remedy on a breach of the Regulations is to prosecute under the following provisions.

Any person who displays an advertisement in contravention **of the regulations** is guilty of an offence under section 109 (2) of the 1971 Act and liable on summary conviction to a fine of such amount as may be prescribed by the regulations, not exceeding £200. On further conviction in respect of a continuing offence a fine of up to £20 a day may be imposed.

The 1969 Regulations prescribe a maximum fine of £100, and in the case of a continuing offence £5 for each day during which the offence continues after conviction.

These maxima were increased by an amendment made by the Local Government and Planning (Amendment) Act 1981 but the Regulations have not to date been amended.

In *Royal Borough of Kensington Chelsea v. Elmton*[1] the Divisional Court considered a case where, after conviction for display of an advertisement board without planning consent, the advertisement was taken down but replaced a week after an appeal against conviction had failed. The council brought a charge of a continuing offence which magistrates had dismissed. The council appealed, but the Divisional Court dismissed such appeal holding that this was a fresh offence and not a continuing one and a new information should have been issued. The Court took the view that it would be an abuse of language to regard the replacement in those circumstances as a continuing offence.

A person who is liable as an owner or occupier, or because the advertisement gives publicity to his goods, etc.,[2] is not

---

[1] (1978) 246 E.G. 1011, D.C.
[2] *See* p. 307, *ante*.

guilty of an offence if he proves[1] that the display was without his knowledge or consent.[2]

Failure to observe any condition relating to the maintenance of an advertisement or a site being used for display, or to the satisfactory removal of an advertisement, does not render such a person guilty of an offence unless he has failed to comply with a notice served on him by the local planning authority under Regulation 8 requiring such compliance within a period (not less than 28 days from service) specified in that notice.

[1] This will be on a preponderance of probability, which is not as onerous a burden as in the case of proof "beyond reasonable doubt". *See R. v. Carr-Briant* [1943] K.B. 607. *R. v. Dunbar* [1958] 1 Q.B. 1.

[2] Section 109.

CHAPTER 11

CONDITION OF WASTE LAND

REQUIREMENT OF PROPER MAINTENANCE

Section 65 of the Act contains provisions enabling a district planning authority or a London Borough Council[1] to deal with any **garden, vacant site or other open land** in their area the condition of which is such that it seriously injures the amenities[2] of any part of their area or any adjoining area. If it appears to them that such is the case they may,[1] serve on the owner and occupier of the land a notice requiring steps to be taken to abate the injury. These steps must be specified in the notice and the period within which they are to be taken must also be specified.[3]

For default powers of the Minister, *see* page 141, *ante*.

Such a notice may be served at any time and takes effect (subject to suspension on appeal)[4] at the end of the period (not being less than 28 days after service) specified in the notice as being that at the expiration of which it is to take effect.[5]

In *Stephens v. Cuckfield R.D.C.*[6] the Divisional Court held that on the true construction of the words "garden, vacant site, or other open land" land within the curtilage of a building was excluded. On appeal, although the decision

[1] Section 65 as amended by the Local Government, Planning and Land Act, 1980 Section 90 and Schedule 15, para. 16.

[2] "Amenity" "appears to mean pleasant circumstances, features, advantages", *per* Scrutton, L.J., in *Re Ellis and Ruislip Northwood Urban District Council* [1920] 1 K.B. 343.

[3] Section 65 (1).

[4] *See post*, p. 322.

[5] *See ante*, p. 116, as to this period in relation to enforcement notices. The same considerations will apply.

[6] [1960] 2 Q.B. 373.

was affirmed, the Court of Appeal decided that whether a piece of land fell properly into either of these categories was a question to be determined with regard to the particular circumstances of each case and that a rule of construction should not be laid down to define "open land" so as necessarily to include all unbuilt on land not surrounded by other buildings, or on the other hand, necessarily to exclude, *e.g.* an area of parkland surrounding a mansion house merely because by being enclosed within a fence it might be described as being part of the curtilage.

In *Britt v. Buckinghamshire County Council*[1] the Court of Appeal decided on the basis of similar provisions contained in the 1947 Act and regulations made under it that the power to serve such a notice as is described above extends to requiring the abatement of an **active use** or a condition brought about by that use, as well as a condition not so attributable, and that, unless planning permission had been granted, a notice may be served notwithstanding that the use is outside the control of other provisions of the Act. This decision is a valuable aid to local planning authorities much troubled by activities such as car breaking in rural areas (which, in fact, was the use which gave rise to the condition complained of in that case), and it would seem that in a proper case action can be taken under the provisions now under discussion where ordinary enforcement action for contravening development is impossible because the use began before the end of 1963.[2]

The relevant provisions of the 1971 Act and the 1962 Act which it re-enacts are in fact different from those of the 1947 Act with which the Court was concerned in this case. In the 1947 Act it was a ground of appeal that the condition of the land to which the notice related was attributable to, and such as resulted from, the carrying on of operations or a use of land for which planning permission **had been granted or was not required**, whereas (as set out hereafter) in the 1962 and 1971 Acts the relevant provision refers to operations or use **not in contravention of Part III of the Act.**

[1] [1963] 2 W.L.R. 722.
[2] *See ante*, p. 130, as to the significance of this date.

Because of this it is sometimes suggested that service of a section 65 Notice is not possible on the basis of the *Britt case* where immunity from enforcement action has been acquired by long established user (in cases before the 1968 Act by the lapse of four years and in cases after it, where the development was begun after the end of 1963).[1] It is submitted, however, that such a notice **can** be served in these circumstances. It is true that in such cases the planning authority is prevented from serving an **enforcement notice** but a use immune from an enforcement notice is still a use **in contravention of Part III**, for it neither has express nor deemed permission. At best it is a user by limitation. Section 65 is contained in Part IV of the 1971 Act (and in the 1962 Act in Part III), whereas enforcement notices were dealt with in Part IV of the 1962 Act and now are dealt with in Part V of the 1971 Act. The provisions are quite separate and distinct and there appears to be no reason why the limitation which Parliament has expressly imposed for exercise of the powers of serving an enforcement notice under Part V of the 1971 Act (or Part IV of the 1962 Act) should have any effect on the exercise of powers under section 65.[1]

Challenge of Notice

A person on whom a notice is served, or any other person having an interest in the land to which it relates may, within the period specified in the notice as the period at the end of which it takes effect, appeal to a magistrates' court for the petty sessions area in which the land is situate.[2] If he does so the notice is of no effect pending the final determination or withdrawal of the appeal.[3]

By section 110 (2), the person appealing and all others are precluded in any other proceedings instituted after the appeal from claiming that the notice was not duly served on the person appealing.

---

[1] This view appears to be strengthened by the decision in *L.T.S.S. Print and Supply Services v. Hackney London Borough Council*, noted at p. 43, *ante*.
[2] Section 105 (2).
[3] Section 105 (3).

Grounds of appeal

The appeal may be made on any of the following grounds[1]:—

(*a*) That the condition of the land to which the notice relates does not seriously injure the amenity of any part of the area of the local planning authority who served the notice, or of any adjoining area.

(*b*) That the condition of the land to which the notice relates is attributable to, and such as results in the ordinary course of events from, the carrying on of operations or a use of land which is not in contravention of Part III of the Act (which relates to the control of development).[2]

(*c*) That the land to which the notice relates does not constitute a garden, vacant site or other open land in the area of the local planning authority who served the notice.

(*d*) That the requirements of the notice exceed what is necessary for preventing the condition of the land from seriously injuring the amenity of any part of the area of the local planning authority who served the notice, or of any adjoining area.

(*e*) That the period specified in the notice as the period within which any steps required by the notice are to be taken falls short of what should reasonably be allowed.

Powers of Magistrates

On an appeal the magistrates' court may correct any informality,[3] defect or error in the notice if satisfied that the informality, defect or error is not a material one.[4]

On determining an appeal the magistrates must give di-

[1] Section 105 (1).
[2] *See ante*.
[3] *See* p. 179, *ante*.
[4] Section 105 (4).

rections for giving effect to their determination, including where appropriate directions for quashing the notice or varying its terms in favour of the appellant.[1]

Further Appeal

The appellant and the authority who served the notice have a right of appeal from the magistrates to the Crown Court,[2] and the usual right of appeal on a point of law by case stated to the High Court will apply.

Restriction on further challenge

Section 243 (3) of the Act provides that the validity of a notice under section 65 **which has been served on the owner and occupier** of the land shall not be questioned[3] in any proceedings whatsoever on grounds (*a*) to (*c*) above except by way of appeal to the magistrates. This provision does not, however, apply in the case of a prosecution brought against a person who had an interest in the land since before the notice was served on the owner and occupier of the land, but who was not served with a notice and who did not appeal to the magistrates against it.

The discussion in Chapter 4 as to the possibility of challenging a notice on grounds other than those specified above would appear to be relevant.

Registration as Land Charge

A Notice as to maintenance of waste land is registrable as a Local Land Charge.[4]

Enforcement

The local planning authority have two means of enforcement:—

(*a*) prosecution;

---

[1] *See* p. 169, *ante*.

[2] Section 106 and Local Government Act 1972, Schedule 16, para. 30.

[3] *See* pp. 197 to 201, *ante*, as to challenging validity of enforcement notice. Similar considerations will apply.

[4] Local Land Charges Act, 1975 and Local Land Charges Rules 1977 (S.I. 1977, No. 985).

(*b*) execution of work themselves.

Prosecution

Prosecution of an offender was originally provided for in Section 104 (2) of the 1971 Act which provided that if after the expiry of the specified period for abatement of the injury to amenity **any person** did anything which had the effect of continuing or aggravating the injury caused by the condition of the land he was guilty of an offence. In *Red House Farms (Thorndon) Ltd v. Mid Suffolk District Council*[1] the Divisional Court held that it was not an offence under that section as originally enacted merely to do **nothing** on response to a notice. Some positive act was required which either "continued" or "aggravated" the injury already caused by the condition of the land. The section has now been amended by the Local Government and Planning (Amendment) Act, 1981[2] in two respects. Firstly liability to prosecution now falls on any owner or occupier who fails to take steps required by the notice and secondly it is no longer necessary for there to be some positive act to continue and aggravate the injury to amenity for there to be an offence.

The amended section now provides for a maximum penalty on summary conviction of £200 (formerly £50). It also provides for an owner or occupier who is prosecuted to defend by showing that it is not he, but a subsequent owner or occupier who is responsible. The machinery is the same as for an enforcement notice.[3] In the case of an occupier, where he has ceased to be the occupier at some time before the end of the period allowed for compliance and nobody then became the occupier (*i.e.* there was no subsequent occupier) he may have brought before the court under the "third party" procedure described *ante*, p. 217 the person who was the owner of the land at the date of the notice.

If after conviction a person does not as soon as practicable do everything in his power to secure compliance with the notice he is guilty of a further offence and liable on summary

---

[1] (1980) 40 P. & C.R. 119.

[2] Section 1 and the Schedule para. 13.

[3] *Ibid.*, sub-para. (7).

conviction to a fine of up to £20 for each day following his first conviction on which any of the requirements of the notice remain unfulfilled.[1]

Execution of work by authority

In default of compliance within the specified period or such extended period as the local planning authority may allow the local planning authority may take the specified steps themselves and have the same power to recover their expenses from the then owner, as they have in relation to certain enforcement notices. The owner and occupier have a right of recovery of expenses in the same manner as in respect of these enforcement notices, exercisable against the person who caused or permitted the land to come to be in the condition in which it was when the notice was served.

[1] Section 107

Appendix

LIST OF FORMS AND RECORDS
relating to
Town and Country Planning

LIST OF FORMS AND RECORDS
relating to
TOWN AND COUNTRY PLANNING
published by Shaw & Sons Ltd.

Cat. No.	Description	Reference to Act
	TOWN AND COUNTRY PLANNING ACT 1971	
	PART III	
	GENERAL PLANNING CONTROL	
	APPLICATIONS FOR PLANNING PERMISSION	
TCP 1	Application for permission to develop land, etc.—Model form contained in DOE Circular 23/72.	s. 25
TCP 2	Additional information required in respect of application for industrial, office, warehousing, storage or shops.	
TCP 3	Notes for Applicants, incorporating information regarding Community Land Act 1975 as recommended in DOE Circular 23/76.	
TCP 16	Acknowledgement of Receipt of Application for permission to develop land.	
	OUTLINE APPLICATIONS FOR PERMISSION TO ERECT BUILDING	
TCP 72	Outline Application for Permission for Erection of a building.	
TCP 76	Notice to Applicant that Authority is unable to entertain Outline Application without further information.	
TCP 74	Grant of Permission subject to subsequent approval of matters relating to siting, etc.	
TCP 75	Refusal of Permission on Outline Application.	

Publication of Notices of Applications

TCP 89	Notice under Section 26 (2).	s. 26
TCP 109	Notes for Applicants as to certificate required under Section 26 (2) incorporating Certificates A, B and C.	
TCP 88	Notice under Section 26 (3).	
TCP 90	Notes for Applicants as to certificate required under Section 27 incorporating Certificates A, B, C and D.	s. 27
TCP 95	Notice under Section 27 of application for planning permission (for service on individuals).	

Determination of Applications

TCP 19	Grant of Permission for Development.	s. 29
TCP 22	Refusal of Permission for Development.	

Registers of Applications and Decisions

TCP 25	Shaway Vertical Filer, printed to form Part I of the register of Applications for Planning Permission.	s. 34
TCP 24	Register of applications for Planning Permission and Decisions thereon. Columnar Form. Loose Leaf Sheets, size 13 × 22½ or half bound book.	
TCP 18H	Do. Alternative pattern. Half bound book.	
TCP 24A	Do. Arranged to use a separate page for each application. Loose Leaf Sheets, size 8⅜ × 14.	
TCP 18AH	Do. Alternative pattern. Loose Leaf Sheets, size 11¼ × 9¼.	

Revocation or Modification of Planning Permission

TCP 69	Revocation Order.	s. 45
TCP 70	Modification Order.	
TCP 71	Notice to Owner, etc., that Order has been made and submitted to Secretary of State for confirmation.	s. 45 (3)
TCP 108	Notice under s. 46 (3) of making of Revocation or Modification Order.	s. 46 (3)

Applications to Determine whether Permission Required

TCP 26	Application to determine whether Planning Permission is required.	s. 53
TCP 16	Acknowledgement of Receipt of application for determination.	
TCP 27	Notice of Determination.	
TCP 148	Register of applications for determination under s. 53.	

Part IV

ADDITIONAL CONTROL IN SPECIAL CASES

Buildings of Architectural or Historic Interest

TCP 121	Notice by Council that a building has become listed.	s. 54
TCP 122	Notice by Council that a building has ceased to be listed.	
TCP 123	Application for listed building consent, incorporating Certificates under Schedule 11, para. 2.	s. 55
TCP 124	Acknowledgement of receipt of application.	
TCP 125	Notification to specified body, and local amenity society, of application to demolish listed building.	
TCP 126	Notice to applicant of decision on application for listed building consent.	
TCP 129	Building preservation notice.	s. 58

Trees

TCP 38	Tree Preservation Order.	s. 60
TCP 142	Notice of making of T.P.O. for service on owner, etc.	
TCP 143	Do. do. for service on Conservator of Forests and D.V.	
TCP 145	Notice of Confirmation by Council of Tree Preservation Order.	
TCP 59	Register of Tree Preservation Orders. Loose Leaf Sheets, sixe $8^3/_8 \times 14$, or half bound book.	
TCP 81	Application for Consent to cut down, lop, top, etc.	

TCP 146	Consent to cut down, lop, top, etc.	
TCP 147	Refusal of Consent to cut down, lop, top, etc.	
TCP 77H	Register of Applications for consent. Loose Leaf Sheets size $11^1/_4 \times 9^1/_4$.	
TCP 78	Register of Notices of Intended Works on Trees in Conservation Areas. Loose Leaf Sheets, size $13 \times 22^1/_2$.	s. 61A

Advertisements

TCP 42	Application for consent to display advertisements.	s. 63
TCP 43	Acknowledgement of Receipt of Application for consent to display advertisements.	
TCP 46	Consent to Display of Advertisement.	
TCP 47	Refusal of Consent to Display of Advertisement.	
TCP 152	Application for temporary display of advertisements for travelling entertainment.	
TCP 153	Consent for temporary display of advertisements for travelling entertainment.	
TCP 53	Register of Applications for consent to display advertisement and decisions thereon—columnar form. Loose Leaf Sheets, size $13 \times 22^1/_2$, or half bound book.	

Waste Land

TCP 68	Notice to Owner requiring proper maintenance of Waste Land, etc.	s. 65

Part V

ENFORCEMENT OF CONTROL UNDER PARTS III AND IV

Enforcement Notices

TCP 107	Enforcement Notice—breach of Planning Conditions to which the four-year Rule applies (Operational Development or Preventing Change of Use to Single Dwellinghouse)	s. 87
TCP 104	Do. —breach of Planning Condition to which the four-year Rule does not apply.	
TCP 105	Do. —material change of use.	
TCP 106	Dp. —Operational Development.	

TCP 200	Letter to accompany copy Enforcement Notice.	

Stop Notices

TCP 137	Stop Notice.	s. 90
TCP 160	Register of Enforcement and Stop Notices. Loose Leaf Sheets, size 13 × $16^1/_2$.	s. 92 A

Certification of Established Use

TCP 136	Application for established use certificate.	s. 94 Sch. 14
TCP 131	Notes for applicants as to certificate required under Article 18 (2) in relation to application for established use certificate, incorporating Certificates A, B, C and D.	
TCP 154	Notice under Article 18 of application for established use certificate (for service on individuals).	
TCP 132	Notification to applicant on receipt of application for established use certificate.	
TCP 134	Established Use Certificate.	
TCP 135	Notice of refusal of Established Use Certificate.	

Listed Buildings

TCP 127	Listed Building enforcement notice—unauthorised works.	s. 96
TCP 128	Do. do. failure to comply with conditions of consent.	

Advertisements

TCP 149	Informal notice to comply with condition prior to taking legal proceedings.	s. 109
TCP 150	Statutory Notice to comply with condition, where person is deemed to display advertisement by virtue of s. 109 (3).	
TCP 151	Notice to discontinue display with deemed consent.	

Part VI

ACQUISITION AND APPROPRIATION OF LAND

The Compulsory Purchase of Land Regulations 1982

CP 1	Compulsory purchase order (Form 1).	s. 112
CP 11	Compulsory purchase order providing for the vesting of exchange land (Form 2).	
CP 2	Newspaper notice concerning a compulsory purchase order (Form 3).	
CP 3	Notice to owners, lessees and occupiers of land comprised in a compulsory purchase order (Form 4).	
CP 3x	Do. do. incorporating additional provisions with respect to listed buildings.	
CP 5	Notice of confirmation of a compulsory purchase order (Form 6).	
CP 10	Newspaper notice of the giving of a certificate under Part III of Schedule 1 to the Acquisition of Land Act 1981 (Form 7).	
TCP 113	Statement concerning general vesting declaration, with form for giving information attached (Form 9).	
TCP 110	General Vesting Declaration (Form 8).	
TCP 111	Notice stating effect of General Vesting Declaration (Form 10).	
AL9	Notice to Treat.	
AL 10	Claim for Compensation by Owner, Mortgagee, Lessee or Occupier.	
TCP 112	Claim for Compensation arising from the making of General Vesting Declaration.	
AL 11	Notice of Entry.	
TCP 130	Repairs notice preliminary to compulsory acquisition of listed building.	s. 115

Part VIII

PROVISIONS ENABLING OWNER TO REQUIRE PURCHASE OF HIS INTEREST

Interests Affected by Planning Decisions or Orders

TCP 66	Purchase Notice.	s. 180
TCP 99	Notice accepting a Purchase Notice.	s. 181 (1) (*a*), (*b*) s. 181 (1) (*c*)
TCP 67	Statement of information to accompany Purchase Notice transmitted to Secretary of State.	s. 181 (1) (*c*)

Interests of Oowner-Occupiers Affected by Planning Proposals

TCP 97	Blight Notice.	s. 193 (1)
TCP 97A	Mortgagee's Blight Notice.	s. 201 (1)
TCP 98	Counter-notice objecting to blight notice.	s. 194 (1)

Part X

HIGHWAYS

Stopping-up or Diversion of Highways

TCP 138	Public Path Stopping-up or Diversion Order.	s. 209
TCP 139	Public Path Extinguishment Order.	s. 214
TCP 140	Notice of Public Path Order, with tear-off slip for return.	
TCP 141	Notice of Confirmation of Public Path Order.	

Part XV

MISCELLANEOUS AND SUPPLEMENTARY PROVISIONS

CONSERVATION AREAS

TCP 155	Direction controlling demolition of buildings in Conservation Area.	s. 277 A
TCP 156	Notice to owner or occupier of making of direction under section 8 (2) containing a declaration under section 8 (4).	

TCP 157	Notice of decision by Secretary of State on direction under section 8 (2) containing a declaration under section 8 (4).	
TCP 158	Notice to owner or occupier of making and confirmation by Secretary of State of direction under section 8 (2).	

RIGHTS OF ENTRY

RF 4	Authority to Enter. Folding card, cloth covered, to be carried by Officer.	s. 281
RF 9	Do. do. (with provision for photograph).	
RF 10	Do. do. (as RF 9 but for issue under seal).	

POWER TO REQUIRE INFORMATION AS TO INTERESTS IN LAND

TCP 32	Notice requiring person to state nature of interest in premises, with reply form attached.	s. 284

LAND COMPENSATION ACT 1961

PART III

CERTIFICATION BY PLANNING AUTHORITIES OF APPROPRIATE ALTERNATIVE DEVELOPMENT

TCP 101	Application for Certificate of appropriate alternative development.	s. 17
TCP 102	Certificate of appropriate alternative development.	

INDEX

A

B

C

F

G

P

V

W